William Cullen Bryant
and His America

Hofstra University
Cultural & Intercultural Studies: 4

ISSN 0195-802X

William Cullen Bryant and His America

Centennial Conference Proceedings 1878-1978

Editorial Board

Stanley Brodwin   Michael D'Innocenzo

Joseph G. Astman, Director
University Center for Cultural
& Intercultural Studies

AMS PRESS, INC.
New York, N.Y.

Library of Congress Cataloging in Publication Data
Main entry under title:

William Cullen Bryant and his America.

(Hofstra University cultural & intercultural studies,
ISSN 0195-802X; 4)
Bibliography: p.
Includes index.
1. Bryant, William Cullen, 1794-1878—Congresses.
2. Poets, American—19th century—Biography—Congresses.
3. United States—Intellectual life—Congresses.
I. Series.
PS1181.W5   811'.3   82-45233
ISBN 0-404-61654-2   AACR2

The publication of these proceedings has been made possible
by a generous grant from the Nassau County Office of Cultural Development (Roslyn, New York). Special thanks go
to Mrs. Marcia E. O'Brien, Director.

MANUFACTURED IN THE UNITED STATES
OF AMERICA

CONTENTS

Introduction

One summer day in 1850, Hawthorne and Melville (meeting for the first time), joined with other literati for a picnic on Monument Mountain. There, over iced champagne, Cornelius Mathews, noted in his time but now all but unread, recited yet another poem Bryant had written connected with his visit to that famous mountain, "The Story of the Indian Girl." The location no doubt necessitated some recognition of Bryant—it was the subject of one of his more powerful poems—but it is hard not to see in the event a valedictory gesture also, an act of homage for the by now "ancient" Father of American Poetry from those artists announcing a newer, darker, more fully blossomed romantic version of the "American Experience" than a young Indian Maid committing suicide over an "unlawful passion."

Perhaps the reports of Bryant's poetic death were greatly exaggerated. After all, he had another twenty-eight years to live—years in which he remained active as a poet, journalist, art sponsor, abolitionist, translator of Homer, and general sage for his time, even as Emerson was to become. The Civil War, destined to be the great watershed in American history and culture, also loomed in his and the country's future, but the dangerous rumblings anticipating the conflict could already be heard. In short, Bryant still had much work to do, and his career was inevitably shaping itself into one of those patterns which define our image of a *representative* man of his Age. Spanning ante and postbellum America, Bryant's career embodied, as few American lives have done, the great struggles and transitions in esthetics, politics, and society that marked the period.

It is from this perspective that we have tried to portray Bryant in the following essays. Our purpose has been to recapture Bryant not as a half-forgotten "pre-romantic" poet whose popular reputation rests upon the slender thread of one poem, nor as a figure patronizingly "re-evaluated," but as a groundbreaking poet and national figure in whose achievements still lurk the original forces that brought him eminence in the first place. Our purpose has been to *rediscover* rather than simply to re-evaluate, a distinction which we believe the *Proceedings* of this Conference have implicitly absorbed and hopefully justified. Indeed, we feel that these essays largely attest to Bryant's achievement as one richly textured enough to deserve profound critical respect and analysis. The old valedictory critical gestures still present in many an anthology or history of American literature and culture must be swept away, as, in fact, several contributors to this volume have long recognized.

It is our conviction that, with critical and historical hindsight, Bryant can be viewed as a man in whom the student of American culture will find the trenchant lineaments of a national *ethos* strikingly and vitally revealed. For, like most representative figures, Bryant integrated within himself the contradictions and tensions with which America was—and still is —burdened: its puritanism and secular "paganism;" its political conservatism and radical democratic impulses; its romantic love of an epic landscape; and the imperatives of urban struggle and sophistication. He could support passionately workers' rights to strike for higher wages and also give his countrymen their first translation of Homer by an American. The two acts are not incompatible, of course, but they do reflect Bryant's extraordinary range of sensibility and values. Surely he had as complex a fate as Henry James could wish, despite his image of a seemingly monolithic romantic-Puritan whose central purpose in life had been to teach people how to die with stoic resignation.

The essays in this volume, then, are testimony to that fated complexity and, above all, to the continuity of the Bryant legacy itself. We are especially proud that our opening essay should be by William Cullen Bryant II, who provides us with an initial, perceptive overview of that legacy. In his statement, "William Cullen Bryant After 100 Years," we grasp the main outlines of Bryant's achievement and are apprised of the many interesting opportunities and needs in Bryant studies still beckoning to scholars. Indeed, we feel the critical essays following his statement illuminate in some detail Bryant's varied creative and public activity from the fresh perspectives Professor Bryant calls for.

A good start is made in David J. Baxter's "The Dilemma of Progress: Bryant's Continental Vision," which shows that Bryant was an early and ardent promoter of the nation's westward expansion, calling for a giant step to the Pacific as early as 1826. Bryant's views on railroads, Indian policy, speculator and squatter rights provide insights into the social nature of his poetry as well as into America's notable era of "manifest destiny," a destiny not every writer of the period embraced. Baxter depicts Bryant as a "poet of contradictions,"one who celebrated the beauty of nature, but who also envisioned America as a great commercial nation. Ambivalent in resolving his continental vision, and yet affirming his poet's love of the unspoiled landscape, Bryant's central perspectives were shaped by his cyclic theory of history which served to resolve many of those contradictions.

In " 'The Prairie' and 'The Prairies': Cooper's and Bryant's Views of Manifest Destiny," Paul A. Newlin pursues the theme comparatively and concludes that both writers saw the culmination of Manifest Destiny as an affirmative development, although the Eden of the West was despoiled in the process. Bryant is portrayed in this essay as being even more democratic and optimistic in his vision than Cooper, and as a man of letters who celebrated the grandeur of the American Western Landscape more than he lauded the progress of man and society.

"Bryant and Dana: The Anatomy of a Friendship," by Bernard Weinstein, examines the fifty-seven-year association between two significant men of different backgrounds and interests. Weinstein demonstrates the deepening of a friendship which emerged from early bonds of poetry and experiences with personal grief. Over time, the two men offered support to each other as they individually grappled with frustrations, aspirations and clarification of their values, while they considered the place of art, poetry and literature in a democratic, materialistic society.

Michael D'Innocenzo's "William Cullen Bryant and the Newspapers of New York" assesses Bryant's editorial career in the context of the remarkable journalists of his era (James Gordon Bennett of the *Herald,* Horace Greeley of the *Tribune,* and Henry Raymond of *The New York Times*). Bryant had extraordinary staying power and was widely respected for the independence of his views, but his personality may have limited his overall impact and his desire to be innovative.

"William Cullen Bryant and the Early Sketch Club" by James T. Callow provides a glimpse of notable New York urbanites whose personal associations have often eluded scholars. These men lived in such proximity to each other that they exchanged little correspondence. Relying on the minutes of the Sketch Club, whose meetings spanned forty years, Callow depicts Bryant as a moving force in a Franklinian junto-like endeavor which informally brought together artists and amateurs to mix "conviviality and productiveness." This essay provides us with a view of the light side of Bryant's nature, while at the same time it explores the context in which a number of public-spirited

New Yorkers reenforced each other's efforts to be of service to their city.

William Cullen Bryant's presidency of the American Art Union and his encouragement of painters like Durand, Church, and Bierstadt are examined by David Shapiro. Here we see Bryant as a major figure in antebellum America —tastemaker, popularizer, catalyst. Shapiro explores Bryant's ideal of "a democratic art for a democratic people," but his essay also places the endeavors of the Art Union and of Bryant in an international context.

Gaines McMartin suggests that Bryant's was a poetry "of gentle reminding" which reflects a coherent and ordered world. The images of enclosure in nature which dominate Bryant's poetry are, according to McMartin, "symbolic of Bryant's own safe enclosure in a world of fixed moral ideas." McMartin compares Bryant's techniques with those of Whitman, and emplasizes that the former relied on carefully circumscribed metaphorical images.

In "The 'Denial of Death' in William Cullen Bryant and Walt Whitman," Stanley Brodwin examines the similarities and differences in the modes and strategies of denials fashioned by each poet as the existential terror of annihilation. Brodwin contends that Bryant "deserves a fresh and sympathetic re-reading for this authentic struggle to come to terms with his death-suffering." Bryant's philosophical complexity is revealed in a wide range of poems, some showing hope only through God's merciful judgment, others suggesting that love transcends death and hence contributes to an "Eternal Present" which cannot be separated from its parts.

Whitman achieved a radical sense of independence from any outside force limiting the Self; his pantheistic imagery glorified "undifferentiated Oneness" in which life and death mysteriously embody each other. On the other hand, Brodwin concludes, Bryant "forever remained anxiously dependent on a Power outside of himself to deny death, whether through Divine love or Grace of a beneficent Nature teaching resignation."

In "'Thanatopsis' and the Development of American Literature," R. Rio-Jelliffe investigates Bryant's theory of poetry and language. She argues that Bryant anticipated the romantic movement in America by more than a decade. Rio-Jelliffe analyzes the language, tone, and structure that distinguished "Thanatopsis" from the work of other poets of Bryant's era and shows that this poem embodies considerably more tension and emotional complexity than criticism has usually accorded it.

Bryant's sense of ambiguity, and his personal and artistic changes over time are considered by Albert McLean in "Progress and Dissolution in Bryant's poetry." While Bryant's poetry taught "the lessons of hope," emphasizing the possibility rather than the assurance of progress in an hospitable environment, McLean underscores the poet's growing appreciation of the "heightened complexity of human experience in an evolving urbanized and cosmopolitan society." Bryant's use of nature in poetry tempered his basic optimism because "nature in her various voices told men of decay and dissolution as well as rebirth." McLean contends that Bryant's sophistication has not been sufficiently appreciated because his was "an art that conceals art."

Another neglected side of the multifaceted Bryant is presented by Donald A. Ringe's fresh analysis in "Bryant's Fiction: The Problem of Perception." Although Bryant based his poetry on Sensationalist theory, he was also concerned about resolving problems about human perception beyond the "rational," of situations in which experience contradicts logic. According to Ringe, the philosophical questions raised in Bryant's prose foreshadowed the direction of American fiction later shaped by Poe, Hawthorne, Melville, and James.

"Anglo-American Encounter: William Cullen Bryant, Dickens, and Others," by Robert Sargent explains that Bryant's role in an emerging American literary culture was unique because he was simultaneously the nation's leading poet and an editor of one of the preeminent newspapers in the United States. This dual fame elicited special note from European observers of the American scene. Sargent discusses the assessments of Bryant by these European travelers to America, and explores their perceptions of the man who was emerging as a major spokesman of American literature in his day. The relationship between Bryant and Dickens, Sargent argues, was more complex and significant than scholars have hitherto acknowledged.

At the age of sixty-nine, William Cullen Bryant began his translations of Homer, an "exercise" that would last nearly nine years. In "'Not the Highest Praise': A Brief Reintroduction to William Cullen Bryant as a Translator of Homer," Thomas G. Voss explains Bryant's preparation for this enterprise, compares his endeavors to those of other scholars, and assesses the contemporary reviews of Bryant's translations.

In "William Cullen Bryant and the Suggestive Image: Living Impact," David Moriarty underscores Bryant's inherent modernity and challenges many of the critical cliches about his work. Building on Albert McLean's interpretations, Moriarty persuasively argues that

Bryant's particular sensitivity to discord and conflict gives his work contemporary appeal. Bryant, this essay contends, must not be read merely as the first American to capture the spirit of English Romanticism, but as a poet whose imagery embodies a startling range of living feeling and thought.

These short summaries are of course meant only to suggest the variety of critical interest in the volume as a whole. We believe that each individual study offers fresh ideas or perspectives which will contribute to an understanding and appreciation of Bryant, the poet whom Whitman honored for creating the "first interior verse-throbs of a mighty world . . . ."

Stanley Brodwin
Michael D'Innocenzo
Hofstra University
Hempstead, New York

William Cullen Bryant after 100 Years

BY
WILLIAM CULLEN BRYANT II
Oakland University, Rochester, Michigan

Seeing the all-too-familiar Nestorian image of Bryant at the top of our program, I was as diffident as Mark Twain on a New York lecture platform in 1876. He was going on "with flying colors," he told Annie Fields, when he detected, near the front of his audience, the "noble gray head and beard" of Bryant. "Nobody told me," he said, "that William Cullen Bryant was there, but I had seen his picture and I knew that was the old man. I was sure he saw the failure I was making, and all the weak points in what I was saying, and I couldn't do anything more—that old man just spoiled my work. Then they told me afterward that my lecture was good and all that; I could only say, 'No, no, that fine old head spoiled all I had to say *that* night!'"[1]

Here Twain reflected, perhaps, a grudging admiration then accorded by young writers to an older generation of classical authors, among whom Bryant was the senior, who still dominated American letters. But Bryant's was a very special case, for by the 1870s he was widely considered, not simply a poet and a journalist, but America's first citizen. Six years before Bryant died, John Bigelow called him "the only man in the United States who cannot be replaced, whose death would leave the country substantially poorer in genius, in character, in moral courage and purpose."[2] And at one of the many commemorations after his death in 1878 George William Curtis said of him, "No man, no American, living or dead, has more truly and amply illustrated the scope and the fidelity of Republican citizenship. . . . Whoever saw Bryant saw America."[3]

Fifty years later Vernon Parrington wrote, "For upwards of half a century now too much of Bryant has been obscured by the brightness of his early fame. Since his death a serious injustice has been done him

1

by the critics, who have dwelt too exclusively on his work in the field of verse to the neglect of other work in field perhaps quite as significant. . . . He is scattered piecemeal through his occasional writings, . . . and the task of piecing him together and visualizing his work as a whole has not yet been done. It will not prove an easy task."[4]

Bryant's work in fields other than poetry has not been wholly ignored in this century. Before Parrington's comment, William Ellery Leonard wrote of Bryant, "No such man ever sat, before or since, in the editorial chair; in no one other has there been such culture, scholarship, wisdom, dignity, moral idealism."[5] Much later Perry Miller commented, "His magnificent editorials during the Civil War are as fine utterances as the ordeal produced—and he was a power in politics as long as he lasted."[6] Allan Nevins, Arthur Schlesinger, Jr., and others have credited Bryant's great influence on the times of Andrew Jackson and Abraham Lincoln. Yet no substantial selection from his fifty years of *Evening Post* leaders has ever been published.

Bryant's "Lectures on Poetry" in 1826 were called a "landmark in our criticism" by Arthur Hobson Quinn,[7] who felt that Bryant's critical writing had long been slighted, because no collection of his literary essays and reviews—which we now know to have numbered more than one hundred—had yet been gathered.

Historians have credited Bryant's catalytic importance to American art. His "sentiment of nature," wrote Wolfgang Born thirty years ago, "was eminently suited to stimulate a landscape painter, and, in fact, the first generation of American landscape painters found him a source of inspiration."[8] My own checklist indicates that more than half a hundred works of art found their themes in one or another of his poems, quite apart from the many illustration his verse collections. Bryant was a personal friend of many nineteenth century artists; he was probably the subject or more portraits than any other American writer. He supported art institutions and activities, from the National Academy of Design and the Sketch Club in the 1820s, and the American Art Union and the Century Association in the 1840s, to the Metropolitan Museum of Art in the 1870s, and his newspaper was always active in their interest. He collaborated in the artists' publications, from *The Talisman* in 1828 and *The American Landscape* in 1830 to *The Crayon* in 1855 and *Picturesque America* in 1874. In 1864, forty-one artists gave him a collection of pictures painted for his 70th birthday celebration at the Century Club;[9] this collection has only recently been opened to public view, in various museums.

But Bryant's achievements in journalism and the arts—as well, of course, as in poetry—will be treated later in these conference proceedings, which seems to be the first serious effort, and an admirable one, to visualize Bryant as a whole since Parrington's challenge of a half century ago. I shall not encroach further on the topics of my fellow conferees. There are, however, several other aspects of Bryant's work to which I should like to call your attention.

Although not a biographer in the strict sense of a "historian of the lives of individual men," Bryant was long the commemorator of his fellows in literature and art. His discourses on Thomas Cole, Fenimore Cooper, Washington Irving, Fitz-Greene Halleck, and Gulian Verplanck, spoken between 1848 and 1870, were judicious appreciations rather than uncritical eulogies.[10] Felicitous in language and tone, they remain models of their kind. After the Cooper address in 1852 Charles Sumner wrote, "It was a truthful, simple & delicate composition; and much as I value sculpture & [Horatio] Greenough, I cannot but add that it will be a more durable monument to Cooper than any other."[11] This was prophetic, for, though Greenough didn't live to complete his Cooper statue, Bryant's discourse, as Quinn noted, "has been the source both for the facts of Cooper's life and for a keen analysis of his writing, to reappear in every important biography of Cooper."[12]

We may not be surprised, then, to learn that soon after Lincoln's assassination in 1865 Bryant was the choice of many prominent Americans to undertake his biography. "I should read it," wrote George Bancroft, "as I read everything you write, with delight and instruction." And Oliver Wendell Holmes pleaded, "No man combines the qualities for his biographer so completely as yourself, and the finished task would be a noble crown to a noble literary life."[13] But Bryant declined, and his tribute to Lincoln remains the short elegy, written for Lincoln's funeral procession in New York, which begins,

Oh, slow to smite and swift to spare,
   Gentle and merciful and just!
Who, in the fear of God, didst bear
   The sword of power, a nation's trust![14]

Bryant's commemorative discourses should be studied in relation to his entire performance as an orator. For several decades he was New York's most courted occasional speaker and chairman of public meetings, giving at least 125 recorded speeches. After a score of these had appeared in his *Orations and Addresses,* published in 1873, James T. Fields called them "the most beautiful speeches in the English language."[15] Earlier, Evert Duyckinck had commented, "Bryant appears frequently at public dinners and meetings at which he always makes the best speech of the evening . . . for he looks straight *into* the subject in hand and his mind once within explores the dormant material in brilliant fancies."[16]

Other studies suggest themselves. We might, for instance, examine Bryant's long activity as statesman without portfolio. His entry into politics at thirteen, with his boyish attacks on Jefferson and Madison in *The Embargo,* was an exercise he was reluctant to acknowledge in maturity. As a young lawyer in Great Barrington he held town offices and was secretary of a Federal-Republican convention. But by his arrival in New York in 1825 he had become a democrat in conviction and utterance. Thereafter, though he consistently avoided political office—even to the point of declining to serve on the state board of regents—his influence as publicist and civic leader grew steadily. His newspaper managed to secure and publish, in 1844, a proposed secret treaty adding Texas to the Union as a slave state, effectively blocking its passage by the United States Senate.[17] He was an architect in 1848 of the Free Soil Party, and when it re-emerged in 1856 as the Republican Party, he was influential in its decisions. He played an important part in the nomination of Lincoln in 1860, and in the choice of his cabinet, as well as in his conduct of the Civil War. During the gloomy and indecisive months of 1862 a national magazine suggested that the *Evening Post's* "clear and able political leaders have been of more service to the government in this war than some of its armies."[18]

In 1857 a federal jurist wrote of Bryant, "What a glory it would be to our country if it could elect this man to the Presidency--the country not he would be honored & elevated by such an event."[19] This isolated opinion won wider currency fifteen years later, when dissatisfaction with President Grant's first term, and disgust with the candidacy of Horace Greeley, his opponent, led several editors to propose Bryant as an alternative. Then in his 78th year, Bryant printed a reply which equaled in finality the famous refusals of Calvin Coolidge and General Sherman, and surpassed them in grace. "The idea is absurd enough," he wrote, "not only on account of my advanced age, but of my unfitness in various respects for the labor of so eminent a post. I do not, however, object to the discussion of my deficiencies on any other ground than that it is altogether superfluous, since it is impossible that

I should receive any formal nomination, and equally impossible, if it were offered, that I should commit the folly of accepting it."[20]

Bryant's competence in four or five modern foreign languages, both in their spoken and written forms, and his numerous prose and verse translations from these, would surely offer fruitful study, as would his legal practice, which would be greatly furthered by the New York Public Library's recent acquisition of a ledger docketing the cases he handled in Berkshire County during a ten-year period. His theory and practice of what he termed the "luminous style" seems to me an important subject for study. His contemporaries, such as Poe and Whitman, had much to say of this: Whitman spoke in 1888 of the "marvelous purity of his work in verse. It was severe—oh! so severe!" he said to Horace Traubel "never a waste word—the last superfluity struck off; a clear nameless beauty pervading and overarching all the work of his pen."[21] Bryant's impatience with fine language was often expressed; once, when his voluble spinster friend Eliza Robbins reported, "The mechanic has returned your chair, and expressed the hope that its equilibrium had been properly adjusted," Bryant insisted on knowing what the man had really said, forcing the confession, "Well, if you must know, he said he guessed the rickety old concern wouldn't joggle any more."[22] He deplored the "hackneyed phrases" and "awkward distortions resorted to by those who thought that by putting a sentence out of its proper shape they were writing like Milton."[23] The so-called *"index expurgatorius"* which he drew up for the guidance of young writers on his newspaper, condemning such loose evasions as "inaugurate" for "begin," would in itself bear serious scrutiny.[24]

There are three subjects to which Bryant gave meticulous attention, and of which no coherent account has been written. The first of these is horticulture.

In the summer of 1978 the Horticultural Society of New York designed its display at the annual flower show in in Bryant Park around Bryant's interest in gardening and fruit culture. In an autobiographical article he had said that from his earliest years he was a "delighted observer of external nature," and that in the spring of his fifteenth year, as a diversion from studying Latin under his uncle at a distance from his Cummington home, he carefully studied the trees and field flowers that were new to him, and waited excitedly for an elegant meadow lily to bloom. Later, he and his bride studied with the eminent naturalist Amos Eaton, and the young poet-lawyer became known in Great Barrington as a "passionate botanist" who "knew the name of every tree, flower, and spire of grass."[25] As a city-bound editor he escaped for long tramps in the country, alone or with friends such as Thomas Cole, Robert Weir, and William Gilmore Simms. When in 1842 he bought the Roslyn property which would eventually comprise 170 acres, he passed much time cultivating fruit trees and rare plants. "His delight," Parke Godwin wrote, "was so great that it is doubtful whether any shrub or tree, fit for planting in the soil of Long Island, of which he happened to hear, escaped his experiments."[26] Friends sent or brought him specimens from abroad. Andrew Jackson Downing, whose influential books on horticulture Bryant praised in the *Evening Post,* said of his friend, "No visitor brought such a discerning and discriminating eye to an inspection of [my] plants and culture as Mr. Bryant. Nothing . . . escapes him."[27]

When Bryant crossed the desert from Egypt to the Holy Land in 1853, one of his companions recalled later, his botanical observations, underscored by apt verse quotations, made the journey rather more delightful than monotonous. On the same trip he had a long conversation with the British botanist Robert Fortune on the advisability of importing into the United States grapes and fruit trees from China, a conversation reported in one of his letters to his newspaper, and reflected two years later in his speech to the New York Horticultural Society on "The Improvement of Native Fruits."[28]

When Bryant repossessed his boyhood home in Cummington in 1865, and in 1871 added the farm of his grandfather Snell, he owned an additional property of 465 acres. Here he planted extensive orchards, in which he set out at least six varieties of cherry, ten of plum, and fourteen of pear trees, as well as hundreds of ornamental trees, including a stand of pines about five hundred feet long which now tower over one hundred feet high. Doubtless none of the original fruit trees survive, but some of their scions may be found among a second growth of hardwood and evergreen, and at the edge of a thirty-acre virgin forest, untouched since Bryant composed "Thanatopsis" and " A Winter Piece" in its dim shade 160 years ago.

Bryant is credited with giving the first impetus to the development of Central Park in New York City,[29] but it is not commonly remembered that he was a friend of Frederick Law Olmsted, first superintendent and designer of that great urban nature preserve. Bryant supported Olmsted's appointment in 1857 and sought to prevent his removal four years later from position in which he had antagonized the park board.[30] In 1858 he printed Olmsted's and Calvert Vaux's *Greensward Plan for Central Park* on his newspaper press, and in 1866 their designs for a San Francisco park and the University campus at Berkeley.[31] He admired Olmsted's books, particularly *The Cotton Kingdom*,[32] a study of the planter-slavery system in the old South. After its author became secretary to the United States Sanitary Commission in 1861, his letters from the war front appeared in the *Evening Post*. Bryant's high regard for his friend's abilities was expressed in a letter to his brother John in 1859, where he wrote, "Frederick Law Olmsted, the Superintendent of the Central Park in our city, who is a man of great administrative capacity, who selects all his subordinates and agents with an instinctive wisdom, and who does not allow a dollar of the public money to be paid out except for value received, would be an infinitely better President than we have had since Van Buren, but nobody will think of nominating him, and few would know whom they were voting for."[33]

Another of Bryant's lifelong concerns was health. He was a sickly child, and had throughout his youth a tendency toward tuberculosis, from which his father and his favorite sister Sally suffered early deaths. Perhaps Dr. Peter Bryant wished his second son to become a doctor, for he named him for a distinguished Scottish physician whose books were required reading for the many medical students he trained as Cullen was growing up. The boy's grandfather Bryant and great-grandfather Howard had been doctors, and Cullen wrote that before he began to study law he read medical and chemical books in his father's library; but, he added, "The hardships of a physician's life, as I saw in the case of my father, disinclined me from making medicine my profession."[34] Yet his early frailty, and the loss of his father's care and counsel, impelled him toward a strict regimen of diet and exercise. Bryant neither smoked nor drank coffee or tea—though he enjoyed a good wine—ate sparingly of meat, and was almost fanatical in his devotion to fruit and berries as essential to digestion and general good health. He continued almost until the end of life to take strenuous exercise in long walks, and as he grew older he set himself a regular daily series of calisthenics, lasting as much as an hour and a half each morning, during which he exercised with dumbbells and a chairs, chinned himself on a bar in his bedroom, and vaulted over his bed with a pole. He was the first among his New York acquaintances to take daily showerbaths. Walking over the Cummington hills in the last decade of his life, he was often seen to place one hand on the top of a wall or fence and vault over it.[35]

Soon after Bryant came to New York he was attracted by the rational medical system of the German Samuel Hahnemann, which was then finding adherents in America. About 1836 he joined the New York Homoeopathic Society, founded by his friend and physician John Franklin Gray, and in 1841 he became its president, publishing his inaugural address, *Popular Considerations on Homoeopathia.*[36] Thereafter he made frequent reference in his letters to recommended medications, and to treatments he had applied to himself and others. Visiting Savannah in 1843, he was asked by its mayor, a practicing doctor and later a founder of the American Medical Association, to recommend medicines for the treatment of his wife's lung trouble. After Frances Bryant had been critically ill at Naples in 1858, Bryant credited her recovery to homeopathic treatment. And there is an amusing letter from Bryant to a young man in Ohio who had written asking his advice in controlling "excited passions." "Keep the thoughts always occupied," Bryant replied, together with "early rising, allowing no time to be passed in bed except for necessary sleep; bathing the small of the back and loins every morning in cold water; chest exercise with ample inflation of the lungs, the avoidance of bad company and of such reading as excites the passions. Some recommend what the Germans call the sitz-bad and electricity. Spiritous liquors and excess in eating should be carefully avoided. Sleep on a hard bed and cultivate hardy habits."[37]

In 1860 the present New York Medical College was founded by Dr. Gray and other homeopathic physicians, and two years later Bryant was elected president of its council. For ten years he presided over its commencements, conferring as many as one hundred M. D. degrees annually, and during his tenure the faculty established the Hahnemann Hospital, which later became the present Flower and Fifth Avenue Hospitals.[38]

Finally, a little-known Bryant activity—book publishing —worthy of notice. Bryant was very active in securing for American writers a fair copyright law. His persistence with Harper Brothers finally secured their publication of Richard Henry Dana, Jr.'s *Two Years Before the Mast.* As president of the American Copyright Club, together with Evert Duyckinck, Bryant launched a series of cheap paper books which within two years published new titles by Poe, Melville,

Hawthorne, Simms, and Margaret Fuller. In 1842, he commented to Richard Dana, Sr. that he was printing his own new book, *The Fountain and Other Poems,* on the Evening Post presses.[39] His occasional imprint, "William C. Bryant & Co," may be seen on some older books. In August 1854 Bryant wrote to Orville Dewey, "My brother John is here, and I, the printer, am putting in type for him a little volume of his poems. I hope there is nothing vulgar or mechanical in being a printer. Horace Walpole, you know, the most fastidious of men, had a press at Strawberry Hill, and printed there the Odes of Gray."[40]

As early as 1835, during Bryant's absence in Europe, his partner William Leggett reprinted on their press a recent book of great influence on Andrew Jackson's financial policies, William M. Gouge's *A Short History of Money and Banking.* Although Bryant at first deplored such an expenditure of his firm's funds, he kept the book in print until, in 1840, he established a separate printing office for commercial paper and inexpensive books and pamphlets. During the succeeding thirty years the variety of publications struck off by this office is suggested by some of their titles. In addition to Cullen's and John Bryant's poems, and the park plans of Olmsted and Vaux named earlier, they included Bryant's discourses on Halleck and Verplanck, and his *Reminiscences of the Evening Post;* the *Transactions of the American Art Union;* a history of the Century Association; catalogues of the Cummington Library, which Bryant gave the town in 1872, of the Dusseldorf Academy of Fine Arts, and of the Homoeopathic Medical College; a defense of Downing's book on lanscape gardening and rural architecture; a manual of the New York City Board of Education; and a number of books and pamphlets on political subjects, such as a history of the *Free Soil Question in the United States,* an annual *Democrat's Almanac,* and the speeches and letters of prominent statesmen.[41] My incomplete checklist of these publications runs to over thirty titles; I should be most grateful to hear of additional ones.

I have attempted in this paper to offer further bits and pieces toward the rounded whole necessary for the eventual assignment of Bryant to his rightful place in American letters. When that time comes, we shall be better able to appraise the validity of an opinion expressed in 1856 by Benjamin Franklin Butler, President Van Buren's attorney general, of Bryant: "Posterity, I think, will place him on the same roll with the Miltons, Hampdens, and Jeffersons of the last two centuries."[42]

NOTES

1. M. A. Dewolfe Howe, *Memories of a Hostess; A Chronicle of Eminent Friendships Drawn Chiefly from the Diaries of Mrs. James T. Fields* (Boston: Atlantic Monthly Press [1922]), pp. 256–57.
2. Margaret Clapp, *Forgotten First Citizen: John Bigelow* (Boston: Little, Brown, 1947), p. 322. from Bigelow's manuscript journal.
3. George William Curtis, *The Life, Character and Writings of William Cullen Bryant . . .* (New York: Scribner's [c1879], quoted in Parke Godwin, *A Biography of William Cullen Bryant, With Extracts from His Private Correspondence* (New York: D. Appleton, 1883), II, 418–19.
4. Vernon Louis Parrinton, *Main Currents in American Thought* (New York: Harcourt, 1930), II, 238–39.
5. William Peterfield Trent, et al, *The Cambridge History of American Literature* (New York: Macmillan, 1917–1921), I, 276.
6. Perry Miller, *The Raven and the Whale; The War of Words and Wits in the Era of Poe and Melville* (New York: Harcourt Brace [1956]), pp. 340–41.
7. *The Literature of the American People; An Historical and Critical Survey,* Arthur Hobson Quinn, ed. (New York: Appleton-Century-Crofts [1951]), p. 385.
8. Wolfgang Born, *American Landscape Painting; An Interpretation* (New Haven: Yale University Press, 1948), p. 36.
9. See *The Bryant Festival at "The Century,"* November 5, MDCCCLXIV (New York: D. Appleton, 1865), pp. 4, 39–40, 87; Charles Downing Lay and Theodore Boston, *Works of Art Silver and Furniture Belonging to the Century Association* (New York: The Century Association, 1943), pp. 43–46.
10. William Cullen Bryant, *Orations and Addresses* (New York: Putnam's, 1873), pp. 1-258, passim.
11. Sumner to John Bigelow, March 2, 1852, quoted in John Bigelow, *Retrospections of an Active Life* (New York: Baker & Taylor, 1909–1913), I, 125–26.
12. *Literature of the American People*, p. 258.
13. Bancroft to Bryant, April 26 [1865], and Holmes to Bryant, April 27, 1865, in the Goddard-Roslyn Collection, New York Public Library. Others who wrote similar letters to Bryant were Theodore Tilton and John Greenleaf Whittier; see *loc. cit.*
14. "The Death of Lincoln," *Poems by William Cullen Bryant. Collected and Arranged by the Author* New York: D Appleton [1876]), p. 446.
15. Godwin, *A Biography of Bryant,* II, 328.
16. Duyckinck to William Gilmore Simms, February 2, 1869, Columbia University Library.
17. See New York *Evening Post* for April 27 and May 2, 1844.
18. Quoted from *Littell's Living Age,* in Allan Nevins, *The Evening Post; A Century of Journalism* (New York: Boni & Liveright [1922]), p. 340.

19. John Curtis Underwood to Eli Thayer, March 11, 1857, Brown University Library.
20. "Card" over Bryant's signature, in New York *Evening Post* for July 8, 1872.
21. Reported by Horace L. Traubel in *With Walt Whitman in Camden* (Boston: Small, Maynard; New York: D. Appleton, M. Kennerley, 1906-1914, II, 532–33.
22. Godwin, *A Biography of Bryant,* I, 339.
23. *A Library of Poetry and Song, Being Choice Selections from the Best Poets, With an Introduction by William Cullen Bryant* (New York: J. B. Ford, 1874), pp. xxx–xxi.
24. Nevins, *The Evening Post,* p. 348.
25. Godwin, *A Biography of Bryant,* I, 25, 31, 203.
26. *Ibid.,* II, 214.
27. Quoted in Donald G. Mitchell, *American Lands and Letters; The Mayflower to Rip Van Winkle* (New York: Scribner's, 1901), p. 392.
28. Godwin, *A Biography of Bryant,* II, 74–75, 68–69; Bryant, *Orations and Addresses,* pp. [269]–282.
29. See, for instance, Henry Hope Reed and Sophia Duckworth, *Central Park; A History and a Guide* (New York: Clarkson N. Potter [1972]), pp. 3–4; Elizabeth Barlow, *The Central Park Book* ([New York] Central Park Task Force [1977]), p. 21.
30. Laura Wood Roper, *FLO; A Biography of Frederick Law Olmsted* (Baltimore and London: Johns Hopkins University Press [1973]), pp. 129, 361.
31. *Preliminary Report in Regard to a Plan of Public Pleasure Grounds for the City of San Francisco* (New York: William C. Bryant & Co., 1868); *Report Upon a Projected Improvement of the Estate of the College of California at Berkeley, near Oakland* (New York: W. C. Bryant & Co.; San Francisco: Towne & Bacon, 1866).
32. *The Cotton Kingdom; A Traveler's Observations on Cotton and Slavery in the American Slave States . . . ,* 2 vols. (New York: Mason Bros., 1862).
33. Bryant to John Howard Bryant, n.d. [1859?], in Knox College Library.
34. Godwin, *A Biography of Bryant,* I, 36.
35. For a description by Bryant of his systematic habits of diet and exercise, see ibid., II, 297–99.
36. *Popular Considerations on Homoeopathia . . . , Delivered before the New York Homoeopathic Society, December 23, 1841* (New York: Wm. Radde [1841]).
37. Draft letter from Bryant to A. S. Wallace, October 22, 1862, Goddard-Roslyn Collection, New York Public Library.
38. Leonard Paul Wershub, *One Hundred Years of Medical Progress; A History of the New York Medical College Flower and Fifth Avenue Hospitals* (Springfield, Illinois: Charles C. Thomas [1967]), pp. 31, 45, 78, and *passim.*

39. *The Letters of William Cullen Bryant,* William Cullen Bryant II, and Thomas G. Voss, eds., vol. II (New York: Fordham University Press, 1977), 176.
40. Bryant to Dewey, August 15, 1854, in Godwin, *A Biography of Bryant,* II, 77–78.
41. These were, in the order named: *Some Notices of the Life and Writings of Fitz-Greene Halleck, Read before the New York Historical Society, on the 3d of February, 1869, by William Cullen Bryant* (1869); *A Discourse on the Life, Character and Writings of Gulian Crommelin Verplanck, Delivered before the New-York Historical Society, May 17th, 1870, by William Cullen Bryant* (1870); *Reminiscences of the Evening Post: Extracted from the Evening Post of November 15, 1851. With Additions and Corrections by the Writer* (1851);*Transactions of the American Art Union, for the Year 1845* (1846); John H. Gourlie, *The Origin and History of the "Century"* (1856); *Catalogue of the Cummington Library* (1873); *Catalogue of a Private Collection of Paintings and Original Drawings by Artists of the Dusseldorf Academy of Fine Arts* (1850); *Seventh Annual Prospectus and Announcement for 1866 and 1867 of the New York Homoeopathic Medical College at 116 East 20th Street, New York City* 1866?); H. J. Ehlers, *Defense against Abuse and Slander with Some Strictures on Mr. Downing's Book on Landscape Gardening* (1852); *Manual of the Board of Education* (1851); Oliver Cromwell Gardiner, *The Great Issue; or, The Three Presidential Candidates; Being a Brief Historical Sketch of the Free Soil Question in the United States from the Congresses of 1774 and '87 to the Present Time* (1848); *The Democrat's Almanac and Political Register for 1839 [-1840, -1842; various titles]* (1838, 1839, 1841).
42. Benjamin Franklin Butler to Martin Van Buren, November 21, 1856, Library of Congress.

The Dilemma of Progress:
Bryant's Continental Vision

DAVID J. BAXTER
Walsh College

William Cullen Bryant died on June 12, 1878, five months short of being eighty-four years old. His long lifetime spanned the era of greatest western expansion in America. When he was born, the western frontier was just pushing across the Alleghanies into the Ohio territory; by the time of his death a continent had been settled. He was ten when Lewis and Clark opened up the Louisiana territory. Two years before his death Colorado became a state, and Denver was a city with over 100,000 people. In 1832 Bryant made his first visit to Illinois when Indian attacks were still a very real threat and the prairie was yet largely unbroken by the plow. On a visit to Chicago in 1841 Bryant noted the small size of the frontier town, but only five years later on a second visit he remarked that "anyone who had seen this place . . . when it contained less than five thousand people, would find some difficulty in recognizing it now, when its population is more than fifteen thousand."[1] Of a visit to another city on the same tour of the Great Lakes in 1846 Bryant wrote: "Farther on we came to Milwaukie, which is rapidly becoming one of the great cities of the West. . . . Milwaukie is said to contain at present, about ten thousand inhabitants. Here the belt of the forest that borders the lake stretches back for several miles to the prairies of Wisconsin. 'The Germans,' said a passenger, 'are already in the woods hacking at the trees, and will soon open the country to the prairies.'"[2] The hacking at the forests, the land, the Indians, and the bountiful wildlife continued unabated for another fifty years until, shortly after Bryant's death, the buffalo were almost extinct, the Indian wars were over, the land was no longer cheap, and the forests were still virginal only in remote sections of the country.

Millions of people felt and followed the lure of the West, literally everyone who emigrated from the Old World westward across the Atlantic to the New. As the Atlantic seaboard became settled and rural villages grew into towns and cities, always a certain portion of the population would feel the overcrowding and move to the West. Inevitably all of the land was bought, taken, sold, bought again, taken again, sold again in an endless transfer of ownership until America's vision of Manifest Destiny was realized, and the West was no longer viable except as the subject for nostalgic musings.

The Bryant family contributed to the movement of population across the continent. By 1835 all of William Cullen Bryant's brothers had emigrated to Illinois from their western Massachusetts home at Cummington. William seriously considered joining the westward migration as he became more and more dissatisfied with his strenuous editorial duties for the *New York Evening Post*. In 1833 he contemplated someday buying a farm in Illinois near his brothers, hopefully upon his return from his first visit to Europe planned for the following year. He and his wife wanted the farm, Frances Bryant wrote, "in order that we may have a place *where on* to rest (if we need one) when we return."[3] William did eventually buy hundreds of acres of land in and near Princeton, Illinois, although he never moved there.[4] The idea of moving westward was strong in Bryant again in 1836. He wrote to his brother John, "I think of making some disposition of my interest in the "Evening Post" and coming out to the western country with a few thousand dollars to try my fortune. . . . I have had my fill of town life, and begin to wish to pass a little time in the country. "[5] William's "a little time" was to have been a year, but the urge was dissipated. He knew he would be bored away from the cosmopolitan surroundings of New York City.

Even if William Cullen Bryant never went West to live, he certainly prompted others to do so. He was caught up in the westering spirit that characterized his century. Bryant's response to the American West, however, was not as simple as his most frequently anthologized poems and the cursory treatment scholars have given the matter would seem to indicate, especially with regard to the American Indian.[6] The complexity of Bryant's view of the West lies in the many seeming contradictions exhibited between his literary, editorial, and personal treatments of the subject. On the one hand he supported legislation regulating speculation in western lands by eastern capitalists, yet, he was a speculator himself, investing in Illinois real estate. The Indians of his poems and tales are often savage, yet, at the same time he emphasized their courage and humanity. He could, in his poetry, see the Indian as closer to God than the white man, yet, in his editorials he endorsed Andrew Jackson's harsh Indian policies governing the removal of Indian tribes from their eastern homelands to the unfamiliar prairies west of the Mississippi. The dominant theme of his poems reflects, above all, his love for the beauty of the natural landscape, yet, he entertained visions of America as a great commercial nation, and supported the rapid settlement of the continent which led to the destruction of the landscape. William Cullen Bryant believed in and contributed to the growth of the myth of America's Manifest Destiny.

As early as the 1820s, Bryant began to publish responses to various proposals, reflecting advanced thinking concerning the future of the West. On December 19, 1820 Dr. John Floyd, congressman from Virginia and later governor of the state, first moved for the appointment of a select committee to 'inquire into the situation of the settlements upon the Pacific Ocean and the expediency of occupying the Columbia River.[7] In January, 1823 Dr. Floyd finally got his bill for the annexation of Oregon up for a vote in the House of Representatives. But Floyd's bill was as yet too visionary for a Congress that by and large could see only as far as the Mississippi River, and it was resoundingly defeated, 100–61.[8] During the decade of the 1820s, with the country barely pushing across the Mississippi, many politicians in Washington were claiming there was enough unsold land east of the great river to absorb settlers for the next seventy years.[9] Explorers were sending back reports that everything between the Mississippi River and the Rocky Mountains was a vast, arid desert, unsuited for civilization.[10] Dr. Floyd, however, during the 1820s, continued to push for the passage of an Oregon bill, citing the tremendous natural wealth in the area, and the need to establish safe routes of travel across the plains to explit this wealth.

In 1825 Floyd's bill was defeated again, but Congress did agree to permit further inquiry into the practicability of Oregon settlement by establishing a committee, headed by Francis Baylies of Massachusetts, to garner more accurate information about the Far Northwest. Early in 1826 Mr. Baylies published his report of the committee. Of Oregon's climate, soil, navigable rivers, and timber resources, the report had nothing but praise, extolling all the virtues of the area Dr.

Floyd had been promoting for six years. But even Baylies's report prompted no legislative action. Congress would remain silent on the issue for over two years.

William Cullen Bryant foresaw and supported the penetration of the nation through to the Pacific. He had every hope that America would become a great commercial nation, and he felt the same excitement in a vision of an enlightened people spreading westward across the continent, changing the natural resources of the country into goods for both domestic and world trade, as did the most imaginative of his contemporaries. In the March, 1826 issue of the *New-York Review and Atheneum Magazine,* Bryant commented upon Baylies's report, and in prose more exuberant than that of Baylies, echoed his call for congressional action:

> There are, however, proper subjects of legislation, and cares worthy of a great nation and its government. One of these, it seems to us, is contemplated in the report of Mr. Baylies. It is certainly a matter of some moment, that a nation should be well acquainted with the value of its own territories, and that it should provide means for its citizens to avail themselves safely and successfully of all the natural advantages which they offer.[11]

In the conclusion to his review of Baylies's report, Bryant became more ecstatic in imagining the future growth of his country, and repeated his appeal for the quick establishment of a military post in Oregon to enhance the spread of civilization to the Pacific:

> Already the outposts of our population are nearly midway between the oceans. What is called by an apt metaphor the trade of population, may be delayed awhile by the barren and elevated regions of the central and western parts of Missouri territory, but will find its way along the fertile borders of the rivers, and in the end will penetrate farther on account of the narrow channels in which it is confined. When the train of covered wagons which is continually moving westward shall have passed the Rocky Mountains, it will descend rapidly to the Pacific. That period will undoubtedly be hastened by planting government posts in that territory as the pioneers of colonization. When it arrives it will give the commerce of the United States an immense preponderance and eastern Asia, and western Europe, will exchange their productions through our territories.[12]

In 1826 the country was moving westward, but in small steps. Most Americans were satisfied to let America's destiny evolve gradually. A sudden, dramatic giant step to the Pacific was as yet inconceivable to most. But William Cullen Bryant in 1826 wanted this giant step taken.

Neither Floyd nor Bryant gave up on the Oregon bill. Congressman Floyd reintroduced the bill into the House for the third time on December 23, 1828. Again the bill was defeated, this time by a vote of 99–75.[13] On January 10, 1829, Bryant came out editorially in favor of the bill in the *New York Evening Post.*

The Oregon bill having been defeated three times in seven years, it remained a dead political issue until the 1840s. In 1842 Oregon annexation again became a volatile issue as thousands of American settlers in Oregon or preparing to go there petitioned their government for military protection. During the six years Congress debated the Oregon question in the 1840s, the *New York Evening Post* again called for quick annexation of the area. Finally on August 13, 1848, almost a quarter of a century after William Cullen Bryant's first statement of his dream for Oregon, the dream was realized with the creation of a territorial government. Bryant's continental vision was that far ahead of its time.

To bind Oregon economically and politically to the North and East, in the 1840s Bryant promoted Asa Whitney's plan for a transcontinental railroad. When in January, 1845, Whitney, a New York businessman and China trader, first proposed to Congress the idea of a railroad to Oregon, he was ridiculed and his proposal tabled, but the grandness of the idea caught Bryant's romantic imagination. The first transcontinental railroad, which ended in California, was not completed until May 10, 1869. Bryant again proved himself a visionary expansionist, realizing the economic potential of a railroad to the Far West decades before his countrymen. Characteristically, Bryant's conception of the impact of a transcontinental railroad on the nation was idealistic in the extreme. Bryant saw only a national good ensuing from a speedy access to the newly opened territories as the railroad carried settlers to the West and returned with their agricultural goods and even with goods from Asia. The railroad would be a giant step for America in her passage to India. Bryant reminded cynics who saw immense private fortunes (specifically Whitney's) being made from the railroad, that Whitney was willing "to relinquish every claim to what remains of the land after the railroad is completed, if the government will but allow him to be the instrument for accomplishing this great undertaking."[14] Three years later Bryant had not changed his belief.

He wrote in the *Post:* "Mr. Whitney, for aught we perceive, gets nothing but the glory of having projected the work, and procured it to be carried into execution."[15] On November 18, 1846, Bryant quoted Whitney in the *Evening Post* on the extensive benefits of the transcontinental railroad:

> The opportunity for employment and settlement which will be opened by this great work, will have a tendency to increase emigration, and by consequence increase the demand for ships, and give activity to commerce. In a country now a desert and remote from all communication with civilized communities, and with markets, a population of consumers and producers will spring up which will become the customers of our merchants and our manufacturers.[16]

The article continued with lengthy and detailed descriptions of the vast wealth of the Far West.

Oregon and the transcontinental railroad, however, were not the only issues defining William Cullen Bryant's position as as visionary expansionist. By 1830 when Andrew Jackson's Indian Removal Bill was being debated in Congress, Bryant, who in his early poetry had often dwelt upon the passing-of-empires theme, had reconciled himself to the displacement and possible extinction of the Indians. Jackson's Indian Removal Bill resulted in long and bitter debates over both the morality and practicality of the measure. Throughout the winter and early spring of 1830 as the controversy raged, Bryant continually came to the defense of Jackson and his bill in frequent editorials in the *Evening Post.*[17] The Indian Removal Bill called for the resettlement of all Indians tribes to west of the Mississippi River, ostensibly to protect them from the violence incited by a too close proximity with white civilization, but in reality to open up more Indian land to white settlement and thus promote western expansion. Already having accepted the displacement of the Indians as sad but necessary, Bryant sincerely believed that the Indian Removal Bill of 1830 was a way of impeding temporarily their ultimate eradication.[18]

The passing-of-empires theme is integral to much of Bryant's verse. Progress meant change and change, it seemed, meant the inevitability of the destruction of races. Besides "Thanatopsis," of his early verse both "A Walk at Sunset" and "The Ages" exhibit Bryant's cyclic theory of history. The Indian was the often used symbol of Bryant's theory. His "Indian War Song" dates from 1810. He planned an Indian tale as early as 1816,[19] and returned to the Red man again and again in his poetry and prose tales as in: "The Indian Girl's Lament" (1823), "An Indian at the Burial Place of his Fathers" (1823). Monument Mountain" (1824), "Indian Story" (1824), "The Cascade of Melsingah" (1818, "The Disinterred Warrior" (1828), "The Indian Spring" (1830). "The Prairies" (1833), and "A Legend of the Delawares" (1872). Significantly, the bulk of Bryant's literary interest in the Indians preceded his trips to the West in 1832, 1841, 1846, and 1854, where the only Indians he saw were of the reservation variety and not the stuff of romance. Except for his 1832 trip to Illinois, Bryant's western adventures inspired no poetry, and even "The Prairies" deals with themes and employs images Bryant had long been manipulating. After the Indian Removal Bill of 1830, he ignored the Indians almost entirely as poetic material.

In 1821 Bryant wrote to his friend Richard Henry Dana, Sr., "You see my head runs upon the Indians—the very mention of them once used to make me sick—perhaps because those who took to make a poetical use of them made such a terrible butchery of the subject."[20] It was with poetic butchery that Bryant was concerned, not the actual. His *Evening Post* reported treaties, battles, and smallpox epidemics among the Indians, but never did anything to try to change the government's brutal Indian Policy. The Indians had long vanished from the western Massachusetts hills where William Cullen Bryant grew up, having posed no threat to the frontier communities of the state since their power was broken by King Phillip's War 120 years before Bryant's birth. Tribes that remained and attempted to accommodate themselves to the White man's culture were gradually pushed westward by a series of removals ending in 1785 when the last remnants left Stockbridge to settle in New York.[21] The very absence of the Indians from the eastern states was the crucial factor in the formation of Bryant's complex response toward them. In his poetry and prose tales they were exotic, mysterious, savage, yet, at a distance of both time and place, admirable. The Indians lived to the west fighting an endless series of temporary holding actions against the inexorable progression of European civilization. Such was the theme of Bryant's first Indian poem, "Indian War Song" in which a battle weary warrior shouts revenge upon the White man.

Ghosts of my wounded brethren rest,
  Shades of the warrior dead!
Nor weave, in shadowy garments drest,

The death-dance round my bed;
For, by the homes in which we dwelt,
And by the altar where we knelt,
And by our dying battle songs,
And by the trophies of your pride,
And by the wounds of which ye died,
I swear to avenge your wrongs.

When any Indian tribes attempted to carry out the threat of Bryant's imaginary warrior of "Indian War Song," Bryant used the powerful platform of the editorial page of the *Evening Post* to condemn their barbarisms. The Indians and their predecessors, the Mound Builders, because they were passed or passing, fit nicely into Bryant's new-empires-built-upon-old theory of history. But they existed primarily for Bryant as an abstraction, a poetic motif of melodrama, not real men undergoing a tragedy. In his personal feelings it is doubtful Bryant was ever more than indifferent and condescending to the plight of the Indians in the first half of the nineteenth century.

When the rights of squatters formed a major political issue during the 1830s, William Cullen Bryant also demonstrated his expansionist beliefs. The Whigs and Democrats took opposite sides of the issue: Henry Clay and his party backed the large land companies and branded the squatters as lawless rabble; the Democrats, especially the radical Locofoco wing of the party with which Bryant was sympathetic, supported a squatter's right to buy his farm at the minimum price when his land came into market, even if the government had buyers ready to pay more. The Democrats wanted to insure that a squatter would not be removed from land he might have been working for years simply because he could not compete against corporate money when the land was eventually placed on sale. William Cullen Bryant was well aware of the plight of squatters along the frontier from the experiences of his own brothers in establishing their farms near Princeton, Illinois in the spring of 1833. In the absence of preemption legislation, the brothers stood in danger of losing the land they were working if by chance it was placed on sale before they had the time to raise and sell a crop to obtain the cash they needed to bid for their land on the open market. On April 25, 1833 William wrote to his mother of how his brothers John and Cyrus were out of cash and "in trouble for fear that the land would come into market and find them unprovided with money to purchase it."[22]

The controversy over squatters rights became most volatile in 1837 when the Democrats introduced a bill in Congress permitting settlers to claim a piece of public land by farming it, thus prohibiting any outright sale to land companies or individuals not actually working the soil. While preemption had been practiced in scattered areas of the West for many years, there was in 1837 no national preemption law. The bill became crucial in 1837 because of a severe economic depression. Bryant reported the evils of the western land system to the readers of the *Evening Post* on February 1, 1837 by printing a letter by a writer with the pseudonym Black Hawk which called for the quick passage of a national preemption law. Two days later the lead editorial in the *Post* came pointedly to the defense of the squatters.

No man who has once visited the West, scruples, if his convenience should lead him, to seat himself upon the unoccupied territory belonging to the government, the sale of which is not yet permitted. Here he builds his log cabin, in the edge of a grove, splits his trees into rails, fences in a portion of the wide and rich prairie, turns up the virgin soil, which yields a hundred-fold for the seeds which he casts upon it, and pastures his herd upon the vast, unenclosed champaign before his dwelling. . . . The cabin of the settler is the work of his own hands; and he has made the prairie valuable by surrounding it with fences, and breaking up the green sward. The neighborhoods formed by squatters give value to the unclaimed lands around them which they otherwise would not have. . . . It is just that they who founded the colonies from which lands derive their subsequent value should be compensated in some way or other for the hardships and inconveniences they have undergone. If local and temporary pre-emption laws are just in principle, then is also a general pre-emption law. What is right in one case is right in all.[23]

For William Cullen Bryant the mainstay of the American westward movement was the white yeoman farmer of the Atlantic states, strong and courageous, who out of need or for the adventure of it emigrated to the West to take advantage of vast areas of cheap, fertile land. He continually used the editorial page of the *Evening Post* to gain and protect the rights of these settlers.

Like Crevecoeur, William Cullen Bryant wanted to conceive as idyllic the relationship between the farmer and his land. But Bryant had difficulty in reconciling his progressive continental vision, which had industry and commerce following the farmer on the frontier, with his love for the unspoiled landscape. While a reading of Bryant's political writings on the Oregon question, the transcontinental railroad, the Indian Removal Bill, and the issue of squatter's rights, would indicate that he had no reservations about the rush of population westward, his political writings reveal only part of his response. His editorial positions lack the complexity of the dimension added by his poetry, short stories, and letters. Here the westward migration is often viewed not as a smooth blending of civilization and nature. In Bryant's mythic scenario for America's continental expansion, the untainted nature of the West would absorb the Eastern emigrants, stripping them not of the essence of civilization, only of its artificiality and moral corruption. But the problem for Bryant was how to reconcile his acceptance of the gradual perfecting of American civilization through its encounter with natural America with his instinctive love for the unspoiled landscape. Bryant's poems, letter and short stories often equivocate in their attempts to reconcile opposites.

Unlike Fenimore Cooper who, as Leslie Fiedler has written, "had no especial love for the American woods, in particular, or American landscape in general, "[24] and whose forests tend to be static backdrops for mythic dramas, William Cullen Bryant responded to the American landscape sensuously, poetically, religiously, describing it not only with feeling but with the eye of a naturalist. In the western Massachusetts hills of his boyhood, Bryant learned to love the delicate beauty of the first flowers signaling the arrival of spring, and to stand in awe of the immense power exhibited by nature in storms and mountains. As he wrote in "Thanatopsis," nature spoke to him a various language through her visible forms: from a waterfowl wending its way through the evening sky, to a small rivulet prattling happily in the forest—all indicating a design in nature not to appall but to comfort. Yet Bryant was a poet of contradictions. His nature poems generally function as an act of faith in the goodness of nature and nature's God, but it was a faith not without doubts, felt realizations that all grand hopes were illusory. Hyatt Waggoner has written: "The imagistic incoherence that has often been noted in Bryant's poems parallels if it does not relect the incoherence of a vision of a poet who could write, 'The Ages' celebrating Progress, yet propose a return to Nature as a cure for the 'guilt and misery' of which he found the world full."[25] Bryant lauded progress, but was not always comforted by it, and so he longed for a return to nature—yet nature, too, in Bryant's darker moods, offered no solace. In "The Journey of Life" the landscape is more horror show than pastoral retreat, and in "Midsummer," Nature's power exudes not life and hope, but produces a a landscape of desolation, a wasteland.

The tension between man and nature is manifest frequently in Bryant's poetry. In "Green River," he made it a point to have his murmuring stream wind away from the village toward the "quiet valley and shaded glen," as if thus to remain guiltless and clean. His Cascade of Melsingah has a sound "solemn and eternal," but the voices of men are "voices that have no business there." And in "A Winter Piece," civilization suggests of spiritual degradation, nature of revitalization. Calling to mind his earlier country life, Bryant mused in that poem:

> While I stood
> In Nature's loneliness, I was with one
> With whom I early grew familiar, one
> Who never had a frown for me, whose voice
> Never rebuked me for the hours I stole
> From cares I loved not, but of which the world
> Deems highest, to converse with her.

When nature is valued only for her meditative opportunities, she exists primarily for solitary individuals as a means of escape from civilized life. In such moods Bryant's poetry evinces a sharp division between the city and the country.

Essentially William Cullen Bryant knew that civilization, a powerful force, would threaten the continued existence of the natural. His efforts to have a large part of Manhattan Island set aside for a park and refuge from civilization are indicative of his desire to bring the city and the country into harmony. On May 9, 1833 the *Evening Post* told its readers:

> The sole good of a community does not consist in making every inch of ground produce some pecuniary profit—It is better that it should be a few dollars poorer, than that is beauty should be destroyed, the purity of its atmosphere corrupted, and the shades and walks established for the comfort and recreation of both poor and rich, converted into noisy and dirty streets."[26]

While strolling through Jones's Wood on the upper part of Manhattan in 1836, Bryant remarked to his future son-in-law, Parke Godwin, of the need to preserve the wood. "In a few short years," Bryant well knew, "the city will have grown up beyond this, and then it will be too late. "[27] Bryant foresaw the destructive possibilities of progress when he visited Mackinac Island off the shore of northern Michigan in August, 1846. Bryant lamented in a letter back to the *Evening Post,* "I can not but think with a kind of regret on the time which, I suppose is near at hand, when its wild and lonely woods will be intersected with highways, and filled with cottages and boarding-houses."[28] Without nature civilization would have lost something vital. And as New York City did grow and Bryant had to go further and further for his peaceful walks, he increasingly disliked the disorder of town life. In his later years he escaped to the country as often as possible. He wrote in 1874, "I cannot make people understand the good fortune of those who are more than a hundred miles from New York."[29]

Because Bryant's view of nature was more pastoral and picturesque than primitive and wild, and because the pastoral is never as antithetical to man as the primitive, Bryant tried to bring man and nature into a tenuous harmony. He could, therefore, believe in both the need to preserve the beauty of the natural landscape, and in his vision of America as a continental nation, great commercially and industrially. With Bryant it was never all man versus nature, or nature versus man. He longed for a balance with all civilized men living in contact with nature. The spreading of the population across the continent and the building of towns and cities would not, in Bryant's most idealistic statement of the myth of westward expansion, destroy nature, but bring more of civilization in contact with her, making men better. And if his dream was always and only myth, as he at times must have known, it was nevertheless beautiful. In his literary works the sound of an axe felling the virgin forest was both promising and sad, as was westward expansion itself. And Bryant, like his century, acknowledged the sadness, but exulted in the promise.

NOTES

1. William Cullen Bryant II and Thomas G. Voss, eds., *The Letters of William Cullen Bryant,* 2 vols. (New York: Fordham University Press), II, 446.
2. *Letters of Bryant,* II, 445.
3. Letter from Frances Fairchild Bryant to John Bryant, December 15, 1833. Collected in Keith Huntress and Fred W. Lorch, "Bryant and Illi-

nois: Further Letters of the Bryant Family," *The New England Quarterly*, 16 (December, 1943), 639.

4. David J. Baxter, "William Cullen Bryant: Illinois Landowner," *Western Illinois Regional Studies*, 1, No. 1 (Spring, 1978), 1-14.

5. *Letters of Bryant*, II, 59.

6. In one of the few critical estimates of Bryant's attitude toward the West, Edwin Fussell has written that "Bryant poeticized about the West more than anyone else before Whitman. He especially liked to dwell on the Indian (melancholy and departing), and on the pioneer (self-reliant and arriving), setting them against grandiose backdrops of forest and prairie. . . . Like other minor writers of his age, Bryant was rarely able to fuse his facts with his fancies, and seems especially bifurcated on the subject of the West." Edwin Fussell, *Frontier: American Literature and the American West* (Princeton: Princeton University Press, 1965), p. 135n.

7. Ray Allen Billington, *Westward Expansion* (New York: Macmillan and Co., 1949), p. 510.

8. *Westward Expansion*, p. 512.

9. *Register of Debates in Congress* (Washington, D.C.: Gales and Seaton, 1824-25), I, Part 1, 23.

10. William H. Goetzmann, *Exploration and Empire* (New York: Vintage Books, 1966), p. 51.

11. William Cullen Bryant, "Occupation of Oregon," *New-York Review and Atheneum Magazine*, 2 (March, 1826), 175.

12. "Occupation of Oregon," pp. 284-85.

13. *Debates in Congress*, V, 192.

14. *New York Evening Post*, December 16, 1845, p. 2 col. 1.

15. *New York Evening Post,* May 18, 1848, p. 2, col. 1.

16. *New York Evening Post*, November 18, 1846, p. 2, col. 1.

17. *New York Evening Post*, January 4, 1830; January 7, 1830; January 9, 1830; January 19, 1830; February 22, 1830; March 6, 1830; April 30, 1830; and May 28, 1830.

18. *New York Evening Post*, October 29, 1830, p. 2, col. 4.

19. Charles Brown, *William Cullen Bryant: A Biography* (New York: Charles Scribner's Sons, 1971), pp. 115-16.

20. *Letters of Bryant*, I, 111.

21. Brown, p. 7.

22. *Letters of Bryant*, I, 371.

23. *New York Evening Post*, February 3, 1837, p. 2, col. 1.

24. Leslie A. Fiedler, *Love and Death in the American Novel* (New York: Stein and Day, 1975), p. 183.

25. Hyatt H. Waggoner, *American Poets: From the Puritans to the Present Day* (New York: Dell Publishing Co., 1970), p. 42.

26. *New York Evening Post*, May 9, 1833, p. 2, col. 2.

27. Parke Godwin, *Life of William Cullen Bryant*, 2 vols. (New York: D. Appleton and Co., 1883), I, 322.

27. *Letters of Bryant*, II, 467.

28. Letter from William Cullen Bryant to Dr. Orville Dewey, May 29, 1874. In Godwin, *Life of Bryant*, II, 342.

The Prairie and "The Prairies": Cooper's and Bryant's Views of Manifest Destiny

PAUL A. NEWLIN
SUNY at Stony Brook

There is a troubling paradox about the American concept of Manifest Destiny: early on, the land was so huge and so abundant with beauty and resources that settlers with romantic inclinations and ample capital were convinced, almost empirically, that this was indeed the promised land, and that we were the chosen people; failure seemed out of the question—abundance was the way of life. God's will seemed clear enough; but such an idylic situation was short-lived. More and more settlers came acquiring increasing amounts of land and creating less certainty about their destiny. By the middle of the nineteenth century when the term was coined, Manifest Destiny was a good deal less a proclamation of optimism than a cosmetic phrase covering deep-seated doubts. Perhaps the first pessimistic comment on Manifest Destiny to reach print was made during Reconstruction time by the humorist Josh Billings, who observed that Manifest Destiny is "the science uv going tew bust, or enny other place before yew get thare."[1] By the nineteen twenties D. H. Lawrence could cast his sardonic eye back over a century of great American literature and, with the insight afforded by the distance of time and the Atlantic Ocean, ask us: "Can you make a land virgin by killing off its aboriginies?"[2] No one answered Lawrence directly, but shortly past mid-twentieth century, two American poets of nearly the same age stood at the western limits of the American frontier and declared America's destiny now as manifested beyond the limits of its shore: Allen Ginsberg, spokesman for certain disillusioned sons of Walt Whitman, looks eastward from Berkeley and rhetorically asks, "America when will we end the human

war?'' And full well knowing the answer angrily responds in the next
line, ''Go fuck yourself with your atom bomb''[3]; and Louis Simpson,
in language more poetic and closer to the American Dream looks westward from the Golden Gate and cries out:

> Lie back Walt Whitman
> There on the fabulous raft with the King and the Duke!
> . . . . .
> Lie back! We cannot bear
> the stars any more, those infinite spaces.
> . . . . .
> We cannot turn or stay.
> For though we sleep, and let the reins fall slack,
> The great cloud-wagons move
> Outward still, dreaming of a Pacific.[4]

This disillusionment, of course, is by no means confined to the artists mentioned, and though the notion of Manifest Destiny is still deeply ingrained in the American myth, no reasonable person can view it in
contemporary times as more than a romantic illusion at best and at
worst as an insidious deception to legitimize self-doubt. Certainly, the
doubt about Manifest Destiny was felt by William Cullen Bryant and
by a contemporary of Bryant's, James Fenimore Cooper, whose
Leatherstocking Tales provided an international audience with a romantic dream-world of the American frontier. By comparing two
works of Bryant's and Cooper's, which bear similar titles, a clear expression of how Manifest Destiny was dealt with early in our republic's
history can be seen.

Cooper's *The Prairie*, was the third of the Leatherstocking Tales to
be written, but it is the last in the chronology of Leatherstocking's
life—indeed, Leatherstocking, called The Trapper in this tale, dies at
the conclusion of the book. The prairie of Cooper's imagination lies
somewhere in what we today call the plains states, and it is in its description sometimes as incongruous as the image of Somerset
Maugham's demented missionary, Mr. Davidson in *Rain*, who babbles
about the mountains of Nebraska. Nonetheless, Cooper's prairie
serves its author's purpose, and that is to show Manifest Destiny in action at the time of the death of our archetypal American hero, Leatherstocking, a hero whose very existence is antithetical to the concept of
divinely intended expansion westward.

It would be difficult to prove that Cooper and Bryant did not believe in Manifest Destiny, but it can be shown that both men regretted

basic aspects of what was seen as God's intention. *The Pioneers*, Cooper's first Leatherstocking Tale, shows his hero to be driven to lawlessness in his attempts to prevent the white man's expansion from encroaching on those, white-skinned and red, who co-exist in harmony with what is shown as God-given Nature. Cooper is fervent, if not eloquent, in his lament at man's heedless destruction of the forests, and his insatiable blood-lust in blasting flocks of passenger pigeons, now extinct, out of the sky with canon fire; he further castigates man of the settlements for enticing fish at night with torch light and seining scores of them from Lake Glimmerglass, only to have their bodies putrify in great mounds on the shore. Leatherstocking himself is hounded through the forest and is driven from the settlements as a fugitive from progress. Yet through it all, Cooper holds up the "white man's gifts" for honorable destruction of life and limb—both wooden and human—as superior to the skills and instincts of Lawrence's "aborigines," who must be cleared out so the settlements can be purified by aristocratic tastes, virginal blond maidens, chubby-cheeked school children, and hymn-singing gentlemen who only lust after God's approval.

By the time Cooper was ready to do in his hero, in what he then thought was to be the last of his Leatherstocking Tales, Cooper was still searching for a satisfactory way to justify the relentless onslaught of white settlers fulfilling their divine destiny against a magnificent natural landscape and its native inhabitants. The early Puritans had faced the same dilemma and, as Cooper ultimately chose to do, played it both ways: if God ordained that the white man should conquer and settle, then anything that obstructed such a plan must be the work of the devil; thus, calling on ancient simplistic symbols of evil, the Puritans could make the Red Man of the forest into the "Black Man of the forest"—a Devil figure that could be exterminated without compunction—and the forest itself could be destroyed whenever it harbored the Devil Indians or otherwise impeded white man's push for material possession, better known as God's will. For the Puritan white consciousness, the great grandeur of Nature was not as easily obliterated as was the Devil Indian, and the forest which could be identified with evil as a habitat of the Devil, could also be identified with the beauty of God's presence and grace, and as such it was a problem when that beauty had to be destroyed. Cooper's democratic sensibilities are best summed up in the concluding sentence of his "The American Democrat" essay when he says: "He is the purest democrat who best maintains his rights, and no rights can be dearer to a man of cultivation than exemptions from unseasonable invasions on his time by the coarse minded and ignorant.'' [5] This attitude abounds in Cooper's fiction, and it provided him with the way to treat Manifest Destiny and the conflicts such a destiny produced.

In *The Prairie*, Leatherstocking (The Trapper) has moved beyond the furthest fringes of the settlements in order to escape the westward-moving settlers and their laws which restrain his independent relationship with Nature. In one of Cooper's most improbable plots, The Trapper befriends a barbaric figure who epitomizes Cooper's abhorrent ''coarse minded and ignorant''—one Ishmael Bush, a displaced squatter who has fled Kentucky after murdering a process server who had come to evict him from the rightful owner's land. Bush is Cooper's *bête noir*, the fallen outcast of society who can rape the land at the phalanx of progress, so that a cultured God-serving aristocracy can follow the paths of destruction, fulfilling God's will and their destiny by building communities in the eyes of the Lord.

Cooper leaves no doubt as to Bush's role when he gives the reader this initial description of the squatter:

> He was a tall, sunburnt man, past the middle age, of a dull countenance and listless manner. His frame appeared loose and flexible; but it was vast, and in reality of prodigious power. It was only at moments, however, as some slight impediment opposed itself to his loitering progress, that his person, which, in its ordinary gait seemed so lounging and nerveless, displayed any of those energies which lay latent in his system, like the slumbering and unwieldly, but terrible strength of the elephant. The inferior lineaments of his countenance were coarse, extended, and vacant; while the superior, or those nobler parts which are thought to affect the intellectual being, were low, receding, and mean. [6]

Besides Bush, there are his sons and an evil brother-in-law, who match the description Cooper gives the patriarch; and having once described the clan, Cooper in terms to endear him to a modern Freudian critic shows them at their task of revising Nature:

> At length the eldest of the sons stepped heavily forward, and, without any apparent effort, he buried is axe to the eye in the soft body of a cotton-wood tree. He stood a moment regarding the effect of the blow, with that sort of contempt with which a giant might be supposed to contemplate the puny resistance of a dwarf, and then flourishing the implement above his head, with the grace and dexterity with which a master of the art of offence would wield his nobler though less usefull weapon,

he quickly severed the trunk of the tree, bringing its tall top crashing to the earth in submission to his prowess. His companions regarded the operation with indolent curiosity, until they saw the prostrate trunk stretched on the ground, when, as if a signal for a general attack had been given, they advanced in a body to the work; and in a space of time, and with a neatness of execution that would have astonished an ignorant spectator, they stripped a small but suitable spot of its burden of forest, as effectively, and almost as promptly, as if a whirlwind had passed along the place.[7]

The Trapper is disgusted, of course, by what he sees, but he only turns his eyes with a "melancholy gaze" upward toward heaven. Cooper has resolved the dilemma of Manifest Destiny and the destruction of the wilderness, and in case the reader has missed his point, he spells it out in a later chapter:

The march of civilization with us, has a strong analogy to that of all coming events, which are known "to cast their shadows before." The gradations of society, from the state which is called refined to that which approaches as near barbarity as connection with an intelligent people will readily allow, are to be traced from the bosom of the States, where wealth, luxury and the arts are beginning to seat themselves, to those distant and ever-receding borders which mark the skirts and announce the approach of the nation as moving mists precede the signs of day.[8]

Bush and his mob ultimately are replaced on the plains by the Captain Middletons and the Inez de Certavalloses—aristocrats who will refine the paths of Bush's destruction; and The Trapper, the good and faithful servant of God, aristocracy, and the unsullied forest, aged, at peace, and with the corpse of his "Christian" dog Hector at his feet, faces the sunset and dies answering the destined call of the Almighty.

There is little to suggest that Cooper's views in *The Prairie* influenced Bryant's thinking as he composed his poem "The Prairies" in 1833. Bryant, of course, knew and admired Cooper; in 1825 in a review of Catharine Sedgwick's novel *Redwood*, Bryant alluded to Cooper's skill in adapting America's past to the romantic tale,[9] and though he declined a request to review *The Last of the Mohicans* for fear that his praise of the book might be misconstrued as adverse criticism by the hypersensitive Cooper, he did later laud Cooper's narrative powers in *The Prairie* in a review published the *The United States Review and Literary Gazette* in July 1827.[10] Indeed, as Charles Brown has noted in his biography, there were more differences in outlook and character between Bryant and Cooper than similarities: "Bryant was a free-trader, Cooper a protectionist; Bryant was a supporter of the Jacksonian principle of government by the people, Cooper an opponent of such leveling; Bryant was a realist in his approach to economics and politics, Cooper a romantic who still clung to an ideal past."[11] Yet, when in 1839, and after six years of waning popularity, Cooper came under severe attack for his political and social views, especially as expressed in *Home as Found*. Bryant came to his aid in an editorial in the New York *Evening Post* and hailed Cooper as "a fearless accuser of so thin-skinned a nation as ours."[12] Bryant certainly was not blind to Cooper's faults as a writer or a person, yet he was able to place valid criticism into perspective with Cooper's praiseworthy qualities, and because of this fairness in judgment and eloquence in the written word, Bryant was chosen to deliver the eulogy at Cooper's memorial in 1852. Thus, there are many connecting inks as well as basic differences between these two contemporaries, but there is little beyond a general similarity in attitude toward Manifest Destiny to equate the themes of Cooper's novel *The Prairie* with Bryant's poem "The Prairies." As a study of "The Prairies" will show, Bryant's view is more openly idealistic within its romantic poetic tradition, and, paradoxically, more realistic in the psychological reconciliation of the bad with the good in the very essence of Manifest Destiny.

"The Prairies" opens with familiar diction in its depiction of the expanding frontier as the "gardens of the Desert," and in the first thirty-four lines, Bryant skillfully defines an Edenic quality of a land of enormous proportions while developing the metaphor of the sea. Of the prairies he says:

> Lo! they stretch
> In airy undulation, far away,
> As if the Ocean, in his gentlest swell,
> Stood still, with all his rounded billows fixed,
> And motionless forever. Motionless?—
> No—they are all unchained again. The clouds
> Sweep over with their shadows, and, beneath,
> The surface rolls and fluctuates to the eye;
> Dark hollows seem to glide along and chase
> The sunny ridges.
>
> (lines 6-15)

The persona addresses the prevailing winds of the South and asks if they have "fanned/A nobler or a lovelier scene?" The Edenic quality is maintained when the speaker vigorously declares: "Man hath no part in all this glorious work," and goes on to describe the handiwork of God as that of a huge formal garden which serves as the foundation for the "magnificent temple of the sky." At the conclusion of this first long verse paragraph, Bryant introduces the corrupting quality of man in a subtly pejorative way by noting that the great heavens of the prairie-garden

> Seem to stoop down upon the scene in love,—
> A nearer vault, and of a tenderer blue,
> Than that which bends above our Eastern Hills."
> (lines 32–34)

Here is a clear hint of taint—the eastern hills where the settler dwells meets the sky with less intimacy and less love and tenderness than is visible to one viewing the prairies by looking west. It is interesting to note that in his original manuscript Bryant had introduced the corrupting aspect of man as early as the third line; in the final version of the poem, the poet uses the third line to emphasize the native and unique quality of the vista before him by stating "the speech of England has no name" for the prairies—prairie being a French word for meadow adapted to the region by French frontiersmen; but in the original version of the poem, the third line read: "And fresh as the young earth ere man had sinned." Apparently, Bryant felt that introducing the taint of man too early to the Eden he wished to impress upon the reader, would lessen the dramatic quality that man plays in the poem over all, and in this he was correct, because the Edenic quality of the prairies frames the poem and is basic to the regret the artist felt in the inevitable onslaught by the eastern settlers. Thus, the second verse paragraph opens with the speaker no longer a sanitized device of observation, but an active trespasser in the Garden:

> As o'er the verdant waste I guide my steed,
> Among the high rank grass that sweeps his sides
> The hollow beating of his footstep seems
> A sacrilegious sound.
> (lines 35–38)

Here Bryant harkens back to the major motif of "Thanatopsis," where the earth is described as a giant sepulchre; but unlike the earlier poem, man's action upon earth seems to violate the dead, and the speaker speculates on those buried there in terms not of an infinite past but of temporal boundaries limited to man's sense of history.

> Are they here—
> The dead of other days?—and did the dust
> Of these fair solitudes once stir with life
> And burn with passion?
>
> (lines 39–42)

The speaker turns to the burial mounds about him for an answer and develops a speculative case for the "Mound Builders" as being an ancient civilization whose earth works predate the Golden Age of Greece. Bryant cleverly develops a progression of American natives at this starting point, and though the mysterious mounds of earth are primitive and puny beside the Pentelicus, the builders of those mounds are described in terms of such a pastoral appeal as to make them appear as the rightful inhabitants of the Garden before the Fall:

> These ample fields
> Nourished their harvests, here their herds were fed,
> When haply by their stalls the bison lowed,
> And bowed his maned shoulder to the yoke.
> All day this desert murmured with their toils,
> Till twilight blushed, and lovers walked, and wooed
> In a forgotten language, and old tunes,
> From instruments of unremembered form,
> Gave the soft winds a voice.
>
> (lines 50–58)

Alas, Bryant's knowledge of man cannot allow the Mound Builders to live in Eden, and the Red Man, stained by the black brush of the Devil, comes "warlike and fierce" and drives innocent man from the Garden. The pastoral scene gives way to piles of corpses and "brown vultures of the wood . . . unscared and silent at their feast" until one Mound Builder, who, overlooked in the masacre, remains

> Lurking in marsh and forest, til the sense
> Of desolation and of fear became
> Bitterer than death, yield[s] himself to die.
>
> (lines 76–79)

Bryant's dramatic sense of the evolution of American natives will not allow the last Mound Builder to be killed, so he envisions "Man's better nature" triumphing and the Mound Builder being accepted into the red man's tribe; man's evil ways are not easily extirpated, however, and the Mound Builder, though choosing a new bride, is unable to forget

> —the wife
> Of his first love, and her sweet little ones,
> Butchered, amid their shrieks, with all his race.
>   (lines 83–85)

All of this speculation about ancient Americans is set against a scene where the speaker sees only the den of the "prairie-wolf" and the tunneled homes of the gopher; and the third verse-paragraph begins with a summation of man's condition:

> Thus change the forms of being. Thus arise
> Races of living things, glorious in strength,
> And perish, as the quickening breath of God
> Fills them, or is withdrawn.
>   (lines 86–89)

Here the speaker makes no challenge as to the correctness of such a state of affairs, and he documents how the Red Man himself has been pushed far to the west with the beaver and the bison, but at the conclusion of this section of the poem and the beginning of the next a tone of nostalgia and regret is established as the poet makes a transition from the realistic present situation to an interpolated equation with a modern Eden: the speaker notes the movement west of the bison, whom the Mound Builders had domesticated in an earlier fanciful passage of the poem; such a fantasy is not repeated here, but now the bison is seen in the realistic, familiar role of being hunted down, and the tone of the speaker is no longer one of objective commentator, but one who regrets the "majestic brutes'" passing and who is awed by the bison's "ancient footprints [still] stamped beside the pool"; this leads naturally into a vision of the scene as the unspoiled paradise once again.

The final section of the poem opens with a description of the prairies from a close view, as opposed to the great expansive vista described in the poem's opening stanza:

Myraids of insects, gaudy as the flowers
They flutter over, gentle quadrapeds,
And birds, that scarce have learned the fear of man,
Are here, and sliding reptiles of the ground,
Startlingly beautiful.
(lines 104-108)

The speaker then concentrates on the bee, whom he calls "A more adventurous colonist than man,/ With whom he came across the eastern deep." The bee is an excellent creature to center upon, because it not only serves as a metaphor linking the past with the society that is to follow, but it is also appropriate as a familiar and prized insect for the frontiersmen, since its honey served as man's only source of sweets far from the settlements—indeed, one of Cooper's rising middleclassmen in *The Prairie* is Paul Hover, a bee hunter, who epitomizes the best qualities of the genteel common man as opposed to the barbaric dregs of society exemplified by the Bush clan. The speaker in Bryant's poem listens long to the "domestic hum" of the prairie bee, which is transformed into a vision through sound—a vision of "that advancing multitude," as Bryant puts it, "which soon will fill" the prairies:

From the ground
Comes up the laugh of children, the soft voice
Of maidens, and the sweet and solemn hymn
Of Sabbath worshippers. The low of herds
Blends with the rustling of the heavy grain
Over the dark brown burrows. All at once
A fresher wind sweeps by, and breaks my dream,
And I am in the wilderness alone.
(lines 117-124)

The speaker in concluding the poem has come full circle in his observation of the prairies, but in his imaginings and reveries while gazing across "the gardens of the Desert" the whole progression of mankind on the North American contintent has taken place, and the fulfillment of America's Manifest Destiny is completed. As with Cooper, Bryant's view is one of a despoiled Eden, and also as with Cooper the culmination of Manifest Destiny is good, but only in the imaginings of a near-Utopian society. There is, however, a marked difference in the manner in which the destinies are achieved in the two works of these artists. Cooper, in his efforts to lift the burden of destruction of Eden from the shoulders of white European settlers, endorses a romantic view of an ideal past which segregates man into castes and classes: there are the chosen aristocrats—cultured and pious; and then there are the fallen rabble—ignorant and barbaric; and finally, there is an indistinct middle or yeoman class for which Cooper has ambivalent feelings akin to those he expressed for the red man—there are good Indians and bad Indians, but the good Indians (those who have been converted by Moravian missionaries) will never be as good as the best of the white yeoman, and the best of the yeoman will never reach the status of the aristocracy, though Cooper admires their upward strivings. So for Cooper, Manifest Destiny neither began or ended as a democratic enterprise: God is white, and as in the best tradition of Walter Scott, the noble wealthy will inherit the earth—an earth tainted by fallen races and unwashed masses.

If a past which divided men into classes of those "who have" and who dominate those "who have not" and are ignored was seen as ideal by Cooper, no such concept was part of Bryant's backward glance. The mid-western prairies serve as a focal plane for Bryant's muse, and his sense of the past moves from Eden through an evolutionary process of cycles of destruction and savagery which destroy natural beauty and man; but Nature prevails and restores the grandeur of the Garden with but the faintest trace of man's folly. Thus, while Cooper idealized the past in romantic distortion, Bryant viewed it with a more scientific, objective eye, and idealized the future in terms of a democracy. The vision induced by the domestic hum of the bee, which the poet has at the end of "The Prairies" is a marvelous combination of classical pastoral imagery and American Christian wish-fulfillment. What Bryant has done is try to populate the Garden with transplanted Elizabethan milkmaids, elfin children and God-loving happy rustics; all is fecund and pure—it is indeed America the beautiful, America the Democracy. Yet a further ideal still is possible, and that is Eden without man, maid and child. For Bryant no destiny of America can supplant the perceived one-time Eden of the prairie, and God's will, even though it can be idealized as a land of milk, honey, purity and equality, must ultimately be regretted so long as man plays a role.

Massachusetts Bay Colony children learned that the alphabet began with the "A" of Adam's fall from grace—"In Adam's fall, we sinned all"—and the sense of man fouling his own nest has been applied to no country as accurately or as often as it has been to our own. No matter how ideal man can imagine that his condition *might* be, the best of all possible worlds still falls short of Eden's congruity between man and

Nature, and for Cooper—and especially Bryant—the destiny manifested in America forever bears the mark of a curse. Thus Bryant, reveling in the vast beauty of the prairies, could idealize the best of America's potential while regretting the ordained doom of America's frontier:

> All at once
> A fresher wind sweeps by, and breaks my dream,
> And I am in the wilderness alone.

NOTES

1. Daniel J. Boorstin, *The Americans: The National Experience* (New York, 1965), p. 273.
2. D. H. Lawrence, *Studies in Classic American Literature* (New York, 1923), p. 43.
3. Allen Ginsberg, "America," *The Norton Anthology of Modern Poetry* (New York, 1973). p. 1126.
4. Louis Simpson, "In California," *The Norton Anthology of Modern Poetry* (New York, 1973), p. 1047.
5. James Fenimore Cooper, "The American Democrat," *The American Tradition in Literature,* Vol. 1, Bradley, Beatty and Long, eds. (New York, 1967), p. 467.
6. Cooper, *The Prairie* (New York, 1956), p. 4.
7. *Ibid.,* p. 13.
8. *Ibid.,* p. 69.
9. Charles H. Brown, *William Cullen Bryant* (New York, 1971), p. 119.
10. The comment on *The Last of the Mohicans* is contained in a letter to Richard Henry Dana. See Parke Godwin, *Life of William Cullen Bryant,* Vol. 1 (New York, 1883), p. 221.
11. Brown, p. 254.
12. *Ibid.,* p. 255.

Note: The text of "The Prairies" is quoted from *The American Tradition of Literature,* Vol. 1.

William Cullen Bryant and the Newspapers of New York

MICHAEL D'INNOCENZO
Hofstra University

Where does William Cullen Bryant belong on the roster of American newspaper editors? According to John Bigelow, Bryant's partner at the *Post* (who later went on to a successful diplomatic and writing career), William Cullen Bryant deserves to be placed in the extraordinary company of Benjamin Franklin.[1]

Bryant, like Franklin, a transplanted Yankee, has sometimes been depicted as a secular Puritan. One recent history of American newspapers judges Bryant to have been "offensively moral."[2] Like Franklin, Bryant was an active publicist for the general good of society during the span of his long lifetime (both men died near their 84th birthdays; both had been journalists for more than fifty years). Beyond their records of unusual staying power, Franklin and Bryant were among the early editors in American society to lend luster and distinction to the profession of journalism.

It is not necessary to push Bigelow's analogy of Bryant and Franklin too far. It may be that we have never had the equal of a Franklin; indeed, few individuals would look good when measured against the man Carl Van Doren described as a "harmonious human multitude."[3] Nonetheless, those who have studied Bryant's career are also impressed by the multifaceted dimensions of his life.

Despite Franklin's early model as a great editor, a career in journalism was not highly esteemed when Bryant began working for *The Evening Post* in 1826. Poetry and literature were his decided preferences, but these were impractical options in those days for a thirty-year-old man with a wife and children, a man who had already given up the practice of law because he found it dispiriting. Whatever the limitations in his new journalism career, Bryant expressed relief in a letter to his wife, Frances, that he was no longer "plagued with the disagreeable, disgusting drudgery of the law," and that he was freed from its "miserable feuds and wranglings."[4]

For awhile Bryant tried to control his journalistic labors so that he would be free to devote as much time as possible to his artistic endeavors. This strategy proved to be ineffective; newspaper tasks and deadlines were always there. They consumed more of Bryant's time and energy than he wished to give them.

When Richard Henry Dana warned Bryant about being drawn into the "vile blackguard squabble" of politics, Bryant responded: "I do not like politics any better than you do; but they get only my mornings, and you know politics and a bellyful are better than poetry and starvation."[5] Because Bryant borrowed money to become a part owner of the *Post*, as well as its editor, his financial well-being was tied to the success of the newspaper. Dana commented in 1829: "If Bryant must write in a paper to get his bread, I pray God he may get a bellyful."[6] Bryant's effective leadership helped to make the *Post* one of the most prosperous newspapers in America.[7] So successful was Bryant in journalism, that he left the paper in the hands of William Leggett, his assistant, and went to Europe in 1834. He did not return to New York for a year and a half (this was the first of several extended absences from the *Post*). Back in the city in 1836, Bryant wrote to his brother John: "It was not my intention when I went to Europe to return to the business of conducting a newspaper."[8] Bryant expressed displeasure about the New York to which he returned and about the direction of his own life. "The entire thoughts of the inhabitants [of New York] seem to be given to the acquisition of wealth; nothing else is talked of."[9] (This was about the same time when Washington Irving was speaking of Americans' "pursuit to the almighty dollar," and when Tocqueville queried: "Why is it Americans are so restless in the midst of their prosperity?").[10] Bryant further observed: "The city is dirtier and noiser, and more uncomfortable, and dearer to live in than it ever was before. I have had my fill of a town life, and begin to wish to pass a little time in the country. I have been employed long enough with the management of a daily newspaper, and desire leisure for literary occupations that I love better."[11]

At this time, Bryant even considered moving to Illinois, or farther West. He seemed to need a change of life. He was forty-two years old. One wonders if the psychological perspectives on male mid-life crisis are applicable to Bryant's America.[12] It is an interesting coincidence that Benjamin Franklin also announced his retirement from the newspaper business when he was forty-two years old. Franklin wrote to his mother to explain his decision, noting that he would rather have people say of him: he lived usefully than he died rich.

Bryant did not go West in 1836 or in the succeeding year when he still considered a move. He remained, however, a reluctant journalist for some time. He lamented to his brother John: "I am chained to the oar."[13] To his friend Dana, he complained: "Here I am a draught-horse, harnessed to a daily drag. . . . I am too much exhausted to use my wings."[14] On another occasion, he wrote to Dana, "I hope . . . the day will come when I may retire without danger of starving and give myself to occupations that I like better."[15]

Whittier was among the many men of letters who frequently urged Bryant to stop writing his "daily twaddle" on politics and turn his creative energy to poetry.[16] A writer for the *New England Magazine* expressed sorrow that Bryant who was "capable of writing poetry to make so many hearts throb, and so many eyes glisten with delight" should exhaust himself in labors that were inimical to the spirit of a poet.[17] To his friends, Bryant explained: "I have no leisure for poetry."[18]

Bryant applied his considerable skills to restoring the economic well-being of the *Post,* which had declined while he was in Europe.[19] Within a few years, Bryant made great progress in his personal fortune, in leisure time and in gaining a sense of well-being. On July 4, 1836, Bryant wrote to his wife Frances boasting of his capacity to work long hours, but entreating, "I only want you and the children back to be as contented as I can be while harnessed to the wain of a daily paper."[20] Bigelow observes that with Bryant's purchase of Cedarmere (his Roslyn, Long Island estate), "life bloomed with new charms . . . and the toils of his profession were at last 'sweetened to his taste.'"[21] After 1838, when Bryant found able assistants to release him from "the drudgery,"[22] his job complaints became less frequent and less intense. Indeed, it is striking to note how seldom his correspondence includes any references to, or evaluations of his newspaper work.

It is interesting to speculate about the forks in the road not taken as Bryant's financial situation became secure and as his options increased. It seems that he could have devoted more time to poetry. He could have been more creative as a newspaper editor. Despite all of Bryant's achievements, Allan Nevins offers the provocative suggestion that perhaps Bryant was temperamentally not inclined to pursue any profession or enterprise vertically, especially if this meant an exclusion, or even a dimunition, of the horizontal range of life's pleasures, varieties and satisfactions.[23]

Bryant used more of his leisure for gardening, enjoyment of nature, for travel (which he dearly loved) and for public, do-good literary and cultural associations. Bryant may have become so thoroughly engrossed in living a stimulating life that his priority was to do things rather than to write about them.

During the time Bryant was working out his own future directions, American newspapers were undergoing radical changes; scholars even describe this period as representing a newspaper revolution.[24] As so often was, and is, the case, New York City was the center for dramatic, novel developments.

One of the striking things about Bryant was that he was at the helm of the *Post* before the journalistic rush to sensationalism; he was an established editor before James Gordon Bennett founded the *Herald,* before Greeley started the *Tribune,* and well in advance of Raymond's launching of *The New York Times* in 1851. It is also noteworthy that Bryant outlasted all of his famous contemporary editors. But Bryant was much more than a survivor. The causes he embraced, the way he used his newspaper, the responses of his contemporaries to him—all reveal a great deal about the man, his profession, and his significance.

There were nearly a thousand newspapers in America when Bryant became editor of the *Post*. There were fewer than 400 in Britain. More newspapers were printed in New York State than in all of Russia.[25] That perspicacious Frenchman, Tocqueville, observed in the 1830s that in America "nothing is easier than to set up a newspaper, as a small number of subscribers suffices to defray the expense."[26] Seventy-five to eighty percent of most papers consisted of advertisements. Most of the news was produced with scissors and paste as items were taken from other European and American journals. Partisan editorials constituted the small amount of original writing. It is not surprising that, as late as 1842, Bryant had an editorial staff of only three to assist him.[27]

When Bryant became editor of the *Post,* its circulation was approximately 1,700; the nation's largest paper, the *New York City Courier and Inquirer,* was only slightly over 4,000.[28] Papers were relatively easy to start because of the advertising and political patronage available, because of relatively low operating and manpower costs, because of government printing contracts, the benefits derived from free newspaper mail exhanges (some journals were said to receive more exchanges than they had subscribers[29]), and because newspapers were charged low postage rates when sold through the mails. (The charges were actually below the costs of transportation; thus, in effect, the government was subsidizing the press—a practice which had been encouraged by Franklin.)[30]

There were nine daily newspapers in New York City in the early 1830s; despite all the aforecited benefits, few did well financially—most had short lives. One commentator has noted: "Editors seemed to have taken to journalism as they took to their wives, for richer or poorer, but there was usually more excitement in a newspaper office than in the average marriage."[31]

During the presidency of Andrew Jackson—the so-called "Age of the Common Man"—American journalism changed dramatically. There were early signs of what was to come; some papers raced their own newsboats in order to be the first to meet incoming transatlantic ships before they reached shore. The New York City *Journal of Commerce* sought to "scoop" its competitors by getting news from Washington to New York City in the breathtaking speed of twenty hours. The *Journal* hired a special relay team of twenty-four express riders to cut sixteen hours off the normal thirty-six hour journey.[32]

But the greatest changes of all came while Bryant was in Europe on his year and a half vacation. With five hundred dollars and sixteen years of journalistic experience, James Gordon Bennett launched the *New York Herald* in 1835. This new journal was partly modeled on twenty-three year old Benjamin Day's *New York Sun,* America's first penny paper issued in 1833. But Bennett did more than any other individual to foster "the new journalism" of the 19th century.[33] He boasted that his twenty-hour work days were worth such extensive commitment because "a newspaper can send more souls to Heaven, and save more from Hell, than all the churches and chapels in New York—besides making money at the same time."[34]

Prior to 1835, most American papers, including Bryant's *Post* were essentially "special audience papers"—commercial sheets, rather expensive at six cents a copy, and aimed at mercantile readers. The new penny press of Day, and, more significantly, of Bennett, sought news that was "readable, sensational or shocking."[35] Bennett showed that this criteria could be applied to business and political news, as well as crime, adventure, tragedy, suffering, and humorous anecdotes used by Day. Within a year, Bennett's *Herald* reached a circulation of 15,000.[36]

Bennett's editorial audacity, his impudence, mockery, vulgarity and extreme sensationalism prompted people to accuse him of "moral leprosy."[37] He was denounced from pulpits of New York churches. Bennett described himself as "The Napoleon of the American Press," and announced that a newspaper's function "is not to instruct, but to startle." Not surprisingly, Bennett and the *Herald* were sharply attacked; one particularly hostile critic asserted that prostitutes regarded the *Herald* as "their special organ." Another noted that a "gentleman would as soon choose a wife in a brothel as marry a woman who read the Herald."[38]

Bennett so provoked people that he was physically attacked in public on several occasions. In each instance, he gave a full report to his readers of the beatings and how he felt about them.[39] But, no matter how much Bennett was personally despised, his paper soon had the greatest circulation of any daily in the world. Allan Nevins observes that men may have concealed the *Herald* when they saw a friend approaching, "but they bought it and they examined every column."[40]

In the 1850s New York's leading dailies were penny papers—the *Times, Tribune, Sun* and *Herald.* Bryant's *Post* was the only six cent paper with a significant influence, and its circulation was only twenty percent of the *Herald's* 60,000.[41] Before 1860, some of the penny papers raised their prices to two or three cents. Some represented marked improvements over the sensationalism in the *Herald.* Because cheap newspapers reached large numbers of people, editors became less dependent on advertisers. The result was more space devoted to news, and more independent views, since alienation of business groups was not so monumental a concern. Strikingly, the more popular, less expensive dailies were soon outdoing the mercantile press even in their effectiveness of business news coverage.

As the face and body of American journalism was being remade, William Cullen Bryant's *Post* changed too, but with less flamboyancy and more selectivity. Bryant maintained the price of his paper at six cents, and he continued a four page format until his death. The fact that he used a small staff, compared to other leading journals, that he opposed Sunday editions, that he relied on the Associated Press during the Civil War and had fewer correspondents than his competitors may suggest that Bryant had a limited recognition of the increasing significance of news gathering in his day. These and other efforts to keep the *Post* small and manageable may also be signs of Bryant's desire to keep his work and his staff under control.

Bryant did not join six other city dailies in 1848 when they established the New York Associated Press in order to share the costs and reception of news over an exclusive telegraph wire. But Bryant soon had a special column devoted to telegraphic news. With America's rapid westward expansion, one editor "insisted that NEWS was an acronym for the directions from which information came—north, east, west, and south."[42] Bryant moved more deliberately than other editors, but, over time, he establisheed one of the best networks of correspondents throughout America and Europe. (Gideon Welles, Samuel Tilden, Salmon P. Chase and Charles Francis Adams were among his notable contributors.)[43] The *Post* probably gave more space to travel reports than any other American newspaper. Bryant, like Franklin, may well have been the most cosmopolitan of American editors, both in terms of his knowledge of other cultures and with regard to the number and extent of his travels abroad.[44]

Visitors from Europe often described American newspapers as "depraved," but the *Post* was marked apart as an exception. Bryant's journal was admired for its "fairness of argument,"[45] for placing editorial independence above partisan political considerations, and for the excellence and literary quality of its writing. The idea of two poets as editors of the *Post* prompted one journalist to describe Bryant and Leggett as "the chanting cherubs."[46]

Bryant was especially proud of his newspaper's independence; the editor's integrity became his hallmark. Bryant even made it a point to avoid socializing with men about whom he might have to offer editorial comment. When a rival journal taunted the *Post* for not receiving political patronage as a reward for its views, Bryant made a rare response to another editor, emphasizing that his paper "is not a mere party hack—it is not a pipe for politicians' fingers to sound what stops they please."[47] Bryant boasted in 1834 that the *Post,* unlike other newspapers, made no inquiry into the political affiliations of its thirty employees.[48]

William Cullen Bryant took increasingly vigorous stands against the expansion of slavery. And, although Bryant seems always to have been "anti-slavery," he was not an abolitionist. The implications in this distinction warrant greater scrutiny than they have received in Bryant scholarship. We also need more probing assessments of Bryant's views on the place of blacks in American society during and after the Civil War. Without question, Bryant became one of the strongest foes of slavery, but, thus far, scholarship offers little perspective on how his views of free blacks compared with those of other leading editors.[49]

Bryant's views on the unfolding crises during the Civil War decades show him to be an editor who forthrightly and unflinchingly took strong and advanced postions. He deplored the "disgraceful barbarities" of anti-Catholic rioters who were forerunners of the Know-Nothing movement.[50] He consistently supported equal rights for minority ethnic and religious groups.

As an opponent of the annexation of Texas, Bryant drifted away from the Democratic party despite his deep concerns about such a move. On February 7, 1848, he wrote to his brother John that a separate party to oppose slavery "would come to nothing. All parties formed for a single measure, are necessarily short-lived and are as much subject to the abuses and vices of party as any other . . . I never mean to belong to any of them, unless I see some very strong and compelling reason for it." In one of his rare, self-reflective views on his role as a newspaperman, Bryant concluded that "the journalist who goes into one of these narrow associations gains by it no increase of independence in discussion, while he parts with the greater part of his influence."[51]

The political issues were indeed so compelling, however, that Bryant backed Van Buren and the Free Soil Party in the 1848 election.[52] After three decades as a Jackson Democrat this was a painful decision. The Kansas-Nabraska bill of 1854 drove Bryant from his old party permanently and prompted him to take an active role in shaping the new Republican organization. He was critical of Roger Taney's Dred Scott decision,[53] and he was an early and persistent supporter of Lincoln,[54] although he never hesitated in criticizing the president when he believed such an approach was warranted.

During the Civil War Bryant was among the first editors to advocate freeing the slaves. His concern about the welfare of blacks prompted him to become a founder of the National Freedman's Relief Association in 1863.[55]

Very little evaluation has been offered on Bryant and the *Post's* responses to the emerging women's rights movement in mid-19th century America.[56] Bryant's support of laborers and their organizations is an important topic that deserves more attention than it has received so far.[57] We could also be better informed about the posture of the *Post* during the heyday of Boss Tweed in New York City.[58] In short, there is still room for Bryant scholarship. Another very provocative area for further scrutiny is Bryant's associations with a succession of young, reform-minded assistants (most notably William Leggett, Parke Godwin, and John Bigelow). Bryant valued these scholarly, competent aides because they made it easier for him to travel for a year or more at a time. But one wonders about the extent to which the young men influenced the older man's views.

Although the circulation of the *Post* did not come close to that of many other dailies, Bryant earned distinction in other respects. His emphasis on American culture marked the *Post* apart from most journals. Bryant's newspaper gave more attention to book and theatre reviews, and Bryant was especially active in supporting American artists and defending their work against British critics.[59] There was, however, an on going power struggle at the *Post* about whether the paper had too many advertisements and too little reading.

Bryant believed that Garrison and other abolitionists were as "wild as the winds," but he nobly defended free speech and press and use of the mails for "all political questions," including "unpopular opinions."[60] No editor surpassed Bryant in his defensc of civil liberties; he railed against Congress and its use of the "gag rule" to stifle abolitionist petitions.[61]

Beginning in 1845, Bryant published a daily column with the heading "City Intelligence." Increasingly, he focused attention on reform projects needed in New York City. Bryant was one of the pioneer and strongest advocates of a planned city park system before all of Manhattan's land was overrun. His efforts began during a visit to London in 1845; he was greatly impressed by Hyde Park, St. James, Kensington Gardens and Regent's Park. When he returned to New York, he hammered away at the issue and helped the make Central Park a reality in the 1850s. Parks, Bryant wrote, were " the lungs" of the city.[62]

Bryant persistently called for a uniformed police department, professional rather than volunteer firemen, and a more effective sanitation department. In these, and other matters, he often drew upon his travel experiences to measure New York City by the highest standards he observed elsewhere.[63]

The judgment offered of William Cullen Bryant in 1922 by Allan Nevins has, I believe, continued to stand the test of time and scholarship. "No American editor of importance . . . made use of the editorial page [as Bryant did]. He had a love of freedom, a sense of justice, and a shrewd judgment of men and affairs. . . ."[64]

In the final analysis, it may be that Bryant's life was his major contribution to American culture—even more than his poetry or his newspaper editing. Mark Hopkins once observed that William Cullen Bryant had "the wisdom of age in his youth, and the fire of youth in his age."[65] Like Benjamin Franklin, Bryant may have most succeeded in getting so much zest from a life that was vitally active for over eighty years.

NOTES

1. John Bigelow, *William Cullen Bryant* (Boston and New York: Houghton Mifflin and Co., 1890), p. 70.
2. John W. Tebbel, *The Compact History of the American Newspaper* (New York: Hawthorn Books, 1969), p. 117.
3. Carl Van Doren, *Benjamin Franklin* (New York: The Viking Press, 1938), p. 782.
4. Charles H. Brown, *William Cullen Bryant* (New York: Charles Scribner's Sons, 1971), pp. 134, 99, 121-2, 156.
5. Parke Godwin, *A Biography of William Cullen Bryant* (New York: Russell & Russell, 1883), I, 235.
6. Allan Nevins, *The Evening Post* (New York: Russell & Russell, 1922, 1968), p. 121.
7. Brown, *Bryant,* pp. 185, 258, 301.
8. Bigelow, *Bryant,* p. 87.
9. *The Letters of William Cullen Bryant,* ed. by William Cullen Bryant II and Thomas Voss (New York: Fordham Univ. Press, 1977), II, 59.
10. Alexis de Tocqueville, *Democracy in America,* ed. by Andrew Hacker (New York: Washington Square Press, 1964), pp. 205-8.
11. Godwin, *Biography of Bryant,* I, 322.
12. Daniel J. Levinson, *The Seasons of a Man's Life* (New York: Alfred A. Knopf, 1978) argues that male mid-life crises are universal experiences in history.
13. Bigelow, *Bryant,* p. 88.
14. *Letters of Bryant,* II, 64.
15. *Ibid.,* II, 27.
16. Brown, *Bryant,* p. 191.
17. Nevins, *Evening Post,* p. 137.
18. *Letters of Bryant,* II, 97.
19. Sidney Kobre, *Development of American Journalism* (Dubuque, Iowa: W. C. Brown, Co., 1969), p. 270.
20. *Letters of Bryant,* II, 37.
21. Bigelow, *Bryant,* p. 94.
22. *Letters of Bryant,* II, 24, 519.
23. Allan Nevins, "William Cullen Bryant," *Dictionary of American Biography,* ed. by Allen Johnson and Dumas Malone (New York: Charles Scribner's Sons, 1929, 1930), II, Part I, 204.
24. See James L. Crouthamel, "The Newspaper Revolution in New York, 1830-1860, *"New York History,* XLV, 95 (April, 1964) and Robert A. Rutland, *The Newsmongers* (New York: Dial Press 1973), pp. 140-2.
25. Rutland, *Newsmongers,* pp. 124-5.

26. As quoted in Crouthamel, "Newspaper Revolution," p. 93.
27. Nevins, *Evening Post,* pp. 179-181.
28. Rutland, *Newsmongers,* p. 116.
29. *Ibid.,* p. 114.
30. Crouthamel, "Newspaper Revolution," p. 93.
31. Rutland, *Newsmongers,* p. 123.
32. *Ibid.,* p. 124.
33. Nevins, *Evening Post,* p. 157.
34. as quoted by Rutland, *Newsmongers,* p. 142.
35. Crouthamel, "Newspaper Revolution," p. 95
36. Rutland, *Newsmongers,* p. 6.
37. *Ibid.,* p. 142.
38. John J. Turner, Jr. and Michael D'Innocenzo, "The President and the Press: Lincoln, James Gordon Bennett and the Election of 1864," *Lincoln Herald* volume no. (Summer, 1974), p. 64.
39. Robert A. Rutland, *Newsmongers,* pp. 162, 165, notes the "bellicose propensity of many editors," their duels and canings as well as fist fights. In 1853, the *Tribune* reported with satisfaction that Bennett " 'the low-mouthed, blatant, witless, brutal [*Herald* editor] had been horsewhipped nine times and suffered the indignity of having his jaws forced open and his throat spit into."
40. Nevins, *Evening Post,* p. 162.
41. Crouthamel, "Newspaper Revolution," p. 103, and Kobre, *Development of American Journalism,* p. 271.
42. Rutland, *Newsmongers,* p. 166.
43. *Letters of Bryant,* II, 514-5.
44. Robert W. Jones, *Journalism in the United States* (New York: E. P. Dutton & Co., 1947), p. 676.
45. Brown, *Bryant,* p. 248.
46. Jones, *Journalism,* pp. 564-5. and Frank L. Mott, *American Journalism* (New York: The Macmillan Co., 1941), p. 258.
47. Brown, *Bryant,* p.212.
48. *Ibid.,* pp. 220-1.
49. See John J. Turner, Jr. and Michael D'Innocenzo, "The Place of Blacks in American Society," *Pan-African Journal* (Winter, 1972), pp. 429-445.
50. *Letters of Bryant,* II, 191.
51. *Ibid.,* pp. 516-7.
52. *Ibid.,* p. 514.
53. Brown, *Bryant,* p. 389.
54. *Ibid.,* pp. 409-10.
55. *Ibid.,* p. 459.
56. See *Evening Post,* August 12, 1848, September 6, 1848, October 10, 1848, August 23, 1848, and March 27, 1852.
57. Dr. Abraham Blinderman's unpublished address, "William Cullen Bryant and the Workingman," delivered at the Bryant Centennial Conference at Hofstra University in 1978, represents a sound beginning on this topic.
58. Silas Bent, *Newspaper Crusaders: A Neglected Story* (Freeport, N.Y.: Books for Libraries Press, 1969), p. 157.

59. *The Evening Post,* November 13, 1848, July 31, 1849; and see Brown, *Bryant,* pp. 212, 413.
60. *Ibid.,* pp. 249, 264.
61. Nevins, *Evening Post,* p. 171.
62. *The Evening Post,* July 3, 1844; Kobre, *Development of American Journalism,* p. 270; Nevins, *Evening Post,* pp. 193, 196; Brown, *Bryant,* pp. 307–8.
63. Nevins, *Evening Post,* pp. 203–5.
64. *Ibid.,* p. 134; also Kobre, *Development of American Journalism,* p. 119.
65. Quoted by Diane Tarleton Bennett and Linda Tarleton, *W. C. Bryant in Roslyn* (Roslyn, New York: The Bryant Library, 1978), Author's Preface.

Bryant and Dana:
The Anatomy of a Friendship

BERNARD WEINSTEIN
Kean College of New Jersey

The friendship between William Cullen Bryant and Richard Henry Dana, Sr. arched across fifty-seven years of American history that included the Jacksonian era, the Civil War and the democratization of arts and letters. It bound together two contemporaries, largely through written correspondence, whose differences were as great as their similarities and whose origins, manners, and attitudes frequently seemed to represent a polar opposition in the national life of their time. This extraordinarily durable relationship has not been examined for itself; Bryant's friendship with Dana is assessed here from the standpoint of their personal, social, and literary interests and values.

The friendship was anchored in literature, for each man contributed a remarkable measure of talent, devotion, and energy to poetry, although in later years Dana was largely Bryant's chief critic, extoller, and literary prodder. It was Dana to whom Bryant turned in countless letters, charting his poetic progress and soliciting Dana's counsel and criticism. It was Dana's work which Bryant, in his turn, tried to coax into print. Dana's own literary output was slim, and today he goes almost unrecognized but for the illustriousness his son, the author of *Two Years Before the Mast,* has brought to his name—this despite the overall importance of the Dana family to the history of Massachusetts. Besides the periodical called *The Idle Man* (1821–1822), the miscellaneous work done for the *North American Review,* and pieces appearing in a few periodical publications edited by Bryant, Dana, Sr. published only two original American volumes in his lifetime.[1] In contrast to Bryant's poetical career, which came to almost the Biblical three score and ten, Dana's creative career had ended by the time he had reached his early forties.

Although by no means garrulous or extroverted, Bryant remained to the end of his life renowned and popular, the recipient of countless poetic, journalistic, and civic honors. Dana, on the other hand, lived a largely reclusive life. His contemporary, Charles Francis Adams, an inhabitant of the same city as Dana, claimed that, over the span of fifty years, he had seen Dana only five times.[2] Several citations from Dana, Jr. in his *Journal* support the notion of his father as a highly-strung, sickly man for whom vitality was rare and whose moments of happiness in later years centered around family reunions.[3]

The backgrounds of Bryant and Dana were marked by strong contrasts. The gulf between them is evidenced by the entry of Dana, Jr. in the *Journal* of February 25, 1844, following a dinner Bryant, then fifty and the most respected journalist in New York, had hosted for Dana, Jr. at his home. Bryant, four years earlier, had launched young Dana as a celebrity by negotiating for the publication of *Two Years Before the Mast.* In a different context the entry would have implied ingratitude:

> B. is to my mind a standing illustration of the truth that in the intercourse of the world good feelings, good principles and intellectual cultivation are not enough to make good manners. . . . B. has good feelings, good principles and a beautiful mind but I was never in company with him . . . when I have not been made to feel unpleasantly and to wish that he had been taught the artificial, the insincere, if you choose, habits of a gentleman. (*J*, I, 234)

Dana, however, when he wrote this, accepted fully and complacently a social doctrine of natural selection and saw himself as an heir to America's aristocracy, thus endowing the observation with an entirely innocent candor.

Dana, Sr. was born in Cambridge in 1787 into a family that had been among the richest and most prominent in Massachusetts from colonial times. His maternal grandfather, William Ellery, had signed the Declaration of Independence, and his father, Francis Dana, was Chief Justice of Massachusetts. To have been born a Dana at the end of the eighteenth century was to be placed at the hub of power among the princes of the new republic who exercised authority with noblesse oblige and repudiated labor for gain. Gradually as Jacksonian democracy became a *real politik* of the nineteenth century, the power of the Danas, Adamses, Ticknors, and the rest became more symbolic than real, and gradually even Dana, Jr., who had regarded "the artificial habits of a gentleman" as a necessary concomitant to "good feelings, good principles and a beautiful mind," would join the Free Soilers and defend escaped slaves against the Fugitive Slave Law. Still the Danas lived out the dream of a republican aristocracy dominated by leisure and cultivation, identifying themselves with England and with religious Trinitarianism, in opposition to Unitarianism, and separating themselves from the foul and noisy crowd. For Richard, Sr., who had gone to Harvard, practiced law, and represented Cambridge in the legislature, public affairs held little attraction, though oddly enough, the law intrigued him, and, while he said he practiced to keep the family chain of tradition whole, he admitted also to being interested in it as a conductor of the imagination: "Does not the imaginative mind draw more facts which have . . . qualities convertible into poetry, when it reaches through a dry, unimaginative medium than when they are presented to it by some imaginative power in some imaginative form? In the former case the imaginative mind is active and creative, in the latter, more of a mere passive recipient."[4] For Dana, though, everything ultimately led to literature. In 1815 he helped to found the *North American Review* and became, despite the repudiation by his class of the professional writer, one of the first professional men of letters in New England. Breaking with family tradition, he married for love alone an impecunious, sickly schoolteacher, Ruth Charlotte Smith, who died in 1822, and he spent the rest of his life in desultory financial circumstances, forever attempting to untangle his and his family's financial knots and living amid dreams of the past and apprehensions about his own time.[5] Van Wyck Brooks described this cousin of the Channings and brother-in-law of the poet and painter Washington Allston as an old man, "strolling through the Boston streets, a forgotten ghost, or basking in the sunshine of his Cape Ann garden, his silvery curls reaching to his shoulders . . . speaking of the British essayists of old and the charms that lingered around their memory. . . ."[6] If Brooks's portrait seems a picture *in extremis* of the dissociation of the past from the present, Dana's own lines from his essay "The Past and the Present" confirms his estrangement from the contemporary bustle and buoyancy:

What a spirit is there in that world old. Who would live in a world where there was nothing old? Experience would not, could not, nor sedateness, nor reflection, slow and thoughtful. Fancy might perhaps; but not imagination, that deeper part of the soul. And could the heart let go all its old attachments, and yet live?

(*PPW*, II, 15)

Dana's life and thought seemed by its example to negate the notions of democratic progress and the cosmic optimism of nineteenth-century America.

In contrast, Bryant's life affirmed the spirit of the age, that of a society open to individual talents and energy. He was descended from generations of farmers and lower ranking professionals, far removed from the stately Danas. His father, Peter Bryant, was a country doctor, who practiced in Cummington, Massachusetts. Peter Bryant's love of music and the classics, his wife's veneration of rhetoric and morality, the natural beauty of Cummington with its rolling hills, and Cullen's own precocity were factors in arousing his poetic interests, but primarily he was encouraged in his fledgling work by his father, who confidently spurred him on. He produced at fourteen a five-hundred line satire of President Jefferson called "The Embargo," which his father had published and which delighted the Federalists, fearful of another war with England. In his youthful political sentiments, Bryant unwittingly supported notions which Dana and his class espoused, although by the time Bryant and Dana met, little of this mutuality of anti-Jeffersonianism was evident on Bryant's part. Unlike Dana, Bryant nourished a clear dislike of the contentiousness, injustice and pettiness of the law, which he studied and was to tolerate until 1825, but he had the good fortune to find in poetry both congeniality with his temperament and the recognition of his posterity, the second of which Dana did not enjoy. Bryant entered journalism in 1826 to fulfill a temporary service to William Coleman, *Evening Post* editor, and was in the long run so successful that journalism remained his vocation for the next half-century, guaranteeing him financial security. To a great extent Bryant represented the rising aspirations of an energetic, enlightened middle class, while Dana represented the fading dream of a debilitated American nobility.

What drew these two men together? Peter Bryant contributed the opening thrust by submitting "Thanatopsis" to the *North American Review,* which his friend Willard Phillips, along with Dana and Edward Channing, edited. Dana, in typically Anglophilic fashion, dismissed it as something "never written on this side of the water . . . considering what American poetry has been up to that moment." Phillips, thinking that Dr. Bryant had written it, sent Dana to the State House in Boston, where the alleged poet was serving as Senator from Hampshire County. Dana found Peter Bryant to "have a good head . . . but I do not see 'Thanatopsis' in it.'"[7] Four months later Cullen submitted two other poems to the *North American Review,* one of which was "To a Waterfowl," and, following that, a critical essay on American poetry. The standards of verse were now so high that the editors discontinued the poetry department "because they could not hope for equally good verse from other writers. . . ."[8] Direct correspondence between Bryant and Dana began in June 1821, after Bryant had submitted some poems to Dana's fledgling periodical *The Idle Man.* Of one, "Green River," Dana wrote that, with the exception of "To a Waterfowl," "it is beyond anything I have ever read of American poetry" (*L,* I, 107). In August 1821, Bryant was invited to read the Phi Beta Kappa poem at Harvard, the occasion for which he wrote "The Ages." It was here that he met for the first time Dana, Channing, and others connected with the *North American Review,* and here that they insisted he not leave Boston until he had published "The Ages" and anything else poetical he had written. The result was a pamphlet, published in September, that contained, in addition to a revised version of "Thanatopsis," three of his finest lyrics: "Green River," "To A Waterfowl," and "The Yellow Violet." Dana's enthusiasm for Bryant's verse was reflected in a joyous opening to a letter on September 8: "I send you a copy of your poems as a glass for you to look into and see how handsome you are in print" (G, I, 176). He undoubtedly felt that he had discovered an American romantic poet who was the poetical and spiritual heir to Wordsworth.[9] Thus began an era of deep friendship and reciprocal support.

2.

Besides the literary aspect, which is the subject of the last part of this essay, a deeply personal aspect becomes almost immediately discernible. Dana was the only person outside Bryant's immediate family with whom he corresponded so intimately. When they began writing to each other he had only recently overcome the loss of his father, who had been from Bryant's childhood his chief mentor, advocate, and confidant. In his earliest correspondence with Dana, Bryant found someone a few years his senior who was willingly, even enthusiastically, encouraging him to persevere in his poetry and directing his progress. For Dana's part, he had lost his wife in February 1822 and was in search of solace and abiding friendship. In a letter of July 20, 1821, Bryant, an enthusiast for physical fitness, said, "I hope you will get the better of your invisible enemies . . . the nerves. Let me be your physician. I recommend then the air of the fields and exercise in the garden" (*L*, I, 126). Of the two, Bryant almost invariably appeared the more outgoing and vigorous in their correspondence, because he was far more involved than Dana in activities and events of his time, had more outlets for his energies, and, for all his reserve and admitted lack of social ease, was on better terms with the nineteenth-century world.

Dana provided Bryant with an outlet to express his youthful vexations regarding money and vocation. Separated from the law in 1825, Bryant felt little more at ease working on the *New York Review* and *Atheneum Magazine*. "This business of sitting in judgment on books as they come out is not the literary employment the most to my taste nor that for which I am best fitted . . . ," he wrote complainingly to Dana on May 25, 1825 (*L*, I, 125). Doubtless, he feared and disliked, as Dana did, the responsibility of reviewing publicly another's work. He remarked, for example, that Fenimore Cooper was an individual "too sensitive . . . for me to touch."[10] But he found that reviewing was something to which he could adapt himself, however unpleasant and difficult the process seemed to him at first. One of his strongest and most influential book reviews was written to commend Dana, Jr.'s *Two Years*, which he had argued Harper Brothers into publishing.[11] He complained to Dana also in the late 1820s of the dual drudgery of working on the *Review* and the *Evening Post*, a toil necessitated by the desperate need of money to support his growing family. During 1836 and 1837, when he was already established as editor of the *Evening Post*, he lamented being "chained to the oar these twenty years, drudging in two wrangling professions one after the other,"[12] and described himself as "a draft horse harnessed to the wain of a daily paper," who, "if there is anything of the Pegasus in me I am much too exhausted to try my wings" (*L*, II, 64). Yet, by the end of the decade, he was one of the few Democratic editors to take an aggressive stand against slavery, support low tariffs, and champion labor unions without flinching or doubting the nobility of his profession. In the early years of indecision, fluctuation, and desperation, the period when Bryant thought himself too abstract, impatient, and forgetful to succeed at any endeavor, Dana provided him with a sounding board. One of his most frequent plaints to Dana centered around the inability to survive materially as a poet, and in one letter he admitted how glad he was to have something else on which to depend for a living (*L*, I, 324).

In 1838, following a period of serious internal crisis which almost destroyed the *Evening Post*, Bryant was finally able to begin reversing the tide of the paper's financial losses over several years. He wrote to Dana with cautious optimism on June 28 that he would soon be able to put the paper in financial order and retire. None of this would happen, but the struggle to place the *Post* on a surer financial footing, and the vigorous involvement of Bryant in historical struggles promoted in him a greater sense of inner security. He became increasingly interested in travel, in the home he was building in Roslyn, Long Island, in his health, and in nature, and he communicated these subjects to Dana in countless letters. He also turned more directly to easing Dana's melancholy, although he was somewhat apologetic for being too hurried and careworn to write. Even late in life, he encouraged Dana's much belated involvements in the literary and social life of his time, advising him not to look upon life as "a melancholy waste. You have impressed the stamp of your mind upon American literature and have helped to make it what it is and what it will yet be" (G, II, 267).

Dana's personal letters to Bryant are far less available in print, and many of them can only be partially reconstructed based on Bryant's responses. Still, a picture of Dana the man does emerge from what we have. What we see is a largely secluded figure who chided himself for being "idle and useless," yet who chose to withdraw from the world. He was invariably reluctant to leave Boston or Cambridge or Cape Ann—wherever he might be living at the time—although he made rare trips to Newport, and, infrequently, he and Bryant saw each other in New York. In 1826, when Bryant was offered the temporary assistant editorship of the *Post*, a permanent post on the newspaper was proffered to Dana, but he turned it down, as well as an offer from Boston's *Columbian Centinel* (L, I, 212, 227). By this time Dana had probably not decided to seek further newspaper employment. He had projected a life of Washington Allston, about which Bryant had inquired in 1846, but which never reached fruition (L, II, 473-476).[13] Nor did the plan he outlined to Bryant to publish a volume of his reviews and essays.[14] If many of Bryant's letters to Dana suggested a man actively in search of vocation, money, time, and stability, Dana's communication suggests a man frequently subject to illness, inertia, and melancholia, whose very life seemed discontinuous, unnaturally smooth, unmarked by events or milestones. In 1859, reflecting on the 1821 period when they first met, Dana wrote to him: "We look back on such a time, not as if there were any continuity between it and the present, but as if it had broken off just there, and we were now in another state, not able to follow up the tradition where and when it ended and the present one began. Nothing positive, like intervening death, only void unmarked space" (G, II, 126). When Bryant's youngest grandchild died Dana wrote to him both in consolation and in personal pain that "we do not make an intermediate state of continued life real enough to ourselves" (G, II, 137).

Dana's friendship was not unproblematic. His letters are sometimes sardonic, dour, demanding of attention. He responded with inexplicable acerbity to the account Bryant gave of the New York cholera epidemic of 1832: "By this time I suppose your city is as gay as ever, and in full dance over the graves of the thousands who have gone down to death since the plague entered it. As I never dance I shall not visit you for that purpose now . . . " (G, I, 284). Dana's personal involvement with Bryant and his verse prompted a less than temperate response when he learned that Bryant had approved a dedication of the English edition of his poems to Samuel Rogers, a rich English patron and friend of American artists and writers, whose literary judgments were not highly regarded, but who had a unique capacity for arousing Bryant's affection: "I learn by today's paper that the English edition of your poems had made its appearance with a dedication to Rogers by Irving. Samuel Rogers. Never mind, dear sir, it will help the favor."[15] Dana could be possessive, as several letters indicate wherein the passion for communication with Bryant made him overlook his friend's own needs and pressures. A pitiable insistence colors a late letter written to Bryant by Dana on the latter's eighty-fourth birthday: "Not that I believe you have forgotten me, although it is a long while since you have made any sign of recognition."[16] Dana associated Bryant with qualities he denied having himself. Bryant's evident energy, for example, must have been perplexing to him: "I look out upon you from my silent twilight cave with admiring wonder. There you are as if the sun were at high noon upon you, and all around you, and you in the fresh vigor of early manhood. Is the sun standing still with you as with Joshua of old? Is there no declining west for you? Where glow your heavens with the last steps of day?" (G, II, 336)

Bryant responded that he was "uneasy when unemployed. . . . Though while employed I am not much haunted with the consciousness of being old, yet the fact is almost always present to my mind that the time of my remaining here is necessarily short, and that whatever I am to do must be done soon, or it may not be done at all" (G, II, 336). In old age Bryant's youthful desperation flared up briefly again in his effort to retain a hold on life. He approached his translation of

Homer, especially the *Odyssey,* with trepidation, as he had once approached newspaper work, although the work itself raised his spirit and affirmed his still vital spark. Nevertheless, he and Dana were being drawn temperamentally closer. Bryant had nothing left for original composition, and, like Dana, he was becoming preoccupied with the deaths of friends, and the world as "more and more a solitude" (G, II, 215). When his wife died he wrote to Dana in a mood like that of "one cast out of paradise." In the closing words to this letter of September I, 1866, he revealed the absolute value Dana had for him, of acting as a filter through which the reserved, diffident poet could purge his feelings: "there is scarcely any person to whom I would write on this subject as I am doing to you" (G, II, 250). He recognized in Dana the quality of one acquainted with the night, but also of one who had glimpsed something beyond life. In the letter of condolence he had written to Bryant in 1866, Dana spoke with almost transcendental assurance: "And so it is, my dear Bryant, that those who are taken from us do not entirely leave us, but are borne along in this living flow, to be again blended with us in an ever-present" (G, II, 248).

Bryant had once written to his friend: "the things most irksome to me in my transactions with the world are to owe money, to ask a favor and to seek an acquaintance" (G, II, 249). But in his personal correspondence with Dana Bryant made a notable exception.

3.

The most potentially divisive aspect of the Bryant-Dana relationship was the socio-political one. In early 1828, in response to Dana's admonition that he not participate in "vile blackguard squabbles" and the degraded methods of political warfare, Bryant reassured him of his dislike of politics, which "get only my mornings, and you know politics and a belly-full are better than poetry and starvation" (L, I, 262). As editor of the *Post,* however, he could not help but gravitate to the Democratic Party which was supporting Jackson and a loose tariff, and later turned toward the multitude of social movements with which he became identified. Repeatedly Dana warned him to give up reforming the world and to keep his eye on poetry. "Human nature is not fitted for such a social condition as your fancy is pleased with." In the socio-political sphere Dana's view of things was conservative, even monarchical. When the 1848 revolution broke out in France, Bryant in an invitation to Dana to visit him in Roslyn, warned him half seriously "not to make melancholy faces at the news from Europe." Ever the cautions meliorist, Bryant confessed apprehensions at the revolution but prophesied that "in the order of Providence . . . republican institutions will come in with a higher and more general civilization, and that their effect is good and wholesome." Only that obedience, he felt, which was "cheerful and voluntary" could be virtue (L, II, 521).

Dana, on the other hand, expressed a general lack of confidence in the powers of government to bring solutions to human affairs.[17] He found the methods of political warfare to be degraded by their removal from the idealistic sphere and by their constant stress on political compromise. His chief animus was reserved for the more radical wing of the Democratic Party, the very wing toward which Bryant was inexorably moving. Bryant himself was always wary of the tactics of political radicalism, such as those of the Abolitionists, believing for a long time that moderation and high principles would bring an end to slavery. In 1854, however, his vision was put to its severest test. That year the Kansas-Nebraska Bill had been passed by the Senate, thus extending slave territory, repealing the Missouri Compromise, and, as a result, driving Bryant and the *Evening Post* away from the Democrats into a new camp dedicated to the formation of a Republican party. In grief and abjectness, he wrote to Dana on May 26: "What you say of the doings of our Government I am sorry not to be able to disagree with. It seems to me that never was public wickedness so high-handed in our country as now" (G, II, 77).

Between the values of poetry and those of the life of his time, Bryant could exercise little choice. His first loyalty was to poetry, and when the age of progress proved an anathema to it, he decried his contemporaries' standards. Bitter that poetry had little commerical value, he wrote to Dana on October 2, 1833: "The march of the age is in another direction; mankind are occupied with politics, railroads and steamboats" (L, I, 380).

Yet what was best in Bryant's liberalism, his general response to civic reform, his opposition to slavery, prison abuses, flogging, captial punishment, and slums, and his support of conservation, sanitary regulations, and municipal medical facilities, were not to be dimmed by either his own reservations or by Dana's social conservatism.

4.

If Dana was a social conservative and, unlike Bryant, a trinitarian opponent of Liberal Christianity, he was nonetheless a literary radical,

an original American romantic who rejected the traditional doctrine
that the Augustan poets were superior to Shakespeare. Van Wyck
Brooks spoke of him as "born too soon, not strong enough to break
his own path and yet the symbol of a rising world where other poets of
a tougher grain were to find their audience waiting."[18] He wrote a poem called "The Buccaneer," redolent of the atmosphere of the New
England coast and variously suggestive of Byron, Coleridge, Crabbe,
and Wordsworth, and tales like "Tom Thornton" and "Paul
Fenton," works of penetrating psychological insight, resembling those
of Brockden Brown, Hawthorne, and Sherwood Anderson, on the
theme of lost young men. His and Channing's retirement from the
North American Review were forced by a conservative majority, led
by Edward Everett, who saw English poetry as the civilized domain of
Pope and regarded Wordsworth as a barbarian. Bryant said, "if the
Review had remained in Dana's hands he would have imparted a character of originality and decision to its critical articles which no literary
man of the country was at that time qualified to give it."[19] He despised
neoclassical artificialities, accusing even poets like Goldsmith of "dim
generalities, and unmeaning and false elegances of phrase";[20] he
praised the "melancholy powers . . . the gloom, awe and mystery" in
the novels of Charles Brockden Brown, whose talent he regarded as
"genius."[21]

    In Bryant, too, he recognized inspired genius. As early as 1821 he
was cautioning him against the process of revision and the artificialities
of poetic diction, which he deplored as much as Wordsworth did. "I
believe that a poet should not be allowed to alter in cold blood; he
grows finical" (*L*, I, 111). Bryant hardly objected, submitting "as
quickly as you could wish your restoration of the altered passages.
Even in 1870 he accused Bryant of revising his printed works:

> I must scold a little, notwithstanding the warning Wordsworth should
> have been to you, you have in cold blood turned critic upon your
> printed works, the control of which was gone when you handed them
> over to the public; and yet you have treated them just as if you sup-
> posed there were still the same interflow of the warm-life blood that
> there was before the severance.
>
> (G, II, 288)

Dana also insisted from the time he had first heard "The Ages" that
Bryant write a long poem, one that would exercise his strength on a
large scale and demand emotional commitment, rather than the short
pieces evolving from random, detached thoughts. "There are men of

talents enough to carry on the common world, but men of genius are not so plenty that any can afford to be idle, neither can any man tell how great the effect of a work of genius is in the course of time. Set about it in good earnest" (G, I, 186).

But Bryant could never rise to Dana's imperative. First he shared with Poe the notion that a long poem of quality was inconceivable; secondly he thought himself too impatient and undisciplined for the task of writing such a poem; finally whereas Dana stressed intuitive, passionate, flowing composition, Bryant restrained himself by measure, balance, and precision in words, and was sensitive to any violation of poetic decorum. For such as he, the short poem was the only viable form. Yet he shared Dana's advocacy of romanticism. He preferred "an excessive ambition of originality" to "a tame and frigid taste."[22] Although he decried to Dana America's ignorance of versification (*L*, I, 3225), he sometimes admitted preferring Dana's lack of diligence in versification to his own conformity to strict meter:

I have sometimes been conscience smitten at wasting so much time in longs and shorts— spending so many hours to make a crabbed thought submit to the dimensions of the metre, to form a couplet or stanza so that the time of it perfectly pleased my ear at the same time that the expression of the thought was the most perfect that I could command. I fear that the process has been attended with a loss of vigor and freshness in the composition.

(*L*, I, 402)

Dana published Bryant in *The Idle Man* and Bryant published Dana in the *Review and Atheneum*. Bryant helped to place Dana's 1833 volume, and the following year Dana's publisher brought out a volume of Bryant's poetry. Few literary friends had a higher degree of encouragement for each other's poetic and critical faculties. Dana believed himself an awkward poet, who had entered the field too late to be molded into a great one, and invariably, he praised Bryant at his own expense. To him Bryant was "thou veteran in verse" and he the much younger poet. When Bryant showed metrical lapses, Dana wrote him: "I may walk over Parnassus in a shag Petersham—people expect nothing better of me; but it won't do for you my dear sir—nothing short of superfine broadcloth must you be abroad in" (G, I, 302). For Dana Bryant's poetry represented grandeur and calm and "a perfection in the meaning which [his] words gave to things." For Bryant, Dana always seemed more at home in the statelines of blank verse than in rhyme, and he may have gone out of his way to overlook the awkward-ness and lugubriousness of "The Dying Raven," "Thoughts on the Soul,"and "The Husband's and Wife's Grave." But there was indub-itable sincerity in his praise of "The Buccaneer": "It has passages of great power and great beauty and the general effect to my apprehen-sion is very fine" (*L*, I, 241). When Dana's 1827 volume triumphed over the virulence of anti-Romantic critics, Bryant was exhilarated: "As to the great poem of which you speak I must turn it over to you to be written. One who has achieved such triumphs as you have over ill-natured critics . . . should not let his talent sleep the moment it is ac-knowledged" (*L*, I, 325). Yet for most of his life Dana's imaginative talent did sleep. Bryant turned from praise of it to praise of his critical faculties. Frequently he acknowledged Dana's leniency and mercy as a critic. He wrote him on April 6, 1845: "You cannot think how much obliged I am to you for the trouble you have taken with my book. There is nobody else whom I would have asked to do the same thing" (G, II, 16).

But if Dana's devotion to Bryant and his clear-sighted judgment of Bryant's literary efforts were a constant beacon in the latter's pursuit of literary immortality, Bryant nonetheless retained marked independ-ence of judgment when he believed himself right, and no editorial ad-vice from Dana could sway him from a single alteration of what he be-lieved the correct path to follow in each poem. The fact of Bryant's ca-pacity for independent judgment and self-reliance makes his general responsiveness to Dana's critical an aesthetic influence the more re-markable.

The history of Bryant and Dana is the history of two men of differ-ing backgrounds and temperaments, who crossed each other's path at a formative moment in American letters and American history and at that crossing built an edifice of friendship and devotion which ended only with Bryant's death in 1878.

NOTES

1. *Poems* (Boston: Bowles and Dearborn, 1827); *Poems and Prose Writings* (Boston: Russell, Odiorne, and Co., 1833); cited hereafter in text as *PPW*. In England Dana published *The Buccaneer and Other Poems* (London: H. G. Clarke and Co., 1844), and an unauthorized edition was issued entitled *The Poetical Works of Edgar Allan Poe and Richard Henry Dana* (London: G. Routledge, 1857).
2. James Grant Wilson, *Bryant and His Friends: Some Reminiscences of*

the Knickerbocker Writers (New York: Fords, Howard and Hulbert, 1886), p. 180.

3. *The Journal of Richard Henry Dana*, 3 vols. Robert F. Lucid, ed. (Cambridge, Mass.: The Belknap Press of Harvard University Press, 1968), 6, 171-173, 222, 235, 336, 385, 406, 416-417, 479, 489, 494, 607, 667, 685; hereafter cited in text as *J.*

4. Wilson, 186-187.

5. See Samuel Shapiro, *Richard Henry Dana, Jr.: 1815-1882* (East Lansing: Michigan State University Press, 1961), pp. 4, 31, 123.

6. Van Wyck Brooks, *The Flowering of New England* (New York: E. P. Dutton, 1939), 119-120.

7. Accounts of the publication of "Thanatopsis" in *NAR* can be found in Wilson, pp. 37-38, 187-188; Parke Godwin, *A Biography of William Cullen Bryant, with extracts from his Private Correspondence* (New York: Russell and Russell, 1885), I, 149-153, hereafter cited in text as G; Tremaine McDowell, "Bryant and the *NAR*," *American Literature,* I (March 1929) 14-26; Charles H. Brown, *William Cullen Bryant* (New York: Scribner's, 1971), pp. 78-79

8. *The Letters of William Cullen Bryant*, William Cullen Bryant II and Thomas G. Voss, eds., I, 1809-1836 (New York: Fordham University Press, 1975), 63; hereafter cited as *L,* I.

9. The following quotation comes from Parke Godwin: "Mr. Richard Henry Dana . . . says: 'I never shall forget with what feeling my friend Bryant, some years ago described to me the effect upon him by his meeting for the first time with Wordsworth's ballads. He said that upon opening the book, one-thousand springs seemed to gush up at once in his heart and the face of Nature, of a sudden, to change into a strange freshness and life. He had felt the sympathetic touch from an according mind, and you see how instantly his powers and affections shot over the earth and through his kind.' " (G, I, 104).

10. Dana once said to Bryant: "For us poets . . . to be exhibiting ourselves before the public in the character of reviewers of one another, strikes me unpleasantly." (G, I, 302).

11. The review appeared in *Democratic Review*, VIII (October 1840), 318-335. The story of Bryant's participation is recorded in Robert Metzdorf's "The Publishing History of Richard Henry Dana's *Two Years Before the Mast*," *Harvard Library Bulletin*, VII, no. 3 (Autumn 1953), 312-332, and Robert F. Lucid, "The Composition, Reception and Influence of *Two Years Before the Mast*," unpub. diss., University of Chicago, 1958.

12. Bryant *Letters*, II, 1836-1849 (New York: Fordham University Press, 1977), 26; hereafter cited as *L,* II.

13. See Brooks, 169. Allston's official biography was finally written by Rev. William Ware in 1852.

14. See Goddard-Roslyn Collection, New York Public Library.

15. John Bigelow, *William Cullen Bryant* (Boston: Houghton Mifflin, 1890), p. 121. Irving had helped to promote Bryant's poetry in England.

16. Goddard-Roslyn Collection.
17. "We must beware then," he wrote at the conclusion of "Law as Suited to Man," "of that popular but most dangerous creed, that a free country will work off its evils." See *PPW,* II, 98.
18. Brooks, 119.
19. Wilson, 189,
20. "Hazlett's Lectures on the English Poets," in *PPW,* II, 249.
21. "The Novels of Charles Brockden Brown," in *PPW,* II, 328.
22. Brown, 147.

William Cullen Bryant
and
the Early Sketch Club

JAMES T. CALLOW
University of Detroit

The Sketch Club that William Cullen Bryant belonged to for some forty years was a social organization of New York artists and amateurs.[1] From 1829 to 1869 they met in each other's homes on a regular basis, at first once a week, then once every two weeks. Conversation seemed to be the chief activity at the meetings, but in the early days the members also attempted, not always with success, to write and draw. (At one meeting, during particularly inclement weather, "there was no drawing but of corks."[2]) The idea behind the club was to mix conviviality and productiveness. Meetings provided members with regular opportunities not only to perfect themselves in their drawings and writing but also to mingle sociably with fellow artists and authors, with patrons, publishers, and other art enthusiasts. In time they hoped to produce a literary annual of their own.

The Club proved itself a very serviceable organization in other ways. Above all it gave men of diverse occupations a chance to broaden their outlook. For at least a few hours every week doctors, lawyers, scientists, ministers, and others could break out of the old environment to seek a welcome change. Certain occupational groups actually found their status raised through the opportunities provided by this novel society. Businessmen like Bryant's friends Charles M. Leupp and Jonathan Sturges became not just *nouveaux riches* but patrons of the arts; while the painters, sculptors, and engravers in the club went from mere craftsmen to respected artists.[3] Furthermore, in the meetings of the club and elsewhere, artist and patron could mingle freely as peers. Here was a rare example in art history of the social nexus replacing the cash nexus.

If the Sketch Club admirably served its members (some seventy-one in all), it had an equally good effect on New York City, for these members were the natural aristocrats who founded and managed some of the city's most important institutions. Bryant, for example, was involved in the operations of The National Academy of Design, The American Art-Union, Central Park, The Century Club, and The Metropolitan Museum of Art.[4] His friend Leupp also served the National Academy and the Art-Union but was involved as well in the House of Refuge and the City College of New York. As might be expected, manuscript evidence indicates that the Sketch Clubbers regarded their weekly meetings as convenient places at which to discuss the business of these institutions.[5] It is possible that one or two of these institutions were even born during the meetings.

The history of the Sketch Club falls into three distinct periods. The first, stretching from 1829 to 1833, was recorded with a great deal of wit by secretaries John Inman and William Emerson and then (with less wit though perhaps more accuracy) by Secretary Thomas S. Cummings.[6] Their minutes, which in some cases read like informal essays, provide us with most of our information on the topics of the sketches, poems, and conversations that marked the meetings. The second period of the club (1834–1843) might be termed its Dark Age, not because the members lasped into an unenlightened state (far from it!) but because no minutes have been found to illuminate the meetings that continued to take place. The third period, beginning in 1844 (when the minutes resume) and ending in 1869 (when the minutes stop), is markedly different from the first. Now the members seem more serious and sophisticated; they have gone farther toward making their way in the world; and they regard the meetings of the club less as a chance to work at their profession than to socialize with people of similar achievement and reputation. The meetings contunued to sparkle with fun, but secreatries John Neilson, Jr. and John H. Gourlie failed to capture it in their minutes, which were seldom more than skeletal in their minutes, which were seldom more than skeletal rosters.[7]

Bryant was a faithful member of the Sketch Club through all three of these periods.[8] As we shall see, his involvement in the club consisted of more than going to 63.6 percent of its meetings, though this was one of the most impressive attendance records in the club's history.[9] He also served, for example, as occasional host and committeeman; but most important, he fraternized with Sketch Clubbers on a daily basis, not just at the weekly meetings.[10] Even when out of the country he spent a great deal of time with the members. Leupp, a wealthy businessman, was his traveling companion on three voyages,[11] while John Gadsby Chapman, William Guy Wall, and other artist-members were visited by Bryant when they were living abroad. The club was seldom far from his mind.

Bryant may well have been a founder of the Sketch Club, though we cannot be certain. When the extant minutes begin, in 1829, his name appears on the rosters.[12] And if the club originated earlier than that date, as seems probable, he was likely to have been a member then, too; for he belonged to most of the groups out of which the Sketch Club grew. To the first of these—James Fenimore Cooper's Bread and Cheese Club—he had been elected as early as November, 1825.[13] And at the second—the National Academy of Design—he had been appointed Professor of Mythology and Ancient History in 1828,[14] delivering a series of five lectures on mythology to the academicians in 1827, 1828, and 1829.[15] Equally important, he was no doubt a friend of all the other early members of the Sketch Club, themselves probable founders. For example, before coming to New York City in 1825 he had corresponded with Guilian Verplanck[16] and had met the poet James A. Hillhouse,[17] and soon after his arrival there he met the painters Samuel F. B. Morse[18] and Thomas Cole.[19] By 1827 he, Verplanck, and Robert Charles Sands began *The Talisman,* a series of gift books embellished by Henry Inman, Robert Weir, Asher Durand, and their other artist-friends.[20] Joining and later superintending the illustrators in this collaboration[21] was Dr. John Neilson, Jr., a skillful amateur artist who had studied under Alexander Robertson.[22] Neilson's friendship with Bryant was closer than has been noted. During the 1830s they spent a great deal of time together, and Neilson's diary abounds with entries recording walks he took with the poet.[23] Nor was it inappropriate that, years later, when Durand painted *Kindred Spirits,* his famous picture of Bryant and Cole, he borrowed some of his design from Neilson's *Devil's Pulpit,* a landscape engraving in *The Talisman* for 1828.[24]

With these and other friends Bryant fully participated in the Sketch Club's first period. Meetings were weekly then, and beginning in January of 1830 they were announced in the *Evening Post,* which Bryant was now serving as editor-in-chief. The *Commercial Advertiser* and *The American* also ran these notices, and the scheme seemed to work well, despite occasional printer's errors, but it was ultimately abandoned, and no announcements have been found in any of these papers after 1833.

Bryant hosted six meetings during the first period. Unfortunately, however, they were not recorded with the fullness that other meetings sometimes received. The first meeting, on Friday evening, April 24, 1829, was attended by ten members[25] and one guest—a "Mr. Aights," probably James Eights, the topographical artist from Albany.[26] For some unspecified reason he irritated secretary Inman with the result that the minutes were cut short with this comment: "By way of a change the Secretary makes no farther minutes of this evening's proceedings. His time having been occupied with reflections upon the inexpediency of admitting strangers to the Noctes of the Club." Yet Inmand did record the topic assigned by Bryant for the evening's sketches: "Subject, a description of the discomfiture of a party of pleasure, upon an island which was overflowed by the tide, their boat having thought proper to travel off without leave or license." The incident was taken from *The Borough* (1810), a group of verse-stories by George Crabbe.[27] That Bryant would have chosen a passage from Crabbe's work is not surprising, for the author was a well-known narrative poet. Whether the choice proved to be wise will not be known until all the resultant sketches are recovered. So far only three—by Weir, Cole, and Ingham—have been located.

With four other meetings hosted by Bryant during this period we are not so fortunate. Two are noticed with a single line in the minutes,[28] and two are not in the minutes at all but are mentioned in contemporary diaries.[29] As a result we cannot determine the topics sketched or the members present at any of these meetings.

At least we have better documentation for the Friday afternoon meeting at Bryant's in Hoboken on October 5, 1832. The minutes tell us that John Howard Payne (author of "Home, Sweet Home") was elected to membership that afternoon, apparently without being nominated at a previous meeting.[30] If this violated the club's rules, it also attests to Payne's great popularity in New York at that time. Only a few weeks later, on November 29, 1832 his friends would hold a successful benefit for him at the Park Theatre. Unfortunately, despite this show of affection on their part, his troubles (financial and otherwise) increased, and he became embittered to the point of alienation. Needless to say, he attended very few Sketch Club meetings.[31]

Bryant, on the other hand, attended many and eagerly participated in the diverse activities. He helped elect at least two dozen new members, including William Dunlap (probably the club's oldest member), Richard Ray Ward (a close friend of Bryant's close friend Robert Sands), Charles Cushing Wright (the medallist), William Emerson, and James Jay Mapes (father of Mary Mapes Dodge).[32] He was there when various nominees were turned down, too, but we cannot discover how he voted in these cases, for while unanimity was required for election, rejection needed only a single blackball.

He also joined in the composition of two poems which have been preserved in the minutes. Bryant, Sands, Neilson, and the Inman brothers wrote the first one, which was simply called "Character."[33] Essentially the poem was a narrative about the termagent Xanthippe and her hen-pecked husband Socrates, but it was the form of the poem as much as its subject that challenged the participants and raised the exercise to the level of a game. The poem was to progress in quatrains, the first two lines to be written by one player, the next two by another. Thus, when his section rolled around, each player had to finish a quatrain started by a previous player and then provide the first half of a new quatrain. Besides, since the predetermined rhyme scheme was *abab*, the player had to rack his memory for words to match his predecessor's, though he could then take sweet revenge on his successor by setting up a still more difficult rhyme of two or even three syllables. Several passages from "Character" will not only show how the procedure worked but will also demonstrate the facility with which Bryant and his fellows played the game. In the following exchange, for instance, both double and triple rhymes are called for and created:

Secretary [John Inman]
The doctor was summoned but came not
Because of her bad reputation;
　　　　　Bryant
Says her husband, your gimlet I blame not
But I hate your damned vociferation.
　　　　　[Bryant again]
So wife you may go for the barber
As the surgeon wont come for a windstopper;[34]
　　　　　Sands
Says she, I'll be damned if I harbour
Such a low lived and beggarly chin-chopper—

In that passage it was Sands who came up with a triple rhyme to meet Bryant's challenge.[35] In the next passage, their roles were reversed, though as before both proved their ingenuity:

> *Sands*
> Of the 17 babes that I'm putative
> Father to, none I acknowledge;
> *Bryant*
> Though I've fed them with food that is nutritive
> And sent all but 16 to college—

Another joint poem, entitled "The Sublime," presented easier challenges and more impressive results.[36] This time there were only three players—Sands, John Inman, and Bryant—and the basic stanza was a sestet rhyming *aabccb*. Once the rotation started, each player was to compose the last three lines of the sestet begun by his predecessor, and the first three lines of the sestet to be finished by his successor. However, this rhyme scheme was less demanding than that of the previous poem, which had kept the players from devoting enough thought to the subject matter. Certain passages in "The Sublime" not only demonstrate the players' adeptness with rhyme and meter but also interest us in other ways. Such a passage is this apostrophe to a mountain:

> *Bryant*
> When'eer I gaze upon you, big and blue,
> I feel myself almost as big as you,
> And swell with proud emotions of sublimity—[37]
> *Sands*
> I think Goliah was a fool to me
> That Magog could not reach up to my knee
> Or Sampson rival me in magnanimity.[38]

Here we find rhyme used for the dual purpose of playing the game and emphasizing key words (the triple rhyme "sublimity" is, in fact, *the* key word of the entire poem), and equally important, we find striking contrasts in diction between, for example, the short, colloquial "big and blue" and the long, scholarly "magnanimity." Most of all, Bryant and Sands have succeeded in giving poetic shape to the abstract ideas and terminology of the eighteenth-century rhetoricians whom they knew so well.

At the many meetings he attended during this first period Bryant may also have joined in the sketching. That he knew how to draw and sometimes drew on other occasions is clearly evident in the recent edition of the Bryant letters, which reproduces several of his sketches.[39] Moreover, the topics chosen by the hosts frequently came from authors in his own literary tradition—such poets, for instance, as Shakespeare, Spenser, Thomson, Byron, and Scott.[40] On the other hand, certain passages in the minutes indicate that he sat these opportunities out, as in the case of a meeting hosted by Hillhouse, where Bryant is listed among the *"non combatants."*[41] Furthermore, though some drawings derived from Sketch Club meetings have been recovered, there are none of his among them.

During this early period several resolutions were brought before the club, and Bryant no doubt voted on them. Most, in fact, concerned the publication of a wished-for annual written and illustrated by the members, probably in imitation of the three *Talisman* volumes (1827–1829) and the *American Landscape* (1830), all of which had been collaborations between the writers and the artists. The first burst of new enthusiasm occurred on March 15, 1832, when it was resolved that "the Sketch Club publish a New York annual for the year 1833; that Mr. Durand be requested to superintend the embellishments & that the corresponding secretary . . . write to Mr. Verplanck, & request his aid in superintending the literary execution. . . ." A few days later John Neilson, the corresponding secretary, did write to Verplanck, who was then serving what proved to be his last term in Congress. After quoting the resolution, Neilson could not resist adding some pessimism of his own:

> Not having been present at the meeting in question I am unable to furnish you with any details of the projected plan, but am sadly afraid it will terminate like all the other magnificent projects of said respectable association. It would not be becoming in me however to throw cold water on the project.[42]

Bryant also wrote Verplanck, in a tone just the opposite of Neilson's:

> The *Sketch Club* have voted to have an Annual,—something more splendid than any which has yet appeared in this country. There are to be six copper plate engravings of larger size than is common in the American annuals—and several more cuts by Mason[43] for head and tailpieces. The book is to have a larger page than any other of our Annuals, and but half the matter. Harper is to be asked to publish it. . . . The plan appears to have been got up by Ingham, Durand, and Weir, who

are full of zeal about it. . . . Write me whether you will undertake the business.[44]

But Verplanck, then serving as chairman of the House Ways and Means Committee, was apparently not to be enticed, and at a meeting on 25 April the *"embryo annual"* was put in charge of a *"Literary Committee"* consisting of Bryant, Neilson, and William Emerson. How much progress was subsequently made is uncertain. Meanwhile in June the Harper Brothers issued *Tales of the Glauber Spa*, written by Bryant, Sands, and three authors who were not members of the Sketch Club. Obviously even this failed to energize the committee, and the new year was almost upon them when at a meeting on December 6 the matter was taken up again. After a speech of "singular impressiveness" by Sands, the members unanimously resolved to appoint a committee of three artists—Neilson, Durand, and Dunlap—to report on "the propriety of publishing" the contemplated book.[45] All these plans came to naught, however;[46] for Sands died suddenly on 16 December, leaving Bryant, Ward, and Neilson, probably his three closest friends, crushed with grief.[47] The members now concerned themselves with various ways of honoring his memory, such as publishing his literary remains[48] or meeting to sketch from his short story "Boyuca,"[49] so that plans for the annual were forgotten, even though this publication was one of the club's major goals.

Conversations at the Sketch Club meetings, which secretaries John Inman and William Emerson heroically attempted to capture on paper, were lively and varied. Certain favorite topics are discoverable, even though we limit our search to passages in which Bryant is specifically mentioned. Politics inevitably came up. For example, on 27 March 1829, while the "paper spoilers" sketched from Scott's *Lay of the Last Minstrel*, "Affairs of the nation [were] settled in solemn conclave by Messrs Verplanck, Hillhouse & Bryant—videli cet Gen Jackson, Van Buren, Swartwout, Tazewell Randolph Webster."[50] Historical topics also appeared frequently and could be argued with great vigor, as suggested by the elliptical style and military metaphors used by Secretary Inman to describe one exchange at the meeting of May 1, 1829:

Idea started by Mr Morse that Tadmor[51] was constructed by the antifloodites—combated by Mr Bryant and the Secretary supported by J. L. Morton and H. Inman. Opposed by DeKay—sustained by H. J.

Morton and Mr Verplanck—assaulted by Dr Neilson and so a *row*—after which a cessation of hostilities upon the arrival of the coffee urn.[52]

Before any new topics could be recorded, Bryant moved the conversation from historical to medical matters, defending his belief that the "perfection of bathing is to jump head foremost into a snowbank."[53] The reaction to this discourse has not been recorded, but at the next meeting Bryant's glibness led him into trouble:

> Thanks of the Club are returned to Mr Bryant for having given an excellent criticism on a College oration, which he had not heard & an admirable account of a dinner which he had not been within scent of. Whereupon—Unanimously resolved, that the said W. C. Bryant be directed . . . to write & publish an account critical, poetical, ethical, didactic metaphysical of the Exhibition of the Nat[ional] Ac[ademy] of Design before seeing the same. Mr B apologized—Modesty—Ignorance—Veneration for the arts—Great respect for Messrs M - I - I - C &c—the whole over ruled . . .[54]

And on the next day Bryant's *Evening Post* carried a full but unsigned review of the exhibition.

The same kind of playfulness marked the miscellaneous activities at meetings which Bryant attended. Minutes were read, approved,[55] and no doubt laughed at: there was "lots of singing";[56] Stephen Gimber strummed the guitar;[57] James E. DeKay stymied the members with a puzzle from *Paradise Lost*;[58] there were visits from a knight in armor[59] and the Prince of Orange;[60] and one night at Weir's "a legitimate & veritable ghost was raised."[61]

What can we learn from this study of the Sketch Club during its playful period? One thing that comes immediately to mind is the value of minutes as a scholarly tool. All too often manuscript letters fail to reveal the day-to-day contacts between close friends if these friends lived in the same city. We can easily document the friendship between Bryant and Richard Henry Dana the Elder, because they wrote lots of letters to each other, since Dana lived in Boston, Bryant in New York. Yet the equally close friendship between Asher B. Durand and Bryant cannot be documented that way, since Durand and Bryant both lived in New York and therefore seldom exchanged letters. The minutes of such organizations as the Sketch Club serve to fill in where correspondence is sparse,[62] and they make a very useful supplement even to model collections of letters, such as the set of Bryant letters now being edited by Professors Bryant and Voss. A dozen references to John Neilson, Jr. for example, appear in the first two volumes of the letters. When supplemented with the hundreds of references in the minutes they give us our first clear picture of a forgotten friendship with a neglected artist.

Bryant's close connection with the Sketch Club in its early period had a lasting effect on his life and career. Of course, the meetings provided him with needed diversion from the tense business of editing a newspaper during the stormy age of Jackson. Bryant learned, as did the other members, to subordinate political and other differences to a common interest in art, and to be convivial even with professional rivals. (Robert Sands and John Inman, for example, both worked for the *Commercial Advertiser* under William Leete Stone, the editor whom Bryant horsewhipped.[63]) Associating so frequently with artists, Bryant learned to understand their thinking, which often agreed with his own. As early as 1826 he was advocating universalism over isolationism in cultural matters, urging Americans to borrow freely from other countries and ages, but to borrow only the best and to adapt these borrowings to the New World.[64] For the next three years, in *The Talisman* series, he and his fellow club members demonstrated how this could be done successfully in the gift book field. Their persona, Francis Herbert, was an urbane cosmopolitan; and his materials were eclectic indeed. Only half the prose dealt with American locales.[65] Even some of this half was set outside the United States or contained foreign characters. (This, too, harmonized with Bryant's theories, for in 1825 he had recommended using immigrant character types as a means of enriching the American novel of manners.[66]) We should recall that cultural universalism was not in vogue at this time, having been subordinated to nationalism, so that the *North American Review* sneered at *The Talisman* for lacking "patriotic incident."[67] But Bryant's connection with the Sketch Club reinforced his stand against such isolationist thinking. A substantial number of the members were emigrés. William James Bennett, Thomas Cole, Thomas S. Cummings, Stephen H. Gimber, Abraham J. Mason, and George Miller all hailed from England. William Guy Wall and Charles Cromwell Ingham came from Ireland, while Joaquim César de Figanière was a Portuguese diplomat.[68] Moreover, out of seventeen topics selected by the hosts for sketching, only four were taken from American authors. Strange indeed, artists with foreign roots working on foreign topics—and yet creating a native school of art! Bryant obviously worried about the process at times, as when he urged Cole in a sonnet not to forget American scenery when he travelled abroad.[69] But on the whole he agreed with the artists and prized foreign travel as decidedly beneficial to their work.[70] He himself was to make no less than six voyages to Europe.

Bryant's early Sketch Club experience also prepared him to help in the marketing and popularization of American art. Weekly contact with artists gave him the confidence to speak for them and to represent their concerns to the public—not just in the columns of the *Evening Post*, but also in the meetings of the Amerian Art Union, on whose Committee of Management he would serve in 1842 and 1843. This grand lottery awarded valuable paintings to the winners, and even the losers got worthwhile premiums, including engravings of works by such Sketch Club members as Asher Durand, Francis W. Edmonds, and Felix O. C. Darley. Bryant served as the Art-Union's president in 1844, 1845, and 1846; and his annual addresses show that he regarded the organization as an important means of getting art into the hands of the people.[71] The Sketch Club by then had elected three enlightened patrons to membership—Luman Reed,[72] Jonathan Sturges, and Charles M. Leupp—so Bryant knew the best side of private patronage. But he knew its worst side as well, for he had heard how highhandedly George Featherstonhaugh and Ithiel Town had treated his friend Cole.[73] And he was certainly aware of his friend Durand's suspicion of the Art-Union, which seemed to threaten the National Academy. Still Bryant saw the Art-Union as a noble manifestation of democracy and a source of income for the artists. Some of the other lay members of the Sketch Club served as agents for the artist members; William Kemble, for example, handled the work of his friend John G. Chapman. But Bryant operated on a larger scale, representing hundreds of artists to thousands of subscribers. Had he not been often in the company of artists, he might never have found himself offered this role or able to accept it.

Finally, he must hope that this paper has helped to change the popular image of Bryant as a white-bearded melancholiac who never had a childhood, who never told a lie, never said anything clever, and never enjoyed a minute of his life but who moped around for years until at the age of 175 he devised a way of torturing high-school students by writing a long, dismal poem about death that their teachers would force them to memorize. Bryant, we have seen, was none of the above, except white-bearded, at any time of his life, and especially during the early years of the Sketch Club. To tell the truth, he disciplined himself more than most and he worked harder than many, but he was also sociable, convivial, and even playful. The Sketch Club gave him a chance to express himself, to enjoy the present, and prepare for things to come.

NOTES

1. For a fuller account of the Sketch Club see James T. Callow, *Kindred Spirits: Knickerbocker Writers and American Artists, 1807-1855* (Chapel Hill: Univ. of North Carolina Press, 1967), pp. 12-29. The author is currently editing the minutes of the club with a research grant from the National Endowment for the Humanities.
2. Entry for Feb. 20, 1829 in the ms. minutes of the Sketch Club at the Century Association, available on microfilm from the Archives of American Art.
3. See John H. Gourlie, *A Tribute to the Memory of Charles M. Leupp: An Address Delivered Before the Column, February 10, 1860* (New York: Printed for the Column by Wm. C. Bryant & Co., 1860, 23 pp.); James T. Callow, "The Art Collection of Charles M. Leupp," *Antiques*, 116 (Nov. 1979), and "Charles M. Leupp: A New York Art patron" (forthcoming); Joanne August Dickson, "Patronage of Nineteenth Century American Painters: Joanthan Sturges and His Associates," Master's thesis, California State Univ. of San Francisco, 1973.
4. See Callow, Kindred Spirits, pp. 31-32, 34-35, 62-63, 8081; William Cullen Bryant II, "Poetry and Painting: A Love Affair of Long Ago," *American Quarterly*,[22] (Winter, 1970), 859-82, esp. 861-71; Robert Bernard Silber, "William Cullen Bryant's 'Lectures on Mythology,'" Diss., State Univ. of Iowa 1962.
5. For example, many entries in the early minutes of the Sketch Club mention conversations about the National Academy of Design. A letter from Jon[a] Sturges to Chas. M. Leupp, no place given, Feby 16th 1854, Rutgers, arranges for meeting at Leupp's to discuss academy matters before the members arrive.
6. John Inman (Henry Inman's brother) took the minutes for 1829-1830; Thomas S. Cummings, for 1831-March 8, 1832; and William Emerson (Ralph Waldo Emerson's brother), for March 15, 1832-April 4, 1833.
7. Neilson took minutes from 1844 through June 24, 1851; Gourlie, from Sept. 27, 1851 through April 9, 1869, the last recorded meeting.
8. In this paper we limit our analysis to those meetings which Bryant attended. For an analysis limited to the meetings attended by another member see James T. Callow, "Robert W. Weir and the Sketch Club," in *Robert Weir: Artist and Teacher of West Point* (West Point: Cadet Fine Arts Forum of the United States Corps of Cadets, 1976), pp. 86-91.
9. Of 272 meetings for which we have rosters he attended 173.

    Part of the author's grant from the National Endowment for the Humanities has been used to analyze the Sketch Club minutes with a compu-

ter. The program facilitates information-trading with interested parties, allows for continuing revision, and reproduces all the rosters for meetings attended by each member and guest of the club. The latest print-out for Bryant serves as the basis of this essay. Of course, the figures given here cannot be final, since hitherto unknown meetings and even lost minutes continue to surface as research progresses.
10. See Callow, *Kindred Spirits*, pp. 63–69, 80–81, 232–35.
11. Bryant himself gave the fullest account of these trips, taken in 1845, 1849, and 1852-1853. See *The Letters of William Cullen Bryant*, William Cullen Bryant II and Thomas G. Voss, eds. (New York: Fordham Univ. Press, 1975-).
12. Though Bryant did not attend the first recorded meeting, he did attend (one week later) the second, on Feb. 13, 1829.
13. Albert H. Marckwardt, "The Chronology and Personnel of the Bread and Cheese Club," *American Literature*, 6 (Jan., 1935), 389–99, especially 392. Other members of the Bread and Cheese who belonged to the Sketch Club in 1829 were Robert Charles Sands, Asher B. Durand, Samuel F. B. Morse, James E. DeKay, Gulian C. Verplanck, Henry Inman, Robert W. Weir, James A. Hillhouse, and William Dunlap. Dr. John B. Stevenson's name first appears on the Sketch Club rosters on Jan. 28, 1830.
14. John L. Morton to Bryant, New York, Jan. 5, 1828, Bryant-Godwin Collection, New York Public Library (hereinafter NYPL).
15. Also later, in 1831. Silber gives the text of the lectures, plus a thorough analysis.
16. Bryant, *Letters*, I, 15, 113-14.
17. Bryant, *Letters*, I, 166; Charles Tabb Hazelrigg, *American Literary Pioneer: A Biographical Study of James A. Hillhouse* (New York: Bookman Associates, 1953), pp. 108-10.
18. *Prose Writings of William Cullen Bryant*, ed. Parke Godwin, 2 vols. (New York: D. Appleton & Co., 1884), I, 279; William Cullen Bryant, "Reminiscences of Miss Sedgwick," in *Life and Letters of Catharine M. Sedgwick*, ed. Mary E. Dewey (New York: Harper & Bros., 1871), p. 441.
19. Callow, *Kindred Spirits*, p. 64; Bryant, "Reminiscences," p. 441.
20. *The Talisman* is given a whole chapter in Ralph Thompson's *American Literary Annuals & Gift Books, 1825-1865* (New York: H. W. Wilson Co., 1936), pp. 56-64.
21. Thompson, pp. 58, 64; Bryant, *Letters*, I, 272 (n. 6), 273.
22. Thomas S. Cummings, himself a teacher of drawing, remarked that Neilson "drew with skill, and his sketches from nature bore marks of ability far beyond the generality of such efforts. He took particular pleasure in the society of artists, and was one of the original members of the old 'Sketch Club.'" *Historic Annals of the National Academy of Design* (Philadelphia: George W. Childs, 1865), p. 229.
23. Margaret Armstrong gives generous samples of this diary in *Five Generations: Life and Letters of an American Family, 1750-1900* (New York: Harper & Bros., 1930).

24. Reproduced as the frontispiece of Callow, *Kindred Spirits.*
25. Verplanck, Cole, Henry Inman, John Inman, Charles Cromwell Ingham, Morse, Weir, Neilson, Sands, and Bryant.
26. See George C. Groce and David H. Wallace, *The New-York Historical Society's Dictionary of Artists in America, 1564-1860* (New Haven: Yale Univ. Press, 1957), hereinafter cited as *DAA.*
27. Source identified courtesy of Professor R. L. Chamberlain. In the minutes secretary Inman ascribed the passage to Crabbe's *Tales of the Hall.*
28. March 4, 1830; Feb. 16, 1832.
29. May 24, 1833, mentioned in the diary of John Neilson for that date, and Nov. 14, 1833, mentioned in the *Diary of William Dunlap,* ed. Dorothy C. Barck, 3 vols. (New York: New-York Historical Society, 1930), III, 757.
30. When the manuscripts at the Century were microfilmed for the Archives of American Art, this single page of minutes was skipped.
31. Grace Overmyer's standard biography of Payne, *America's First Hamlet* (New York: New York Univ. Press, 1957), has nothing on his connection with the Sketch Club.
32. Respectively elected on May 8, 1829, Jan. 21, 1830, Jan. 17, Nov. 17, Nov. 17, 1831.
33. Jan. 28, 1830, hosted by John Inman at the Bank Coffee House.
34. Earlier in the poem Xanthippe had stuck her husband with a gimlet and then "complained that his bowels let wind in."
35. Some may prefer to call *windstopper/chin-chopper* triple assonance. It does seem akin to *mincingly/trippingly,* the example given for this term in Joseph T. Shipley, ed., *Dictionary of World Literature,* New Revised Ed. (New York: Philosophical Libarary, 1953), p. 31.
36. Feb. 4, 1830, at Weir's. For more on this meeting see Callow, "Weir and the Sketch Club," pp. 89-91.
37. This stanza is based on the associational esthetics of Archibald Alison, while the entire poem, with its emphasis on size, makes use of the theory of sublimity expounded by Edmund Burke. Associational psychology in the writings of Bryant is discussed by James T. Callow in his "William Cullen Bryant: Literary Critic," Master's thesis, Univ. of Toledo 1952, chap. 1 and 2.
38. The minutes spell it magnaminity.
39. Bryant, *Letters,* I, after 248.
40. As early as 1806 Bryant was echoing the clichés of James Thomson and was also trying to follow this eighteenth-century poet's practice of looking at nature directly. See Richard E. Peck, "Two Lost Bryant Poems: Evidence of Thomson's Influence." *American Literature,* 39 (March, 1967), 88-94. As late as 1871 Bryant was praising Thomson. See Bryant, *Prose Writings,* II, 321.
41. March 27, 1829.
42. John Neilson Jr. Cor. Sec.ʸ S. C. to Hon. G. C. Verplanck, New York, March 26th, 1832, New-York Historical Society.
43. Abraham John Mason (1794-?), a wood engraver, came from England to New York late in 1829. He was elected to membership in the Sketch

Club on Nov. 17, 1831 and is known to have attended its meetings into the Spring of 1833, the beginning of the minuteless period. In 1839, according to *DAA,* he returned to England.

44. March 30, 1832, in Bryant, *Letters,* I, 322.

45. The sole guest at this meeting was "Mr E. Bliss," certainly the Elam Bliss who had published *The Talisman* series and *The American Landscape.* See the Bryant *Letters,* passim, for numerous references.

46. Ironically, in 1833 the Harpers did publish Verplanck's *Discourses and Addresses on Subjects of American History, Arts, and Literature* (New York: J. & J. Harper).

47. Sands, Ward, Neilson, and Manton Eastburn had been, since 1819, the sole members of a club called The Literary Confederacy.

48. *The Writings of Robert C. Sands, in Prose and Verse, with a Memoir of the Author,* 2 vols. (New-York: Harper and Brothers, 1834). Though the memoir is usually attributed to Verplanck, the entire edition was actually a cooperative effort. The story may be pieced together by referring to Neilson's diary and the ever-helpful Bryant *Letters,* I, 365-66, 367-68, 375, 379, 386-87. Within a few days of Sands' death, Bryant, Ward, and Neilson discussed the desirability of such an edition; and on Dec. 24, 1832 Bryant asked Verplanck to "undertake the work." But without waiting for Verplanck's reply, they readied "subscription papers" which promised an edition prepared by a "literary friend." In a letter enclosing copies to Verplanck, Bryant renewed his request and offered to relieve the harried Congressman of any "drudgery" involved (Jan. 11, 1833). Meanwhile, he noted, Ward was moving easily toward the goal of procuring 1,000 or more subscribers (idem and Jan. 25, June 22, Sept. 10, 1833). No minutes survive to indicate whether the Sketch Club discussed the edition when they met at Bryant's in Hoboken on the afternoon of May 24, 1833, but a few days later Neilson, Ward, and Eastburn were there (or next door at Sands' to make selections for the edition from "some old files of papers" (Neilson's diary for May 29). By the end of the year things had come to a head, Bryant had apparently done most of the editorial writing, and some of the club's artists were involved as well. Bryant's wife clearly assessed the situation in a letter to her brother-in-law: "We miss poor Sands very much, his works will be published soon. Verplanck undertook to arrange them for the press—but has done but little about it. William has had the greater part of it to do. He was also to write a memoir of him, and the printers are now ready for it. Wm. went to see him the other day, he said that he had not begun it—yet, but thought he should have it ready soon. Mr. Weir took Sands's likeness after his death. Durand is engraving it. It will be placed in the book. We think it a pretty good likeness" (Frances Bryant to John Howard Bryant, New York, Dec. 15, 1833). Finally, in 1834, the book was published. As might be expected, a substantial part of the 28-page memoir prefacing the two volumes came from Bryant's pen. Many passages, in fact, clearly derive from a "Memoir of Robert C. Sands" which Bryant had written for the *Knickerbocker Magazine* more than a year earlier: *The Knickerbacker* (sic), 1 (Jan. 1833), 49-56.

No doubt this cooperative venture was also helped along by Robert's sister, Miss Julia Sands, who has been called the only female member of the Sketch Club. Though her name does not appear on the surviving rosters, she was in the habit of referring to certain members as Brother Ward, Brother Neilson, etc.

49. The meeting took place on Jan. 24, 1833, at Ward's. In his invitation to Morse the host specified that "Boyuca" would be the topic for sketching: Ray Ward to Morse, New York, Jan. 22, 1833, Morse Papers, Vol. XI, Library of Congress. Perhaps it was planned to use some of these sketches in the forthcoming edition of Sands' works. After the meeting Neilson wrote in his diary: ". . . passed evening at a meeting of S. C. at Bᵣ Ward's. Subject Boyuca. Some very pretty sketches made." The story, which is set in the exotic West Indies and tells of a search for the Fountain of Youth, would have obviously suited the artists' pencils.

50. Andrew Jackson's administration was less than four weeks old. Martin Van Buren, who had been elected governor of New York only the year before, was now chosen as secretary of state in Jackson's otherwise mediocre cabinet. Samuel Swartwout had been appointed collector of the Port of New York. Littleton W. Tazewell, at that time a U. S. senator from Virginia, was not made a member of the new cabinet, though Bryant had hoped for his appointment, or at least the appointment of others of equal caliber. (See Bryant, *Letters*, I, 277, 278 n.) John Randolph of Roanoke, now nearing the end of a distinguished career as statesman, had recently been defeated in a bid to return to the U. S. Senate but in 1829 was serving as a member of the Constitutional Convention of Virginia. He had backed Jackson in 1828, and the new president would later appoint him minister to Russia. Daniel Webster, who in 1828 had supported the "Tariff of Abominations," was currently serving as U. S. senator from Massachusetts. For his position on the tariff, and for other matters, he was the frequent target of Bryant's sharpest satire. See, for example, "Mr. Webster's Wit," New York *Evening Post*, Nov. 20, 1837.

51. I.e., Palmyra, a city in ancient Syria ruled in the 3rd century, A.D. by Queen Zenobia.

52. Samuel F. B. Morse, Henry Inman, and the Brothers Morton (John Ludlow and Henry Jackson) were artists; James Ellsworth DeKay was a medical doctor and naturalist.

53. Could Bryant have actually been discussing the hydropathic treatment given him at the age of three? "In after years . . . those who had been medical students with his father . . . delighted to tell of the cold baths they were ordered to give the infant poet in a spring near the house each early morning of the summer months, continuing the treatment, in spite of the outcries and protestations of their patient, so late into the autumn as sometimes to break the ice that skimmed the surface." Senator Dawes, quoted in Godwin, I, 5 n.

54. May 8, 1829. The offending "criticism" and "acount" appeared as an article in the *Evening Post* of May 7 describing the anniversary meeting of the Columbia College alumni, during which there was an oration by

Professor James Renwick and a dinner in College Hall. The initials probably stand for Morton or Morse, Ingham and Inman, Cummings or
Cole.
55. For example, on March 29, 1832 and Feb. 21, 1833.
56. April 8, 1830. Also April 17, 1829; March 25, April 1, 1830; and March
15, 1832. On March 29, 1832 A. J. Mason offered the club a song of his
which used the names of all the members. A copy of the text is in the minute book for that year.
57. March 15, 1832.
58. March 29, 1832.
59. April 17, 1829. See Callow, "Weir," p. 89.
60. Jan. 24, 1833.
61. April 17, 1829. See Callow, "Weir," pp. 88–89.
62. When the early minutes of the Sketch Club are published, they will be
seen to have more than biographical interest; for they also qualify as important chapters in the history of American humor and the informal essay.
63. It is even possible that Sands caused this whipping with one of his practi-
cal jokes. See Professor Bryant's interesting comment in Bryant, *Letters,*
I, 302–303.
64. Bryant, "On Originality and Imitation," *Prose Writings,* I, 35–44, discussed in Callow, "Bryant: Literary Critic," chap. 7.
65. Thompson, p. 62.
66. Bryant, "American Society as a Field for Fiction," *Prose Writings,* II,
351-60.
67. Thompson, p. 62.
68. See *DAA* for the artists; for Figanière, see *Grande Enciclopèdia Por-
tuguesa e Brasileira* (Lisbon; Rio de Janeiro: Editorial Enciclopèdia,
1942), XI, 280.
69. Bryant, "Sonnet—To Cole, the Painter, on His Departure for Europe,"
The Talisman for MDCCCXXX, p. 336.
70. See, for example, Bryant's memorial address on Cole in *Orations and
Addresses* (New York: G. P. Putnam's Sons, 1878), pp. 20–22. Other
cultural universalists among the Knickerbockers are identified in Callow,
Kindred Spirits, pp. 138–39.
71. See Callow, *Kindred Spirits,* pp. 32–36.
72. See the *DAB* and John Durand, *The Life and Times of A. B. Durand*
(New York: Charles Scribner's Sons, 1894), pp. 104-30; Lillian B. Miller,
*Patrons and Patroitism: The Encouragement of the Fine Arts in the
United States, 1790-1860* (Chicago: Univ. of Chicago Press, 1966), pp.
151–55, 172, 277–78. Reed, Sturges, and Leupp were all elected to membership at unknown dates, during the club's minuteless period.
73. Bryant discussed Cole's problems with these patrons in his talk on Cole
before the National Academy. See *Orations and Addresses,* pp. 9–11 (for
Featherstonhaugh), 26–27 (for Town).

William Cullen Bryant and the American Art Union

DAVID SHAPIRO
New College, Hofstra University

If one person can be said to have embodied the mainstream of American cultural life during the middle of the nineteenth century, that person was William Cullen Bryant. It was not his poetry alone that gave him that position, nor was it solely his editing of the *New York Evening Post.* He epitomized his time in his character, in his public being. Certainly he was at the center of the nation's culture, and frequently he was the high point around which events flowed.

The years of his presidency of the American Art Union—1844, 1845, and 1846—can serve as substantiation of the premise. During his three years tenure the organization's membership grew from 2,080 to 4,457. It may be said, in fact, that these three years put the Art-Union over the hump. (It had been organized in 1839 as the Apollo Association.) Thereafter the Art-Union became a powerful tastemaker, and by 1847 its membership had increased by more than 5,000 to a total of 9,666. Eventually the Art-Union reached a national roster of 19,000 before it was dissolved by law in 1853, ostensibly for operating a lottery.

What was this organization, the American Art-Union, and how did it come into being? According to its plan: "The American Art-Union in the City of New York is incorporated by the Legislature of New York for the promotion of the fine arts in the United States." It was to be "managed by gentlemen" who received no compensation and who were to be chosen annually by the members. Its aim was to "accomplish a truly national objective, uniting great public good with private gratification at small individual expense [in ways] best suited to the situation and institutions in our country, the wants, the habits, and taste of our people."[1] Bryant, presiding over the annual meeting of December, 1845, put it succinctly: "The plan of our Institution is to collect small contributions into large masses, and to direct them to great results."[2]

The annual five-dollar membership subscription fees were to be divided among several fixed projects. Of first importance was the production of a large and costly engraving from an American painting, of which each member was to receive a copy. Such engravings were expensive to produce, since a craftsman might spend as long as three years to make one. Whenever funds justified it, an extra engraving or work of art was to be furnished to the members.

Each member was to receive the *Bulletin* of the American Art-Union, a monthly publication of sixteen pages, which was to include in each issue an etching or engraving of a painting that had been purchased as well as the *Transactions* of the Art-Union.

Funds received from membership fees were to be applied to the purchase of American paintings and sculptures by native or resident artists. These works were to be publicly exhibited in the Gallery of the Art-Union from the time of acquisition until the Annual Meeting in December, just before Christmas, when all were to be raffled off, each member having one chance for each five dollars paid. The Art-Union was also to maintain an office and a free picture gallery in New York City, where members could see new works of art and receive their engravings, paintings, and reports.

So much for the Art-Union's plan of organization, which of course was further spelled out in detail. The important innovation of the Art-Union was that the patronage of wealthy private individuals was replaced by a membership organization. In numbers, art patrons were multiplied, although none need have been wealthy. Additionally, individual taste was superseded by the judgment of those empowered by the Art-Union to make selections.

This was a novel way of supporting art and artists. By using the large sums of money collected via its five dollar subscriptions, the Art-Union became an educator and tastemaker as well as a patron. It was able to purchase large numbers of paintings that were distributed by means of an annual raffle. Its art journal, the *Bulletin*, kept its thousands of members informed about the art world here and abroad. In each issue an etching or engraving, "suitable for framing," as the saying still goes, was given to the members. By sponsoring a free art gallery, then rare, and perhaps more importantly, by insisting on *Ameri-*

can subject matter in landscape and genre painting, the Art-Union was able to affect taste in the United States.

The *Bulletin* reported from time to time on works of art submitted for purchase by artists and let readers know about those rejected or accepted. In 1850, for instance, 1800 paintings were offered to the Art-Union, of which 460 were purchased. Two years earlier, the *Transactions* noted, the works of art selected had been "painted by 231 different artists, residing in fifty towns in sixteen states and territories, from Maine to Louisiana, [and] in Rome, Florence, Dusseldorf, Paris, and London."³ It went on to report that paintings had been purchased from 145 artists in New York, 27 in Pennsylvania, 10 in Massachusetts, 7 from Ohio, 5 from New Jersey, and 4 from artists who lived in the District of Columbia—and small numbers of works coming from half a dozen other states. Since the membership, too, was national, the result was widespread support for American art to a far greater degree than had ever been known before.

There was a specific procedure artists were required to follow in submitting paintings. Work was entered at the artist's expense; the price of the work was to be stated in writing; work was to be suitably framed, and was to be hung at the discretion of the Committee of Management. All these provisos are similar to those today for work entered in competitive exhibitions, but no competition in recent times has been able to purchase anything like the number of works the Art-Union could afford. Artists were in general pleased with the existence of the Art-Union and the National Academy of Design. But to most of the artists the most important issue was whether their own paintings were selected for purchase and the prices they were paid for them.

The American Art-Union seems at first glance peculiarly American in concept, a matter about which it boasted in the annual report of 1848, saying that the Institution had been created "for the 'greatest good of the greatest number,' [that] it had been modeled after naught but the demands of the age and of the land we love."⁴ But the *Knickerbocker Magazine*, in an article on the history of art-unions, said that these membership art-buying clubs were invented in Munich, Germany, in 1823. An art-union was founded in Berlin in 1825, and by 1839 there were 29 such unions in Germany. Further, the *Knickerbocker* article reported, "the London Art-Union was established in 1837, and Edinburgh, Dublin, Manchester, Birmingham, and other cities of the United Kingdom" followed with similar organizations soon thereafter.[5] They functioned in essentially the same way, with membership fees used for the purchase of engravings for all and for paintings distributed to winners of lotteries. The American Art-Union changed its name from the Apollo Society, in fact, because "the term Art-Union had gained distinctive and universal acceptance."[6]

The American Art-Union felt itself to be in competition with the London Art-Union, Europe's largest. The American Art-Union claimed moral superiority because of its free art gallery, its method of awarding works of art, and because it was designed for the "whole republic." (The London Art-Union awarded money prizes to members, who were thus enabled to select paintings at specified galleries.) By 1849 the American Art-Union had almost twice the membership of its London counterpart, with 18,960 members as against London's 10,391. By November, 1849, the *Knickerbocker Magazine* could say that "so far as the extent of territory embraced in its operation is conceived, all the foreign associations are insignificant in comparison with this, and, in fact, our association [the American Art-Union] is, for our country, the mother of Art-Unions."[7]

The achievements of the Art-Union excited emulation and resulted in the establishment of "five other Art-Unions in different sections of the United States, all engaged in the same cause, and all attended with a good degree of success,"[8] the Art-Union *Bulletin* reported in 1850. These five were the Western Art-Union in Cincinnatti, the Philadelphia Art-Union, the New England Art-Union in Boston, the New Jersey Art-Union in Newark, and the Chicago Art-Union. Public response to all of these resulted in an influx of organizations from abroad hoping to cash in on the market for art.

One of these, the Dusseldorf Art-Union, established an American branch called the Dusseldorf Gallery in New York. But by 1857 the Cosmopolitan Art Association of Sandusky, Ohio, organized in 1854 along the lines of the American Art-Union, (although the latter by then no longer existed), bought out the entire stock of the Dusseldorf Gallery for $180,000. Earlier the Dusseldorf had been accepted by the American Art-Union without demur, though not so the International Art-Union, another new arrival from Europe. The *Bulletin* in October and November of 1849 declared that the International was a front for Goupil, Vibert, a Paris art gallery, and thus a commercial enterprise masquerading as an art-union. Even though it, too, ran a free gallery, the works exhibited there, according to the *Bulletin*, were "faulty in moral tone and in point of technical excellence," and they emphasized "the sensual rather than the spiritual elements of art."[9]

The International Art-Union was the only competitor with which the American Art-Union did not have friendly relations. Each attacked the other, and newspapers and journals chose sides, while the *Bulletin* declared that "no other Art-Union in the world shall excel ours in the quality, the numbers, or the variety of works to be distributed to all its members."[10] The Art-Union believed, furthermore, that its subscription list could not possibly be diminished other than by such a disaster as an epidemic—never by the competition. And as it turned out, no other art-union ever came close to their success, and as for the International, it was never even a serious rival.

This was the proud organization over which William Cullen Bryant presided. His tremendous influence as a public cultural figure made him a good choice, and in his speeches he made the Art-Union "a symbol of democracy, insisting that popular taste can often be good taste and that both artist and public benefit from a wide distribution of original paintings."[11] Bryant also counted artists as close personal friends, among them Asher Durand and Thomas Cole, and he had had contact with art students in the period during which he taught them mythology at the National Academy of Design. As a member of the Sketch Club, where amateurs and professionals in the arts came together, Bryant met frequently with artists and sketched alongside them at meetings. His reviews of art were published in the *Evening Post* and elsewhere. One instance of the artists' warmth toward Bryant occurred on his 70th birthday, when, at a celebration given by the Century Club, he was presented, by Daniel Huntington, President of the National Academy of Design, with a portfolio of works given by such artists as Asher Durand, Daniel Huntington, John Kensett, Eastman Johnson, Fredserick Church, Swain Gifford, Emmanuel Leutze, and Albert Bierstadt among others—as impressive a list of well-known American painters as could have been garnered. Bryant responded by saying, "I prize this gift . . . not only as a memorial of the genius of our artists, but also as a token of the goodwill of a class of men for whom I cherish a particular regard and esteem."[12]

His friendship with artists and his understanding of their problems helped avert open expression of the intense rivalry that existed between the Art-Union and the National Academy. Not so fortunate was his successor, general and poet Prosper M. Wetmore. During his presidency relations deteriorated. But while Bryant was in office the Committee on Management could report in 1845 that "the opinions of artists and connoisseurs justify us in also saying that much good has been realized—that within the sphere of our action and, in part, by our influence, artists of merit are more employed and better paid than ever before; that American art has risen to a position which it never held before, and that in the City of New York, at least, other institutions for the promotion of the fine arts have found in the American Art-Union a valuable coadjutor. The National Academy of Design and its schools of instruction, and the New York Gallery, more recently established, instead of being injured as some people feared they would be, by our prosperity, have really derived some indirect aid from our labors. It is now apparent that we do not occupy a position of rivalry with those institutions. We are only of their sisterhood."[13]

But when Wetmore was president the rift with the National Academy became so intense that the Academy threatened to inaugurate its own "Painters and Sculptors Art-Union," while the Art-Union, in retaliation, warned that it would start a rival art school. Wetmore, speaking for the Art-Union, said that "ours is indeed a free Academy of Art," implying that the National Academy was anything but free.[14] There were concrete reasons for the quarrel. The National Academy, an organization composed of artists only, charged admission to its annual exhibitions. It strongly believed, furthermore, that the Art-Union, as Academy Treasurer Thomas E. Cummings said, "congregated the art patronage in its own hands—it made the demand and furnished the supply," and, it was averred, the Art-Union "had its favorites in the distribution of its favors." It was also said of the Art-Union that it "ruled the artists," that "they became jealous of its power and thus neither the serving nor the intended-to-be-served were satisfied."[15]

It is true that the Art-Union, as an organization buying hundreds of paintings every year, could make or break an artist economically and in terms of reputation by distributing (or choosing not to) thousands of engravings of a painting and by exhibiting original work. Even if not abused, such power can be fearsome. This particular furor between the National Academy and the Art-Union died down, however, after Wetmore was succeeded by Abraham Cozzens, like Bryant familiar with the Academy, indeed an Honorary Member of it—an "Amateur of the Academy" as such non-professionals were termed. Cozzens's policy of rapprochement between the two organizations was effective.

II.

It cannot be denied that many of the works selected by the American Art-Union were influenced by Bryant, either by his poetry or his essays. The greatest words of praise for a painting at that time were that it was "a perfect poem," as was said of Thomas Cole's allegorical series, "The Voyage of Life." Some paintings were inspired by Bryant's poetry or directly illustrated his lines. Asher Durand's "Pastoral Landscape" was exhibited alongside these lines from Bryant's "Fountain":[16]

Blue eyed girls
Brought pails, and dipped them in the crystal pool;
And children, ruddy-cheeked and flaxen haired,
Gathered the glistening cowslip from the edge.

Similarly, Durand's painting, "Thanatopsis," was exhibited by the Art-Union with these lines appended:[17]

The hills
Rock-ribbed and ancient in the sun—the vales, etc.

Yet, if the paintings echoed and sometimes illustrated Bryant, it was because the painters and the poet were at one with their time. Bryant's ideas about taste indicate that he was familiar with Archibald Alison's theories of associational psychology as presented in *Essays on the Nature and Principle of Taste*. "When any object, either of sublimity or beauty," Alison wrote, "is presented to the mind, I believe every man is conscious of a train of thought being immediately awakened in his imagination, analogous to the character or expression of the original object."[18] The artists, like Bryant, hoped to evoke the right reactions in the minds of their audience by presenting objects of sublimity or beauty.

To Bryant, as well as to the Hudson River artists and aestheticians, works such as William Gilpin's *Forest Scenery and Other Woodland Views* also seem to have been important. For all of these poets, critics, artists, and theoreticians, Nature, which was consistent with morality, was God's creation. Bryant's "Forest Hymn" says what each of them said in one form or another.

Father, thy hand
Hath reared these venerable columns, thou

didst weave this verdant roof.
And to the beautiful order of thy works
Learn to conform the order of our lives.[19]

In his essay, "Thoughts on a Rainy Day," published in 1823 in the New York *Mirror*, Bryant explicates his thoughts on the relationship between God and Nature.

> While *nature* holds an instructive volume, while she publishes to the heart *her* religion, a voice is heard from every moving sphere: it addresses itself to the reason of man—it is the voice of divine truth! It commands him to compare the religion of *nature* with the higher and holier system revealed, in beneficent goodness, from Heaven to "Moses and the prophets."

> And, on making the comparison, can no difference be discovered? Yes; the natural religion is but an evidence of the power, the illimitable dominion of God; and, as such, is entitled to the reverence of men; the *revealed* contains the sacred precepts of His grace, His mercy, and His love.[20]

Nature, then, points to God, but revealed religion is a higher manifestation of God. Bryant proposes that evidence of a Creative Being is revealed by our untrammeled natural world, a wilderness "fresher from the hand of him who made it" than the Europe from which our culture had sprung. Such unspoiled nature was itself a manifestation, to Bryant, of a mightier power.

The painter Thomas Cole, in his essays on American scenery, offers similar thoughts. "Perhaps the most impressive characteristic of American scenery is its wildness," Cole wrote. Therefore "the consequent associations are of God the creator—they are undefiled works and the mind is cast into contemplation of eternal things."[21] Although there was still much wildness on the American continent during Cole's time, the Hudson River mountains and valleys that formed his habitual locale were already far from pristine or truly wild.

Bryant's ideas on the sublime and the beautiful reached the artists through his poems. Asher Durand was especially responsive. The art critic Henry Tuckerman wrote in 1847: "Set Durand's 'The Beeches' alongside certain verses by Bryant . . . and in spirit you will find they are identical." George Sheldon, another critic, wrote that "the mention of Mr. Bryant's name suggests the fact of a resemblance between

the aims and the methods of Mr. Durand and the author of 'Thanatopsis.' . . . Mr. Durand's [paintings] 'In the Woods' . . . and his
'Primeval Forest' . . . are [Bryant's] 'Forest Hymns.'" Such reciprocal influence was so evident it need not be further belabored, but it was
not Durand alone who responded in this way. Thomas Cole and a host
of other painters, especially those patronized by the American Art-
Union, can be seen to echo Bryant in their prose, paintings, and in the
verse at which many of them dabbled.

Yet despite his influence on the painters of his age, there was little
original about Bryant. He either followed or emulated ideas found in
Wordsworth, Gilpin, Alison, Channing, and others. Bryant's importance lies in the way he transmitted and focused their thinking in his essays and poetry. Perhaps equally significant was his exemplary role as
a widely respected public figure. This morally engaged man, who attempted to do good only, came to be seen as the prototypical American intellectual. Known throughout the literary and artistic world of
his time, he was the stream on which so many of the intellectual,
moral, aesthetic, and political ideas of the day were carried, the condu-
it that irrigated a thirsty society.

Bryant's role, as transmitter of what was probably the best of Establishment thought, was essential to the Art-Union in its formative
years, and helped to make it the powerful tastemaker it became. If the
list of works purchased and exhibited by the American Art-Union and
the documentation of their distribution during one year of Bryant's
leadership are examined, it becomes evident that an actualization of
Bryant's idea of "a democratic art for a democratic people" was
achieved. Of the 115 works distributed by lot in 1845, the middle of his
three-year presidency, it will be seen that at least half were painted by
artists now acknowledged to have been among our very best. Thomas
Cole's "View on the Catskill" was won by a lucky Joseph Hyde of
New York; Asher Durand's "Study Near Marbleton" went to prize
winner George Eaton of Baltimore, Maryland; Cole's "Deserted
House on Mt. Desert Island" was the prize of a man in Salem, Massachusetts, and George Caleb Bingham's masterpiece, "Fur Traders De-
scending the Missouri," now in the Metropolitan Museum, went to
Mobile, Alabama. John Kensett's "Footpath in Burnham Forest"
went to a member in Detroit.[23] The high level of the paintings and the
widespread membership show that all over the country there were people aspiring for art as a moral and uplifting experience. They seem to
have agreed with Cole's notion, parallel to Bryant's, that "art, in its

true sense, is in fact man's lovely imitation of the creative power of the Almighty."[24]

NOTES

1. M. Bartlett Cowdrey and Charles E. Baker, *American Academy of Fine Arts and American Art-Union, 1816–1852* (New York: New York Historical Society, 1953), p. 114.
2. William Cullen Bryant, American Art-Union *Transactions for 1845*, p. 5. At the Annual Meeting on December 18, 1846, Bryant spoke of the "flattering success" the Art-Union had experienced in the past year. "The season which now closes is altogether the most brilliant," he said, with the number of works purchased and distributed "richest and largest." He continued: "Our artists paint with a freer and happier pencil, they give us more and better pictures, because they know they have a resource in our Institution . . . We may claim, therefore, to have done something to awaken and call forth a genius for Art among our countrymen."
3. Cowdrey and Baker, *American Art-Union*, p. 151.
4. *Ibid.*, p. 133. The authors are quoting from the American Art-Union's 1848 Annual Report.
5. *Ibid.*
6. *Ibid.*, p. 134
7. *Ibid.*, pp. 137–138.
8. *Ibid.*, p. 138.
9. *Ibid.*, p. 145.
10. *Ibid.*, p. 147.
11. James T. Callow, *Knickerbocker Writers and Artists* (Chapel Hill: University of North Carolina, 1967), p. 226.
12. John Bigelow, *William Cullen Bryant* (Boston and New York: Houghton Mifflin, 1897), p. 231. In making this presentation of 43 sketches on November 3, 1864, Daniel Huntington said, "The artists love you very much, and you know it; we claim you as one of us, remembering that you were one of the original members of the old Sketch Club, and a member and founder of the National Academy of Design . . . For many years we have been cheered by your mind pictures of American scenery, and inspired by your sounds of human freedom, and we pray that God may grant you yet many years to charm our hearts with new images of truth and beauty." Bryant responded, "Among the artists of our country are some of my oldest and best friends. In their conversation I have taken great delight, derived from it much instruction." (George Bancroft, *The Bryant Festival at the Century* [New York: Appleton, 1865]), p. 41.
13. American Art-Union *Transactions for 1845*, p. 6.
14. Cowdrey and Baker, *American Art-Union*, p. 188.
15. Thomas S. Cummings, *Annals of the National Academy* (Philadelphia: G. W. Childs, 1865), p. 149.

16. David La Wall, *Asher Durand* (New York: Garland, 1977), p. 234. In an article that appeared in the *Magazine of Art*, October 1952, titled "James Fenimore Cooper and the Hudson River School," Howard Mumford Jones outlined the two fundamental ideas of Hudson River writers and artists. These were 1) the theme of the grandeur of God working in the universe, and 2) the theme of the decay of empire, the assumption that nations, like men, have their childhood, youth, maturity, old age, and death. Thomas Cole's "Voyage of Life" and "Course of Empire" exemplify this idea. Emerson's notion is similar when he states that "the world proceeds from the same spirit as the body of man. It is a remoter, and inferior incarnation of God in the subconscious. Its serene order is inviolable by us. It is, therefore, to us, the present expositor of the divine mind."

17. *Bulletin of the American Art-Union* (May 1850), p. 20. The *Bulletin* for December, 1850, also quotes several lines from the poem.

18. La Wall, *Durand*, p. 242.

19. *Ibid.*, p. 479–480, 500.

20. *Ibid.*, p. 500.

21. Thomas Cole "Essay on American Scenery," *American Monthly Magazine*, New Series, I (January, 1836), p. 5.

22. La Wall, *Durand*, p. 468.

23. *Transactions* of the American Art-Union, 1845, pp. 27–29.

24. Louis L. Noble, *The Course of Empire, Voyage of Life and Other Pictures of Thomas Cole* (New York: Cornish, Lamport, 1853), p. 336.

Patterns of Enclosure:
Unity in the Poems of
William Cullen Bryant

GAINES McMARTIN
Gallaudet College

The poetry of William Cullen Bryant is not fundamentally a poetry of exploration and discovery. Most of the ideas and experiences presented by Bryant's poems were very familiar to his readers. When Bryant used a yellow violet to present a picture of humility, and when he used a waterfowl to present his idea of divine providence, he was neither challenging nor extending the means available for understanding the world. Instead, the best of Bryant's poems serve to reinforce and lend an added measure of form to familiar ideas and experiences.[1] Bryant's poetry presents a coherent and ordered world, a world whose boundaries are understood and accepted on the basis of faith as well as experience.[2]

In addition, Bryant's poems do not seem to have the kind of unified organic and symbolic structure that we often find in poetry of exploration and discovery. Unlike Walt Whitman, Bryant does not use symbolic images that grow in complexity and ambiguity as they become the focal points of a poem's developing meaning. In contrast, Bryant's images, such as that of the yellow violet and the waterfowl, can seem static in their relationships to the abstract statements that follow.

But whether or not we wish to call it a symbolic or an organic unity, many of Bryant's poems have a rather thorough-going unity of their own kind. Much of this unity is centered on patterns of enclosure. Many of Bryant's poems are dominated by images of enclosure in nature, whether on a small scale such as that of the reeds bending over the nest of the waterfowl, whether on a grand scale such as that of the vast prairies hedged round with forests and swelling under the vaulted sky, or whether on a cosmic or metaphysical scale such as that of the encircling expansion of "The Flood of Years" which flows outward forming the boundary of time and existence. Images of enclosure like these often combine with a careful circumscription of the range of meaning of the poem's central metaphors to give the feeling that life has a measure of coherence and can be fulfilled within a recognizable set of boundaries.

Perhaps the basis of the unity in Bryant's poems can be examined best by looking first at a poem that may seem to have an inconsistency or a break in its structure. The first two stanzas of "A Scene on the Banks of the Hudson" present a remarkable series of images of enclosure:

> Cool shades and dews are round my way,
> And silence of the early day;
> Mid the dark rocks that watch his bed,
> Glitters the mighty Hudson spread,
> Unrippled, save by drops that fall
> From shrubs that fringe his mountain wall;
> And o'er the clear still water swells
> The music of the Sabbath bells.
>
> All, save this little nook of land,
> Circled with trees, on which I stand;
> All, save that line of hills which lie
> Suspended in the mimic sky—
> Seems a blue void, above, below,
> Through which the white clouds come and go;
> And from the green world's farthest steep
> I gaze into the airy deep.[3]

In the first stanza the poet finds his way surrounded by "cool shades and dews," the Hudson spread "mid the dark rocks," and the rocks in turn "fringed" by the shrubs, from which drops of dew fall into the river, marking it with circular patterns but not destroying the stillness of the water. There is also a quiet enclosure in sound as Sabbath bells swell over the scene. In the next stanza we find the nook of land surrounded by trees, by water, and finally by the sky, both above and below, as it is reflected in the water. Finally, in spite of, or perhaps because of all this encircling and enclosure, the poet finds himself "from the green world's farthest steep" gazing "into the airy deep." He is somehow freed from all sense of being surrounded.

The next stanza seems to break the unity of the poem:

Loveliest of lovely things are they,
On earth, that soonest pass away.
The rose that lives its little hour
Is prized beyond the sculptured flower.
Even love, long tried and cherished long,
Becomes more tender and more strong
At thought of that insatiate grave
From which its yearnings cannot save.

Instead of following up on the description of his powerful experience of enclosure and escape, Bryant opens this stanza with a statement about mutability, and illustrates it with a rose, an image unrelated to the images in the first two stanzas. He closes this stanza with a moral about the strength of love in the face of approaching death. Certainly the stanza does not seem to grow very directly out of anything in the first two.

The next, and concluding, stanza refers back to the images in the first two stanzas, but it does not seem to be a very strong follow up:

River! in this still hour thou hast
Too much of heaven on earth to last;
Nor long may thy still waters lie,
An image of the glorious sky.
Thy fate and mine are not repose,
And ere another evening close,
Thou to thy tides shalt turn again,
And I to seek the crowd of men.

The series of images of enclosure leading to "from the green world's farthest steep/I gaze into the airy deep" is now reduced to a rather simple idea of repose, a kind of Sunday morning "heaven" free from the cares of the crowd of men. The first two stanzas of this poem seem full of the potential for a mystical experience, or at the very least, for some kind of new understanding or personal revelation. But instead, the third and fourth stanzas introduce a series of conventional ideas presented with a series of brief and equally conventional images unrelated to the earlier images of enclosure.

But from another point of view "A Scene on the Banks of the Hudson" could be said to have a more unified structure. Part of Bryant's feeling of repose may come from the ideas expressed in the third stanza. The development of the poem indicates that these ideas were not derived from the images presented in the first half of the poem, but were understood and accepted long before the poet entered the scene. However, these ideas are, in a sense, part of the enclosure he experiences; by circumscribing the import of the imagery in the first two stanzas they help Bryant to be at peace—if he were involoved in an act of discovery of one kind or another that peace might not be so complete. The images of enclosure, therefore, can be symbolic of Bryant's own safe enclosure in a world of fixed moral ideas. He does not need to make any new discovery or decision about his relationship to nature; the natural world he experiences is a familiar world, and he has always known that he will have to return to "seek the crowd of men."[4] In this light the last three lines are an effective conclusion to the poem—the day will close with evening, the tide will turn again to the sea, and Bryant himself must return to his busy human world. The cycles of the life of nature echo the cycles of the life of man; both nature and man exist within inevitable echoing and cyclic enclosures.

In "The Yellow Violet" we see a somewhat different relationship between image and idea, but the basic strategy of their presentation is similar. Instead of veering away from a more direct involvement with the dominant pattern of images as he does in "A Scene on the Banks of the Hudson," here Bryant carefully circumscribes the central image from the outset. In this poem Bryant expresses his idea about humility by creating a metaphor in which the yellow violet's relationship to the world of nature and other flowers is analogous to man's relationship to society and other men. But Bryant does not first present the flower in its own terms and then draw on the image for analogies that will help reveal the nature of humility; instead, he personifies the flower, describing it as if it were a little humble person. It has a "glowing lip," a "gentle eye," an "early smile," and remains on its low "seat" while other flowers are "flaunting nigh." Thus the yellow violet becomes in part an example illustrating directly an already known idea of humility, instead of functioning as an analogy through which we can discover something new. In contrast, Walt Whitman in poems like "A Noiseless Patient Spider" and section 28 of "Song of Myself" uses the opposite technique—instead of transferring language from the subject of the metaphor to the image, he transfers language from his image to his subject.[6] For example, in "Noiseless Patient Spider" a thought becomes a "ductile anchor"—the image of the spider building a web acts as a metaphor by providing language that can help us better understand the subject of a man seeking to understand and relate to his world. But in many of Bryant's poems, although the metaphorical image seems to come first, and the moral or idea later, in fact the idea is prior to the image and is the source of much of the language that is used in its presentation. This technique can be a way of carefully circumscribing the power of a metaphor to suggest new ways of looking at things. Bryant's images are presented so that they function as reminders of ideas and experiences already known and accepted.

"To a Waterfowl" presents its central image in a way very similar to that used in "The Yellow Violet." The bird is personified, suggesting that its need for guidance is the same as man's. Therefore, instead of serving as an analogy that presents a comparison between two similar yet different relationships, the image is transformed so that it can stand as a direct example. As the final stanza makes clear, man and bird are in fact guided by the same supreme being.[7]

In "A Forest Hymn" and "Thanatopsis" the central images do not really provide opportunities for the kind of analogies we have been discussing, but we see the same basic strategy for controlling their meanings that we saw in "The Yellow Violet" and "To a Waterfowl." "A Forest Hymn" presents the idea that because the forest is a pure creation of God, lacking the evidences of pomp and pride present in cathedrals, it can be an ideal place of worship. This poem can suggest a kind of pantheism as well as other revolutionary ideas concerning the prevailing churches, but Bryant carefully skirts these issues in order to focus on the idea that the forest is in fact a temple. After asking why we worship only "under roofs that our frail hands have raised" Bryant speaks of the "venerable columns," "dim vaults," and "winding aisles" of the forest. Thus the forest is not truly an alternative to a temple as a place of worship; instead, it is transformed so that we can see it as actually being a kind of temple. The forest can provide pure religious influences when we see it in terms of our usual places of worship.

"Thanatopsis has a similar structure in its central metaphor. Although the first verse paragraph presents an image of man in death losing his individual identity when he is "resolved to earth again," the poem turns away from this idea and focuses instead on the concept of the earth as a tomb that provides a magnificent and vast resting place where we will join all the people who have died since the beginning of time. The earth-as-tomb image controls the thought in the poem even to the point of suggesting that geographical features are grand funeral decorations.[8]

All of the poems I have discussed so far have not only carefully circumscribed metaphorical images, but also strong images of enclosure that contribute to their meaning and overall unity. In "To a Water-fowl" the bird's flight "along that pathless coast—/ The desert and il-limitable air" is contrasted with two kinds of enclosure. On the larger scale, the bird is taken up in God's creation when heaven "hath swal-lowed up" its form—the fowler's eye is helpless to harm a bird en-closed in such vastness. And on the smaller scale the bird seeks an en-closure in a summer home, where "reeds shall bend,/ Soon o'er thy sheltered nest."[9] In "The Yellow Violet" the images of enclosure are indirect: the flower is at first exposed and alone, flowering "beside the snow bank's edges cold." Later it becomes surrounded and over-topped by other flowers, but it accepts this enclosure amid the society of others and does not violate its own nature. In "A Forest Hymn" the natural objects underneath the over-arching branches of the forest safely can be "instinct with God;" Bryant carefully avoids expanding his ideas beyond these confines to include a radical pantheism. The im-ages of enclosure in "Thanatopsis" are even more prominent, dominating the development of the earth-as-tomb idea.

But because the morals of these poems are stated so explicitly, and are not always related directly to the images of enclosure, many of these poems can seem to have a division between image and moral that the idea of a comforting enclosure in a world of familiar ideas may not quite bridge. It is one thing to see a unity between an image of enclo-sure and a moral that itself focuses on the idea of rest, comfort, and peace, but it is quite another thing to see a parallel between an image of enclosure and the mere fact that a familiar and conventional moral is provided, having the indirect effect of providing comfort.

However, some of Bryant's poems do not include an explicit moral, and it is in these that images of enclosure often provide their most uni-fied thematic current, one fully a part of the structure of meaning. "An Indian Story" is a short narrative poem of about eighty lines that tells of a young brave's hunt for a deer, the abduction of his bride dur-ing his absence, and her recovery. Bryant does not conclude the poem with an explicit moral, but relies on a pattern of images, including en-closure, to focus his meaning. Instead of describing the central actions of the story directly, the imagery of the poem develops a series of par-allels between Indian and nature. The first three stanzas present young Maquon's song as he goes off to the hunt:

> I know where the timid fawn abides
> In the depths of the shaded dell,

Where the leaves are broad and the thicket hides,
With its many stems and its tangled sides,
   From the eye of the hunter well.

I know where the young May violet grows,
   In its lone and lowly nook,
On the mossy bank, where the larch-tree throws
Its broad dark bough, in solemn respose,
   Far over the silent brook.

And that timid fawn starts not with fear
   When I steal to her secret bower;
And that young May violet to me is dear,
And I visit the silent streamlet near,
   To look on the lovely flower.

The fawn and flower in their enclosures are images of Maquon's new bride whom he leaves enclosed in her own bower, and his specially privileged knowledge of these bowers signifies his harmony with nature. But while the bride, fawn, and flower lie in shaded enclosures, "evil eyes/ Are at watch in thicker shades." When Maquon returns from his hunt carrying the deer, he finds the bower destroyed, his bride gone, and when he calls he hears only "The hum of the laden bee"—an ironic image of himself laden with the red deer, and of his rival who has made off with the young bride. But by autumn Maquon has recovered his bride and left his foe under "a hillock of fresh dark mould,/ In the deepest gloom of the spot." Maquon's foe does not belong with a bride in the shade of a bower, but can live only in "thicker shades," and in death lies under the dark mould. Enclosure to this degree becomes imprisonment. An additional pattern of images associates Maquon, a red man, with the color red—the red deer, the firebird, the red sunset, and the red autumn are all signals of his successes.

Thus, "An Indian Story" presents ideas of good and evil through a pattern of images, without an appended moral. The young brave simply exemplifies life in harmony with nature. "The Murdered Traveller" also makes a particularly effective use of imagery. Again, enclosure is important, but its opposite, exposure, dominates the development of the poem.

When Spring, to woods and wastes around,
   Brought bloom and joy again,
The murdered traveller's bones were found,
   Far down a narrow glen.

The fragrant birch, above him, hung
   Her tassels in the sky;
And many a vernal blossom sprung,
   And nodded careless by.

The red bird warbled, as he wrought
   His hanging nest o'erhead,
And fearless, near the fatal spot,
   Her young the partridge led.

But there was weeping far away,
   And gentle eyes, for him,
With watching many an anxious day,
   Were sorrowful and dim.

They little knew, who loved him so,
   The fearful death he met,
When shouting o'er the desert snow,
   Unarmed and hard beset;—

Now how, when round the frosty pole
   The northern dawn was red,
The mountain-wolf and wild-cat stole
   To banquet on the dead;—

Now how, when strangers found his bones,
   They dressed the hasty bier,
And marked his grave with nameless stones,
   Unmoistened by a tear.

But long they looked, and feared, and wept,
   Within his distant home;
And dreamed, and started as they slept,
   For joy that he was come.

Long, long they looked—but never spied
   His welcome step again,
Nor knew the fearful death he died
   Far down that narrow den.

The imagery is more direct than that in "An Indian Story," describing nothing in terms of something else in the way the Indian brave's bride was described as a fawn and a flower. The contrasts in the scene are presented with a pure simplicity. We see the hardness of winter, the joyful but indifferent spring, and finally the inability of those who find the traveller's bones either to understand his fate, or to notify those people far away who loved him and still expect him amid their grief over his absence. The images of enclosure and exposure subtly vary the images representing comfort and respose in Bryant's other poems. The traveller's bones are enclosed by nature, but this enclosure is indifferent and incomplete. The fragrant birch does not over-arch or embower his bones, which are beyond comfort anyway, but simply "above him, hung/ Her tassels in the sky." This contrasts ironically with the image of his exposure when he faced the fatal attack "shouting o'er the desert snow,/ Unarmed and hard beset;—." Images of enclosure and exposure are fully integrated into the development of the poem.

In several poems, such as "The Journey of Life," "The Unknown Way," and "The Two Travellers," Bryant uses a journey as an allegorical image of life. In those poems Bryant takes an idea of a journey, and then shapes it to conform to the view of life he wants to express. This shaping is not unlike the shaping and circumscribing of the central images of poems such as "The Yellow Violet" and others. But in "The Murdered Traveller" the presentation of the journey has an archtypal integrity; at least it has not been overtly transformed to fit the ideas Bryant wishes to express. A part of its effectiveness is in its spare simplicity—in fact the journey and the murder itself are not really described, and the victim is simply an anonymous traveller with no specific destination, occupation, or home. The poem is an example as parable about man's aloneness both in life and while facing death, and the uncertainties we all must bear in a world where communication fails.

Just as the presence of an explicit moral in poems such as "To a Waterfowl," "A Forest Hymn, and "A Scene on the Banks of the Hudson" could seem to be reflected in their images of enclosure, so in "The Murdered Traveller" the lack of a comforting moral can seem to be reflected in images of exposure and ironic semi-enclosure. "Rizpah," which presents Rizpah's lament during her trials and grief over her dead and outcast sons, has a powerful reflection of its theme in its imagery of exposure. This poem also lacks a comforting moral, ending with:

> . . .But the howling wind and the driving rain
> Will beat on my houseless head in vain:
> I shall stay, from my murdered sons to scare
> The beasts of the desert, and fowls of air.

Many of Bryant's poems which have more extended descriptions of nature are also dominated by images of enclosure. These poems generally review familiar aspects of nature and do not recount the discovery of the particular and concrete. For example, in lines 28 to 50 of "A Winter Piece" Bryant does not attempt to present a specific scene:

Still there was a beauty in my walks; the brook
Bordered with sparkling frost-work, was as gay
As with its fringe of summer flowers. Afar,
The village with its spires, the path of streams
And dim receding valleys, hid before
By interposing trees, lay visible
Through the bare grove, and my familiar haunts
Seemed new to me. Nor was I slow to come
Among them, when the clouds, from their still skirts,
Had shaken down on earth the feathery snow,
And all was white. The pure keen air abroad,
Albeit breathed no scent of herb, nor heard
Love call of bird nor merry hum of bee,
Was not the air of death. Bright mosses crept
Over the spotted trunks, and the close buds,
That lay along the boughs, instinct with life,
Patient, and waiting the soft breath of spring,
Feared not the piercing spirit of the North.
The snow-bird twittered on the beechen bough,
And 'neath the hemlock, whose thick branches bent
Beneath its bright cold burden, and kept dry
A circle, on the earth, of withered leaves,
The partridge found a shelter.

Bryant gives a selection of details ranging easily from the larger perspectives on the village and the valleys in the distance, to the feel of the air and the contrast with summer, and to the buds on the boughs and the sheltered partridge. Bryant does not compose the scene for us—he gives little sense of the specific relationships between its parts, nor does he really describe any of those parts. He simply names things and usually provides each with an adjective. He presents "bright mosses," "spotted trunks," "close buds," and so on, but seldom gives much idea of what these things look like. Descriptive similaries are rare—the frost work bordering the stream is "as gay/ As with its fringe of summer flowers;" however, this is not actually descriptive, but only suggests Bryant's own mood. Bryant does occasionally include some specific detail. The four lines about the partridge finding shelter beneath the thick branches of the hemlock is a good example, but details like this are used primarily to give a sense of the range of things the scene includes, and do not enable us to see things in much particularity. However, if Bryant does not present much specific detail, or define

exactly the sensory aspects of what he describes, he does by careful selection provide an outline of the scene. Not an outline placing things in
relation to one another in a specific way, but one defining the extent of
the scene by touching on the near and the far, the large and the small,
and the senses of sight, sound, and smell,[10] in a manner that clearly reminds us of what is involved—none of Bryant's descriptions leave us
with a sense of confusion; they have clarity throughout.

Bryant's descriptive poems have a special kind of movement that
provides order and helps to develop their themes. Typical of Bryant's
descriptions of nature, "A Winter Piece" moves inward from the general to the more specific, from the far and large to the near and small,
to focus on images of peace and enclosure. The poem is structured
around several movements toward what could be called climaxes of enclosure, two of the most important being the image of the sheltered
partridge and that of the glaze storm's crystal bowers, where one can
enter "the broad arching portals of the grove" into "The spacious
cavern of some virgin mine,/ Deep in the womb of earth," or "the
vast hall/ Of fairy palace . . . Where crystal columns send forth slender shafts/ And crossing arches." The theme of enclosure is prominent also in "The Prairies," where the expanse of the scene might
work against enclosure. But this is an "encircling vastness." Bryant
ends the first verse paragraph with:

> The hand that built the firmament hath heaved
> And smoothed these verdant swells, and sown their slopes
> With herbage, planted them round with island groves,
> And hedged them round with forests. Fitting floor
> For this magnificent temple of the sky—
> With flowers whose glory and whose multitude
> Rival the constellations! The great heavens
> Seem to stoop down upon the scene in love,—
> A nearer vault, and of a tenderer blue,
> Than that which bends above our eastern hills.

Here the progression is the reverse of that in "A Winter Piece," moving away from the specific, and moving outward to larger and larger
encirclements of the prairies' expanse. And poems not emphasizing enclosure specifically often have a generally similar inward or outward
movement, as does "Summer Wind." The sultry still heat stretches
outward from the speaker, followed by a movement inward with the
approach of the wind.

A generality of description contributes to the careful control Bryant exercises over his metaphorical images. In his *Lectures on Poetry* Bryant explains that he "would rather call poetry a suggestive art. Its power of affecting the mind by pure suggestion, and employing, instead of visible or tangible imitation, arbitrary symbols, as unlike as possible to the things with which it deals, is what distinguishes it from its two sister arts, painting and sculpture."[11] A high degree of generality in an image gives a freedom to present like for unlike. Only if we see a forest and a cathedral in very general terms, can we see them to be similar. The same is true of prairie and sea, ice-covered grove and crystal mine, and many of Bryant's other metaphors representing nature. It is this generality of description that enables Bryant to effectively circumscribe the meaning of the central images of poems such as "The Yellow Violet," "A Forest Hymn," and others. The affective association of subject and vehicle actually may be more important than a visual similarity. Thus, while a forest with its trunks and arching branches may generally resemble elements of a cathedral, it is more important that we feel a similar reverence in each.

The generality of Bryant's images does not, however, work to broaden reference, or link things in ways that reveal basic principles not fully realized before. Instead, this generality contributes to a poetry of gentle reminding. To look at an image too closely could hinder the recollection of things already known and felt. If diverse things are linked, the linkage is easy because things are not confronted directly and concretely, but rather through general resemblances and feelings. Bryant introduces little into his poems that could conflict with the goal of providing a kind of gentle reminding. When there could be suggestions of broader correspondences between man and nature, the import of the metaphors is carefully circumscribed.

But the gentleness of the reminding does not preclude images that have real suggestive power. For example, in "Thanatopsis" the lines that speak of "the stern agony, the shroud, and pall,/ And breathless darkness, and the narrow house" have a particularly expressive focus on a few simple but basic images. Rather than describing a funeral, Bryant captures our mind's eye with a few generalized but essential details. "The narrow house" is also an effective metaphor supporting the earth—tomb contrast that is the central theme of the poem. "To a Waterfowl" has similarly effective imagery. In the lines "Soon shalt thou find a summer home, and rest,/ And scream among thy fellows; reeds shall bend,/ Soon, o'er thy sheltered nest," Bryant has typified a perspective on the bird's world, but he has neither described that world nor challenged us to see it in a new way.

Most important, Bryant's poetry has clarity. If Bryant teaches, he teaches us to see, understand, and remember things with clarity and order. If his descriptions do not create specific places for us, they can typify. And Bryant's poems that present ideas often have a unity between mood, image, and idea that gives the poetry a feeling of balance and respose. Bryant's poetry is a poetry of enclosure: the meanings of Bryant's metaphors are carefully circumscribed so that images of enclosure within a familiar natural world can reflect a world enclosed within a framework of familiar ideas and feelings.

NOTES

1. Albert F. McLean believes that in Bryant's poetry nature is a medium for discovery, but he fails to describe precisely the process of discovery and does not explain what genuinely new insights are attained. *William Cullen Bryant* (New York: Twayne Publishers, 1964), pp. 39–64.
2. In "Romantic Coherence and Romantic Incoherence in American Poetry," in two parts, *Centennial Review*, 7(1963): 219–36, and 8(1964): 453–64, Bernard Duffy presents a similar idea of this coherence in Bryant's poetry: "Romantic coherence, I would say, was formed by a common attitude of belief analogous to orthodox religious belief. . . . The poets of the coherence were soul pilgrims to whom poetry was important because it accomodated familiar, extra-natural truth in believeable form" (p.221).
3. All quotations of Bryant's poetry are from *Bryant's Complete Poetical Works*, ed. Henry C. Sturges (New York: D. Appleton, 1908), the "Roslyn Edition."
4. George Arms sees a dramatic element in Bryant's poetry in "William Cullen Bryant: A Respectable Station on Parnassus," *University of Kansas City Review*, 15(1949):215–23, revised and reprinted as the introduction to Bryant in *The Fields Were Green* (Stanford: Stanford Univ. Press, 1953), pp. 9–19. He explains that the dramatization is frequently indirect, often so indirect as to make its presence doubtful in a single poem" (p. 12). Generally, I doubt its presence. Rebecca Rio Jelliffe in "The Poetry of William Cullen Bryant: Theory and Practice" (Diss. University of California at Berkeley 1965) makes a better case by tracing the infusion of emotion into images of nature, as well as shifts in the tone of the voice of the poems. The best example she presents is "A Scene on the Banks of the Hudson." She sees a dramatic unity in this poem's "composite of image—mood—thought. . . . The luminous unreality in the early stanzas and the complete mergence of the poet with scene build up by contrast, the closing tone of sadness. Thought and sensibility are thus

bodied forth, not directly, but obliquely through the parts of the poem"
(p. 259). Although some of Bryant's poems may have a dramatic element, I believe they are essentially non-dramatic.

5. Here I use the term "analogy" to mean a linking of two relationships
that are both similar and different. Thus, in this poem an analogy could
be stated in this way: the yellow violet's relationship to the world of nature and other flowers is analogous to man's relationship to society and
other men—each in its own way maintains its identity (or humility) amid
changing circumstances. An anlogoy in this sense must have four
distinctly different parts, but Bryant blurs or dissolves a necessary distinction by personifying the flower. For a discussion of analogy and its
significance in literature, see William F. Lynch, *Christ and Apollo: The
Dimensions of the Literary Imagination* (New York: New American Library, 1960).

6. In this essay I am assuming that a metaphor has three parts: a vehicle
(here the metaphorical image), a subject (the area of interest the metaphor could be said to be about), and a meaning (the complex of ideas and
feelings that arise from the joining of the subject and the vehicle in the
context of the poem).

7. In a few of Bryant's poems analogies are presented without any circumscribing of their meaning by personification or other aspects, real or im-
agined, or direct resemblance. For example, "The Snow-Shower" draws
an analogy between two snowflakes joined physically as they fall and a
husband and wife joined in marriage as they go through life. The wife
and the husband may be "hand in hand" at times, but this image of
physical joining does not undercut or circumscribe other aspects of the
meaning of the metaphor. However, metaphors such as this seem limited
in meaning regardless of how they are presented, possibly because they
are based on relationships that are not very intrinsic. The fact that two
snowflakes may be joined as they fall does not tell us much about snowflakes and it cannot tell us much about the nature of marriage. Similarly,
I suspect that whether it were personified or not, a yellow violet could not
tell us very much about humility. Analogies such as those in Bryant's
poetry are in sharp contrast to many of the analogies used by Emerson or
Whitman. For example, when Emerson in "Two Rivers" draws an analogy between the flowing of water and the flowing of spirit, it is clear that
flowing is part of the essential nature of water, and we find the idea that
spirit may also flow in its own special way to be spilling over with meaning. But Bryant's metaphors in their use of relatively extrinsic relationships seem well adapted to simply reminding us of familiar ideas.

8. An additional aspect of enclosure in this poem is that the lines enclosing
the central portion—the poet's introduction to the voice of nature and
the last 15½ lines—were written at a later time. These lines reinforce the
comforting sentiments of the poem. See Tremaine McDowell, *William
Cullen Bryant: Representative Selections, with Introduction, Bibliography, and Notes* (New York: American Book Company, 1935), pp.
389–91. For a more detailed discussion, see William Cullen Bryant III,

"The Genesis of 'Thanatopsis,'" *New England Quarterly*, 21(1948): 163-84. Hyatt Waggoner in *American Poets: From the Puritans to the Present* (Boston: Houghton, Mifflin, 1968), pp. 75-83, sees a disunity between the ideas expressed by the voice of nature and the comforting conclusion of the poem, which he believes is a return to the poet's own voice(also see Arms, "William Cullen Bryant," pp. 220-22). Although Waggoner does not analyze the poem's imagery in detail, his criticism suggests that the earth-as-tomb image does not circumscribe sufficiently the implications of man's return to the elements.

9. The pictoral aspect of this poem, with its feeling of vastness and its images of enclosure, suggests some parallels between Bryant's view of nature and that of Thomas Cole and other representatives of the Hudson River School of landscape painting. The relationship between Cole and Bryant has been discussed in several articles, including Donald A. Ringe, "Kindred Spirits: Bryant and Cole," *American Quarterly*, 6(1954):233-44. Ringe emphasizes a similarity between Cole's and Bryant's feelings for the immensity and majesty of God's universe. See also, Charels L. Sanford, "The Concept of the Sublime in the Works of Thomas Cole and William Cullen Bryant," *American Literature*, 27(1957):434-48. Sanford discusses some of the same subjects as Ringe, but emphasizes a similarity in the presentation of nature as refuge. A more specific similarity between Bryant's descriptions and the paintings of the Hudson River School generally, and which can be connected to the idea of refuge, is the images of encirclement and enclosure, often with a vanishing point in the distance as a focus of the encirclings, as is suggested in "To a Waterfowl" and is prominent in Asher B. Durand's painting "Kindred Spirits."

10. See Evans Harrington, "Sensuousness in the poetry of William Cullen Bryant," *University of Mississippi Studies in English*, 7(1966):25-42. Harrington emphasizes Bryant's use of detail related to all the senses. See also. Donald A. Ringe, *The Pictoral Mode: Space and Time in the Art of Bryant, Irving, and Cooper* (Lexington: Univ. Press of Kentucky, 1971). In chapter 2 Ringe emphasizes Bryant's use of specific detail and, I think, exaggerates its concreteness. In *William Cullen Bryant*, McLean's claim that Bryant presents, for example, the "immediate experience of the present" in "The Prairies" also seems to me to over-state the case. Norman Foerster, in *Nature in American Literature* (New York: MacMillan, 1923), pp. 7-19, emphasizes most of the important aspects of Bryant's use of the concrete.

11. *Prose Writings of William Cullen Bryant*, ed. Parke Godwin, Vol. 1, *Essays, Tales, and Orations* (1884; rpt. New York: Russell and Russell, 1964), p. 5.

The "Denial of Death" in William Cullen Bryant and Walt Whitman

STANLEY BRODWIN
Hofstra University

The denial of death: the phrase is Ernest Becker's, and I propose to use it as a critical entry point into Bryant's and Whitman's explorations of mortality.[1] That both poets struggled to deny death is by now a commonplace in any study of them. Charles H. Brown, Bryant's most recent biographer, states unequivocally that the poet was "appalled by the sense of death and gropingly sought some belief that would deny what he knew to be a universal truth, or if not this, a way in which man could approach it with equanimity."[2] And Stephen E. Whicher claims that "the thought of death was clearly the chief threat [Whitman's] . . . vision had to overcome." For Whitman, "death simply *was not.*"[3] The fear of death began early in both poets' lives—as with most of us—and was expressed in this 1847–48 notebook entry by Whitman which can speak for Bryant, too:

> I am not glad tonight. Gloom has gathered round me like a mantle tightly folded. Yet I know not why I should be sad. Around me are my brother men merry and jovial. No dear one is in danger. . . . Thus comes that I am not glad tonight. I feel cramped in these coarse walls of flesh. The soul disdains. . . . O mystery of death I pant for the time when I shall solve you.[4]

To "solve" death, i.e., deny it, does not mean, I think, a conscious or unconscious obliteration of the fact of death itself; rather, it is an impulse which alerts us to the many strategies humanity has developed to find a creative *modus vivendi* with the pervasive psychological terror death represents. Death becomes that "complex symbol"[5] to which each individual adjusts and for which the artist finds his own

113

cluster of emotionally charged symbolic forms. For the death-obsessed poet, metaphor and symbol, the authentic moment of terror recollected in tranquillity, serve primarily as imaginative explorations of finitude, a way of capturing the consciousness of non-being, and only secondarily as fixed icons of doctrinal belief. The poetic process itself, therefore, may function to render death terrorless. The dread "separation anxiety" death imposes can, through the poetry, either transcend or merge painlessly into the structures of Time, Space, and Nature, those life-controlling and limiting contexts of the Self. They must be "translated," to use a Whitmanesque word, into poetry which would embody the various personal or cosmic relationships the poet experiences. Read in this way, Bryant's and Whitman's familiar dialogues with death can take on fresh meaning and interest for us. And, seen from this angle, our poets make an especially appropriate pair for contrast and comparison. Together they spanned almost the entire nineteeth century producing poems, which both in their striking similarities and radical differences, project images of terror and affirmation, ranging from the most traditional Judeo-Christian verbal iconography, to the most unorthodox mystical pantheism.

Of course, other American poets are equally revelatory in this respect, e.g., Bradstreet, Poe, and Dickinson, but Bryant and Whitman share a special historical and poetic kinship which illuminates their individual quests to deny death. The historical connection, while significant, is not, however, necessarily crucial. Enough to say that they were both journalists, though Bryant achieved great fame and influence in that career; both shared a Long Island background and similar Jacksonian principles; both spoke out for a distinctively national literature; and, above all, they knew each other personally. In Tremaine McDowell's words, "each respected the other as a democrat and lover of nature."[6] To be sure, Bryant understandably could not give the first edition of *Leaves of Grass* his unqualified praise, as did Emerson, but this did not prevent Whitman, in 1881, from glorifying Bryant as the poet "pulsing the first interior verse-throbs of a mighty world—bard of the river and the wood," who was always "lurkingly fond of threnodies—beginning and ending his long career with chants that contained morals "grim and eternal, if not as stormy and fateful, as anything in Eschylus" (*SD & Collect*, p. 180).[7] And in *Goodbye My Fancy* (1891), Whitman praised Bryant's "The Battle-Field" and "A Forest Hymn" as "magnificent," prompting him to give "the file-leading place for American native poesy to W.C.B." (*SD & Collect*, p. 496).

Such overpraise cannot be attributed to their personal and political connections; it is more likely that Whitman saw in Bryant an earlier if conventional version of himself: a singer of the "first interior verse-throbs of a mighty world." Certainly their love of nature is a clear affinity, too, but for Whitman there were other poets—Emerson primarily—who shared the same passion. Or perhaps Whitman divined what Donald A. Ringe points to as the central artistic affinity relating them: that "in their imaginative grasp of the nature of the external scene and man's place in time . . . Bryant and Whitman are most alike." Furthermore, "each sought in his verse to connote the expansiveness of his vision through the evocation of the great reaches of the universe and the majestic sweep of centuries."[8] To this insight I would add that perhaps the greatest affinity between them was that Whitman saw in Bryant a fellow death-sufferer, who, like himself, persistently followed the track of that most personal and profound theme. Indeed, both their preoccupations with nature, time, and space, may be seen as individual poetic struggles to create metaphors whose essential power could confront and deny the master complex symbol.

Now by his own autobiographical testimony, Bryant's anxiety over death began early in his life. He alludes to his immersion in Old Testament thought and Calvinist theology, particularly stressing his reaction to the plea, "Let not our feet stumble on the dark mountains of eternal death," a line, he says, which "forcibly affected" his "childish imagination."[9] And in 1815 in an untitled quatrain beginning, "Not From Life and All its Woes," he speaks of the " . . . sacred dread of death/Inwoven with the strings of life," and the "eternal doom of heaven/That man must view the grave with fear."[10] Thus, as much of his other poetry attests, the metaphorical synthesis between death and nature became the medium through which his personal anxiety could pass and find expression. His fear of death was always to be viewed as "sacred," demanding, as in Whitman, sacramental imagery and tone. Absorbing both the influence of Wordsworth's romantic sublimity and the gothic horrors of "graveyard poets" like Robert Blair and Henry Kirke White who, as it were, midwifed "Thanatopsis," Bryant was able to exploit creatively a new if not always acceptable kind of romantic sacramentalism. This helped him to translate his anxiety into forms of "symbolic immortality," i.e., poems that communed through Nature with a Divinity who would ensure his life after death. At the same time, early nineteenth century New England culture underwent important changes in attitudes toward death. The dominant change was, as David E. Stannard has shown,[11] the gradual softening of terror-ridden imagery in poetry, painting and tombstone art, into more "cherubic" forms of quiet resignation or sentimental joy for the dead "in heaven." More significantly, the eighteenth and nineteenth centuries also saw the development of a new attitude toward death which Philippe Ariès has described as a romantic and rhetorical treatment of *la mort de toi*—the death of the "other"—an attitude that joined with the oldest existing one in Western culture, *et moriemur*, we shall all die. Finally, there was the more troubling preoccupation which appeared in the twelfth century and without doubt the most important contemporary concern, *la mort de soi*, one's own death.[12] Into this complex there emerged, according to Ariès, the idea of death as "rupture" or break, shattering man's struggle to treat it as something unfrightening because so familiar; indeed, Western iconography, beginning in the fifteenth century, gradually equated death with a kind of rape and took on that distinctive tension with which Freud grappled, the conflict of Thanatos with Eros. Though Eros is fairly well sublimated in Bryant—unlike Whitman—his poetry will move through all these dispositions, delineating them in "communions"—a word carrying sacramental meaning in itself—with Nature, time, and space. His characteristic tropes and figures of cyclical changes may be seen as his attempt not only to capture the sublime in the American landscape and culture, but also to release a death-suffering ego from a closed world of mortality to an open, ever-changing one. As Ernest Becker points out, basic anxieties are not only controlled by repression; there is also a "healthy-mindedness" that absorbs fears and expresses itself by "unfolding one's capacities into the world . . . in feeding on its limitless experience."[13] Bryant was just such a healthy-minded poet whose energetic public career may be viewed from this perspective as a psychological compulsion to fulfill the active life of experience countering his richly poetic inner one. Significantly, two years after the publication of his first version of "Thanatopsis," Bryant wrote an essay "On the Happy Temperament" (1819), in which he apparently came to terms with mutability, change, and death, rejecting the superficiality of the "Addisonian" man of an "unbroken cheerfulness." But in one key statement, I believe we have a vital clue to the relationship between Bryant's anxiety over death and his preoccupation with Nature, change, and time. He writes: "As awful as the prospect of death justly is, he, who has thought of it most, will perhaps recollect, that he has sometimes felt a thrill or wild and strange delight as he contemplated this great change of being.''[14] Here is an attempt to capture a mode of denial located in a sense of exultation; a way of investing the concept of change with an emotional thrill incarnated in his own Self's transfiguration. It is important to recognize that that state with its potential for Dionysian imagery is submerged by his Apollonian contemplation of the awesome changes in Nature and time in poems like "The Ages," "The Past," "The Fountain," "The Prairies," and others. In confronting death the possibility of "wild and strange delight" becomes muted and calm, repressed in the consolatory, collective sleep imagery of "Thanatopsis," which he was revising from 1818 to 1820. In the end, it would be Whitman who celebrated the Self's transfiguration into Nature making death, in a poem like "Scented Herbage of My Breast" (1860), "exhilarating." This ecstatic note is sounded from "Song of Myself" to the poems of "Whispers of Heavenly Death" (1871). The opening poem of that cluster, "Darest Thou Now O Soul," gives us a Whitman who could "loosen . . ./All but the ties eternal, Time and Space," in an epiphany of joyous freedom from all "bounds . . . them to fulfil O/soul" (*LG*, pp. 441–42).[15] By contrast, Bryant could imagine himself and history swept up into the cycles of Time expanding in Space, but never mystically "loos'd" beyond them. He may have achieved his final "mediation" between Puritanism, romanticism, and stoic classicism, as Tremaine McDowell says,[16] but his communion was always from the position of a threatened observer clinging to personal identity. Even his identifications with Time-Past and Time-Future reminded him of death. So, for example, in his final version of "Thanatopsis,"[17] after stressing the "voice of gladness" and "healing sympathy" communion with Nature brings, the "still" voice offers its *memento mori* sermon reminding us that roots shall "pierce thy mould." In the next section, however, the "visible" forms of Nature—hills, woods, rivers, ocean—Sun and planets—dramatically lose their healing qualities, to become "but the solemn decorations all/Of the great tomb of man." Consolation now does not come through Nature but through sharing death with the "Fair forms, and hoary seers of ages past,/All in one mighty Sepulchre." This middle section originally ended with the sentiment that everyone at last "shall come,/And make their bed with thee," the familiar *et moriemur*. But a final seven-line addition, though ostensibly reinforcing this idea, subtly undercuts its consolatory tone by reflecting the melancholy stimulated by brooding on Time-Past: "As the long train/Of ages glide away, the sons of men,/The youth in life's green spring, and he who goes/In the full strength of years . . ./Shall one by one be gathered to thy side,/By those, who in their turn shall follow them." And that is why the final section almost inevitably had to begin with the strong admonition, "So live, when thy summons comes to join/The innumerable caravan . . .," so that we may go to our deaths not like a "quarry-slave at night,/Scourged to his dungeon . . ." This last image actually reintroduces the terror against which Bryant must counter with the philosophically weak plea for an "unfaltering trust." The famous last simile of lying down to "pleasant dreams" seems more a tired release than firm philosophic acceptance. The "trust" that presumably Nature's visible forms are supposed to instill in us—the lessons of eternality, moral harmony, common destiny, a sustained universe—do not neutralize the underlying fear of "the mysterious realm." Though I accept Albert F. McLean Jr.'s insight that, for Bryant, the forms of Nature teach humanity "the limitation of human understanding" and to "abandon its presumptuous claims to uniqueness and autonomy,"[18] there is a strange lack of philosophic joy coming from such wisdom in the poem. A brief passage from Wordsworth's "The Excursion" (1814) may, simply by contrast, help clarify this point. Wordsworth writes that the spirit who "communes with the Forms of nature" will not only find "joy," "the good," and a "holy tenderness," but also will, "by contemplating these Forms/In the relations which they bear to man,/He shall discern, how, through the various means/Which silently they yield, are multiplied/The spiritual presences of absent things" (Bk. IV, 1230-55). If "Thanatopsis" does not yield "spiritual presences" of joy in its attempt to control the fear of death, nevertheless its imagery and theme are charged with a subtle tension created by the Self's awareness that the visible forms of Nature are controlled by time and death, too.

Not surprisingly, Bryant's best nature poems of this period do yield those presences and general laws. "The Yellow Violet," "To A Waterfowl," or even the long but less successful "A Winter Piece," manage to evoke through their analogies felt moral and natural laws. When, in "A Winter Piece" Bryant describes a small protected windflower "blue as the spring heaven" . . . "Startling the loiterer in the naked groves/With unexpected beauty," even as the storm clouds come again to "buffet the vexed forest," the reader does for the moment feel the surprise and hope. The presence of death can only disturb the harmony of these communions, cannot be "absorbed" or neutralized no matter how spiritually uplifting Nature may be to the poet. Thus, "fixed tranquillity" of an unfallen Nature celebrated in "Inscription For the Entrance To A Wood" (1817) heals the despair of those hurt by the "guilt and misery" of human affairs, but death itself is directly avoided in this Arcadia. "Thanatopsis," however, was a fine and courageous attempt to deny death, a direct confrontation, as it were. Significantly, in a poem like "A Forest Hymn" (1825), Bryant again avoided an attempt to make a "definitive" statement about "spiritual presences" in Nature. Going into God's "first temples" to hold "Communion with his Maker" Bryant again finds "That delicate forest flower" which will teach him the law of "upholding Love," which is the "soul of this great universe." In the forest, "Life mocks the idle hate/Of his arch-enemy Death—yea, seats himself/Upon the tyrant's throne—the sepulchre,/And of the triumphs of his ghastly foe/Makes his own nourishment. . . ." The final stanza shows the poet retiring to those solitudes to face the moral chastisement God employs with his dread whirlwinds and storms. But the poet wishes to be spared from the "sterner aspects" of God: "Be it ours to meditate,/In these shades, thy milder majesty,/And to the beautiful order of thy works/Learn to conform the order of our lives." Here are Wordsworth's "general laws" which also reflect a Nature divided between "storm" and "calm" or good and evil in a romantic version of biblical prophesy. Moral categories still divide the world, death and life are still enemies, and we pray to escape the one to find peace in the other. Death and the whirlwind cannot be accepted as part of God's or Nature's ultimate design. There is not even an attempt—as in "Thanatopsis"—to conform to this aspect of His Being. But the tension in Bryant between denial and acceptance necessarily continued. This tension can be seen, for example, in two other works he wrote during this period. The first is a prose narrative called "The Whirlwind,"[19] and the second is a long poem, "The Hurricane" (1828), both of which use this biblical imagery to explore the problem. The poem powerfully describes the storm as prefiguring death, "the dark eternity to come," tragically alienating the poet from the world. In the Irvingesque sketch, the narrator meets a travelling preacher who tells him the story of how a whirlwind—really a humbling theophany—destroyed his family, even killing his father as he was reading the Bible. Echoes from the *Book of Job* and *Ecclesiastes* abound throughout the story as we learn of the lone survivor escaping to narrate the tragedy. He speaks of his wild mourning and "moaning of agony" which could not be moderated until, growing up under a benign guardian, he realized that the "chastisement, though severe, was meant for good" (p. 175). Cheered, he goes West to spread the gospel. The rationalization through religion is transparent, of course. And the narrative may well have been Bryant's personal catharsis and psychological projection concerning his own father's death in 1820 although he did not morbidly grieve, then, according to Charles H. Brown.[20] It appears that Bryant swung between the need to accept the idea of death (symbolized by storms) as chastisement, and at the same time to avoid it by contemplating Nature's "milder majesty." The presence of these attitudes and their correlative images inform poems like "The Burial-Place" (1818), "Hymn to Death" (1820), and "The Two Graves" (1826). Ostensibly depicting the shift of burial customs from Old to New England, "The Burial-Place" actually dramatizes the Self's psychological reaction to the death of the "other" as it is memorialized through the transformation of the grave as bed-garden into "naked rows of graves." In this poem, the imagery of "Thanatopsis" is translated into a brief example of a ritual change that is overwhelmed by a larger cosmic pattern. The opening lines tell of English "sires" who soothed "the natural dread of man's last home, the grave. . . ," by dressing it with the flowers and trees of immortality—the yew, the willow, the "ancient ivy." There are sentimental allusions to the deaths of sweet maidens and infants, the mourning of "childless dames" and orphans. The second stanza describes the loss of this tradition by the Puritans who now leave "naked rows of graves/And melancholy ranks of monuments . . . where the coarse grass, between,/Shoots up its dull green spikes. . . ." This image is reinforced with another, more significant one: bramble bushes that grow by the graves offer their berries to a "schoolboy's hand,/In vain—they grow too near the dead. . . ." Wild Nature and the loss of custom both serve to complete the distancing in man's relationship to death. Unapproachable and guarded, as it were, by green spikes, the grave stands as a symbol of vanity and therefore punishment, too, as it had been in the Middle Ages and in the starker aspects of Protestant theology. But if man cannot pluck the berries of immortality (cf. Milton's "Lycidas"), then Nature, "rebuking his neglect," will transcend this historical change by planting on the grave its brier roses and the strawberry plant with her "ruddy pouting fruit. . . ." While this is yet another poetic cliche of Nature's immortality, in the context of the poem the image escapes this charge by dramatizing the failure—perhaps unwillingness—of the poet's own society to deny death. The vast ontological gulf between Nature's eternality and humanity's mortality abides.

In the "Hymn to Death," we see a fascinating poetic and psychological drama unfold. Here the terror of death is transferred to a grand personification: Death avenges the oppressed and destroys the evil— atheists, extortioners, perjurers, and the like. This traditional imagery may have owed something to Rembrandt Peale's immensely popular painting of 1820, "The Court of Death," which showed a blackrobed figure dispensing justice to a variety of evildoers, all painted in a mixture of gothic and "sublime" neo-classical poses.[21] But Bryant realizes that he may be too quick to sing death's praises, and so he psychologically protects himself at the start with a statement of humility and fear: "True it is, that I have wept/Thy conquests, and may weep them yet again,/And thou from some I love wilt take a life/Dear to me as my own. . . ." The poem then thunders on, picturing death reforming the world and punishing the wicked. Almost as a self-fulfilling prophecy, news of his father's death causes the poem to suddenly break and turn into a lament. All Bryant has left is his "faltering verse" to offer at his father's grave. He bids his father rest until the "brief sleep of death is over," and to await resurrection. The lines are drained of force and seem merely a conventional epitaph, for there is the deflating realization that evil men still live. The situation is there for a Job-like *cri di coeur,* but Bryant is not equal to it. The death of the "other" has chastised him and his vengeful posturing now seems just that. The last lines of the poem are, however, remarkably honest and revealing: "Shuddering I look/On what is written, yet I blot not out/The desultory numbers; let them stand,/The record of an idle revery." It is a complete statement of defeat—a surrender to despair—that significantly renders poetry, of all things, meaningless, an "idle revery." Creative activity has universally been a crucial way to deny death, but here it is taken by surprise and loses its self-justification. Death penetrates Bryant's neo-classical posture and brings it literally and literarily down to earth. And yet, because of the drama it enacts, the poem stands in spite of itself as an authentic experience against the sentimental rationalizations with which early Victorian art and poetry, including Bryant's, were saturated. Later, in 1839, Bryant would protect himself somewhat better against false optimism. In "The Fountain," he again takes us through the passage of history, the fountain itself a powerful symbol of dynamic change which nourishes war and peace, love and hate. Yet its "eternal change" need not necessarily be eternal. Chastened by his knowledge of geology,[22] Bryant is able to project any number of ends for the fountain. Man can "deform" the landscape it makes green, or its own veins can be "choked in middle earth," or perhaps great changes in the earth's crust will make it gush "midway from the bare and barren steep." Still, this knowledge of "death" or uncertain change in Nature could not resolve the terror within. But in the small and sturdy blue autumn flower he could create a metaphor consonant with his sense of being. That is why "To The Fringed Gentian" (1829), despite its tacked-on moral, is an effective poem. The flower is an image of brave isolation, its blue heart part of the blue heaven. Bryant can only hope to absorb its quiet hope when his "hour of death" draws near. He can hope for "Hope, blossoming" within his heart as he departs. Hoping for hope: here is perhaps Bryant's deepest level of doubt and death-suffering.

The last two poems I wish to discuss, though separated by forty years, are significantly linked death poems. "The Two Graves" is yet another meditation on death and nature but here given a kind of legendary or folkloristic quality by romanticizing the graves of an old couple buried fifty years before the poet's time. "October, 1866" is an elegy on the death of Bryant's wife. Ostensibly different kinds of poems, they both grapple with the themes of age, separation, and hopes beyond the grave. In "The Two Graves," the old couple are buried in a "bleak wild hill, but green and bright," a delicious pastoral plot where there is "nothing . . . that speaks of death." Only in the town are there graveyards speaking of the "strict and close" ties that bind us all in death. As usual, the nature imagery serves to poeticize death and make it seem quiet and beautiful. But the grave always points to the "still and dark assemblies below." The graves of the old couple are, however, gone, though the poet once discovered them eighteen years ago. They had died alone, their family scattered, yet leaving the memory of a fertile farm life. A symbol of the perfect natural life in a Jeffersonian and Wordsworthian mold, the couple's life and anonymous death cause the poet to philosophize on the question of the soul's "banishment" from its body. For Bryant, it is a "cruel creed, believe it not!" It is as if, projecting his soul's separation from both his own body and the eternal presence of his beloved, he must find some way of stilling the anxiety this thought presents him. His desperate need to believe that death does not separate is embodied in the repetitive intensity of his emotional assertion: "They are here,—they are here,—that harmless pair,/In the yellow sunshine and flowing air." He imagines their souls together haunting their old cottage ground and woods, waiting and lingering "Till the day when their bodies shall leave the ground." It is clear that Bryant is less interested in Christian eschatology than he is in denying the trauma of separation. Here there is no attempt to deny or neutralize death itself, only the wrenching from love that death brings. Indeed, this poem rebels against what Ariès calls the "new intolerance of separation" with its wild grieving, lugubrious mourning pictures and ornate tombs. It is true that the poem does use the nineteenth century notion of death as a "milder lot" to the "good," but this brings no real consolation. The separated soul will yearn for the "rock and stream it knew of old." Like Whitman or Unamuno, other great death-sufferers, Bryant sees that creeds and doctrine mean little in the face of death. Only the heart's need matters. The old couple's graves objectify that need. Bodily resurrection is there not primarily to join man with God and eternity, but to join man and wife, and still the primal agony of separation.

In "October, 1866" Bryant again confronts the full reality of the death of the "other" and its trauma. Indeed, his concern with this problem signals a shift from his earlier preoccupation with death itself, as I have suggested. In "The Two Graves" he was able to create an effective poetic mood through his legend-like story; in the elegy he must examine his own feelings of loss. He cannot enjoy the beauty of nature now; its quieting and even salvational lessons fail. In "what fair region dost thou now abide?" is the anguished question. The language and tone of the poem, though traditional and uninspired, does carry an emotional sincerity in the poet's refusal to rationalize the problem away with pretentious theological concepts. "Nay, let us deem that thou dost not withdraw/From the dear places where thy lot was cast . . .," he writes. Let us believe what we must believe, in order to carry on. Still on earth where once "Walked God's beloved Son,"—his token theological allusion in the poem—his wife will see the beauty denied to humanity's "dimmer sense" and will continue to minister Bryant's moral needs, turning him from paths that end in sin! Not only is the poet's separation psychically denied, but he also retains the beloved as a guiding moral spirit, psychologically absorbing her into his very moral life where he could experience her "reality." His wife's spirit, and not her death, will be his final chastener. However much the poem reflects a conventional attitude, it contains, with an almost childlike openness, a significant emotional strategy toward death. Still, there is no breakthrough or surrender to an all-absorbing love-passion that subsumes and then transcends death. But in "The Flood of Years" (1876), he returned to his true poetic passions, Nature and Time, for one last assault. Only in the endless forward movement of Time could that primal terror possibly lose its specific identity. Thus, "A mighty Hand, from an exhaustless Urn,/Pours forth the never-ending Flood of Years." Time not only brings death but also *is* death; ontologically they are one. But since Time cannot die—is eternal—the death it carries within itself, slaying the "brood of Hope," must be swept over a "belt of darkness" into eternity, as well. The "bright river" of Time broadens into a "sea," all its eddies bringing together old friends in "joy unspeakable." Bryant's powerful trope bears its own paradox: the Self keeps its personal immortality *and* is seamlessly woven into "eternal Change." This romantic Unitarian pantheism may be a theological impossibility, but for Bryant it was a necessary psychological and poetic resolution. And when questioned as to whether these lines represented his "final" belief, Bryant wrote that he could not have written them unless he believed in the "everlasting life of the soul; and it seems to me that immortality would be an imperfect gift without the recognition in the life to come of those who are dear to us here."[23] We note here the emphasis on the immortality of the beloved "other," and not on his own, though that is implied. Psychologically he has established his freedom from anxiety on the conviction that love of our "tender-ties" can never be withdrawn; therefore, the mighty "Concord" or *Logos* that controls the flood of years in the Eternal Present cannot be separated from *its* parts. All goes "hand in hand," soul and matter, mortality and immortality.

Was this, then, Bryant's final metaphor of dependence and hope? Or was his "true" faith in the many church hymns he wrote declaring the salvific power of Jesus' love and God's merciful judgment? Perhaps because they are hymns fashioned for a specific purpose, they never reach the kind of emotional pitch which characterizes the best of his other work. Belief here still seems qualified by hope. More significantly, the idea of death as degrading man is still present. A year after he published "A Flood of Years," he wrote the hymn "A Captive Loosed," which describes the Apostle Peter, doomed to death in Herod's dungeon-cell, freed by a messenger from God. The Saint is saved, but "Chains yet more strong and cruel bind/The victims of that deadly thirst/Which drowns the soul, and from the mind/Blots the bright image stamped at first.'' We, the victims, are back in the desperate fallen human condition. The final quatrain implores God to send his ''gracious Spirit'' to lead ''the captive forth to light,/A rescued soul, a slave no more.'' Words like *implore, beg, pity, fatal, slave, chains,* and *bind* may be conventional Christian language; nevertheless, they breathe forth the tensions of Bryant's original drama: a lifetime of confrontation with and spiritual enchainment to the terror of death. Despite his flight into Nature and Time, Homer's world or Wordsworth's, Bryant raises up St. Paul's cry: '' . . . who shall save me from this body of death?'' (Rom.7:24).

In turning to Whitman, we meet a poet who, as I have already suggested, saw death as an ''unloosening'' of the individual soul into the mystic ''float'' where all things are held in some divine ''solution.'' As in ''Crossing Brooklyn Ferry,'' his pantheistic imagery creates and then annihilates Time and Space into a reality of ''undifferentiated Oneness'' where death and life mysteriously embody one another. The very process of this fusion is what makes death ''exhilarating'' and why, in ''Scented Herbage of My Breast,'' Whitman cries:

> Give me your tone therefore O death, that I may
> accord with it,
> Give me yourself, for I see you belong to me
> now above all,

for death is ''real reality'' and dissipates ''this entire show of appearance . . .'' (*LG*, 115). Erotic calamus leaves grow from his breast infusing death with ''exhilaration'' which begins with birth and sexuality. Such poems are, finally, parts of Whitman's ''great poem of death,'' the poem he also wished to evoke from other poets. The next great ''literatus'' must achieve in a positive way what Lucretius ''sought most nobly'' for his culture: the denial of death. This declaration from ''Democratic Vistas'' (*SD & Collect*, p 255) envisions the coming American Bard as confronting Nature, time, and space in order to become ''master of fortune and misfortune,'' so giving the ''ship that had it not before in all her voyages . . . an anchor.'' This, then, is Whitman's astonishing strategy for his and future democratic epics: *only a denial of death will create a spiritual stability that can release all the natural optimism and energy inherent in a democratic humanity.* That is why he writes that, ''In the future of these States must arise poets immenser far, and make great poems of death'' *(SD & Collect,*

p. 254). I call this an astonishing strategy because I do not know of any major poet—except perhaps Lucretius—who posits a vision of the denial of death as a spiritual prerequisite for a liberated and healthy social order. But Lucretius did it "negatively," as Whitman points out, no doubt alluding to the lack of a transcendental ideal in *De Rerum Natura*. And, despite Whitman's frequent personal identification with Christ as one who suffers the agony of the human condition for all, Christianity itself, even with its doctrine of resurrection, did not adequately deny death or its terrors for him. Rather, as we saw in Bryant, death remained the punishment that shakes our faith and affirms our temporal and sinful insignificance. With such attitudes Whitman had little to do. We need only recall canto 32 of "Song of Myself" which glorifies the animals who "do not sweat and whine about their condition" or "weep for their sins." Only in the Old Testament did Whitman see a National Epic that contained no "hair-splitting doubts, no sickly sulking and sniffling, no 'Hamlet,' no 'Adonais,' no 'Thanatopsis,' no 'In Memoriam'" (*SD & Collect*, p. 397). It would be difficult for us today to characterize this remarkable list of works as "sickly sulking and sniffling," Hamlet's soliloquies to the contrary notwithstanding. But from Whitman's psychological and poetic vantage point—despite his generous comments on Bryant's Aeschylean power—"Thanatopsis" would be "sniffling" if only for acknowledging a fear of death Whitman seemingly had obliterated, at least in his own poetry. In "To Think of Time" (1855, 1881), Whitman reveals to us the terror implicit in even allowing for the *possibility* that the soul is not immortal: "Do you suspect death? if I were to suspect death I should die now,/Do you think I could walk pleasantly and well-suited to annihilation?" (*LG*, p. 439). Psychologically, such an attitude may represent a form of "protesting too much" in order to deny a genuine anguish. Whitman is, of course, given to posturing and flinging his "barbaric yawp" at the reader; yet, in his most familiar and great lyrics on Nature and death—cantos 5 and 6 of "Song of Myself," "Out of the Cradle Endlessly Rocking," "When Lilacs Last in the Dooryard Bloom'd," "Scented Herbage of My Breast,"—the posturing is replaced by a remarkable lyric sensitivity and control that reflect an authentic integration of philosophical with aesthetic vision. He is able to convince us through that vision that death is, indeed, "luckier" than what we suppose; that its "bitter hug of mortality" cannot "alarm"; and that a corpse is but "good manure" feeding an erotic Nature: "I smell the white roses sweet-scented and growing,/I reach to the leafy lips, I reach to the polish'd breasts of melons" (*LG*, p. 87). Death is always "sane," "blissful," "beautiful," "sacred." The anxiety that normally attends a profound contemplation of death is absorbed into images of penetration and expansion, ultimately circling the individual "knit of identity" and universe itself. In "When Lilacs Last in the Dooryard Bloom'd," we find this all-enveloping image:

> Then with the knowledge of death as walking one side of me,
> And the thought of death close-walking the other side
>   of me,
> And I in the middle as with companions, and as holding
>   the hands of companions,
> I fled forth to the hiding receiving night that
>   talks not. . . .

There in the night "by the swamp in the dimness," Whitman meets the bird who sings to him the carol of death for the "comrades three," i.e., the poet and his two death companions. As "one" they heard the song that will deify the horrors of the Civil War and Lincoln's martyrdom:

> *Come lovely and soothing death,*
> *Undulate round the world, serenely arriving, arriving,*
> *In the day, in the night, to all, to each,*
> *Sooner or later delicate death.*
>
> (LG, p. 335)²⁴

These lines begin an apostrophe to death which is but a poetic extension of the final coda in "Out of the Cradle Endlessly Rocking" where death, "The word final, superior to all," is sent up by that old crone, the sea, to lave ecstatically the "outsetting bard" (*LG*, p. 252). These passages may be considered as Whitman's paradigms on the theme. It is clear that their "purport" is to deny death by making love to its maternal-erotic energy, and by envisioning it as the Ground of Being itself. Whitman's imagery grasps death phenomenologically as a "solution-like" reality, i.e., the *real* reality, and perceives it aesthetically as a delicate "float" or blissful primal rhythm. Though springing from the same sources and imagery as Bryant's, Whitman plunges us into a radically different world. For Whitman, the very categories of the death of Self, the "other" and humanity (*et moriemur*), are no longer meaningful in any traditional terms, although some of his juvenile poems poorly imitate their standard emotions and Bryant's forms. Whitman's mature Self or ego does not confront reality "apart" from itself. Its "real" relationship is with the "soul," that undying psychospiritual presence "in" him and part of the All. That this metaphysical structure had its roots in a very real psychological experience is suggested in one of his early notebook entries: "I cannot understand the mystery, but I am always conscious of myself as two—as my soul and I: and I reckon it is the same with all men and women."[25] The "I" and its physical identity (as with all matter) is subject to death, but the "soul" is not. By a psychological mechanism not clearly understood even by critics who have studied Whitman's poetry psychoanalytically, Whitman has "invested" the soul with an immortality that is not—*cannot*—be dependent on a pre-existing God. From a Rankian perspective, Whitman massively "transferred" all his anxieties to a Power that can subsume them and never die itself. But this Power, unlike the Judeo-Christian God, is ontologically part of the "I" yet capable of dialogue with it. And since Whitman reckons it is the same with others, he is assured of both personal and collective immortality. Such a construct, once psychologically "worked out" and given its metaphysical labels, could then become available, as it were, for the basis of a grand poetic dialogue embracing life without death. In the end, Whitman experienced a radical sense of independence from anything "outside" limiting the Self. He was after all, "Divine" inside and out. By contrast, Bryant forever remained anxiously dependent on a Power outside of himself to deny death, whether through Divine love or Grace or a beneficent Nature teaching resignation. The different strategies of our poets toward death do not merely represent a simple shift in literary culture from pre-romanticism to romanticism; rather they epitomize a profound polarity between those enduring "puritan" and "pagan" strains so evident throughout American literature. And yet, paradoxically each poet's individual need to deny death helps us to grasp a basic affinity between them exacerbated by the encroaching doubts and spiritual crises that have particularly marked the last two centuries. There is no doubt that these crises, either caused or intensified by factors as diverse as the Industrial Revolution, the breakdown of traditional Christian values and faith, intellectual and social revolutions initiated by Darwin, Freud, Marx, and Einstein, and the rise of modern existentialism with its explorations of the "Absurd," have all given the problem of death and dying a new urgency. Stripped of his traditional supports, modern man, unlike past generations, has had to learn to face annihilation alone, or at least with unsettled beliefs and convictions. In this admittedly generalized context, Bryant deserves a fresh and sympathetic re-reading for his authentic struggle to come to terms with his death-suffering. Controlling and controlled by a rhetorical language and poetic form that did not allow a self-indulgent release of his existential anxieties, he was able to create a personal drama that lends his work a power and philosophical complexity often lacking in many of his popular contemporaries: Longfellow, Whittier, Holmes, and James Russell Lowell. Only Poe, Melville, and Dickinson, with their obviously more original genius, created profounder visions, and their dominant status in American literature is due, in part, to their remarkable explorations of man's struggles with religious doubt and death. Whitman's unique epic vision of the American Self has earned him the title of National Poet for many, though we have come to place more and more stress on his elegiac power. But in the final analysis Whitman's own praise of Bryant's "threnodies" as "grim and eternal" may well alert us to a striking critical truth.

NOTES

1. Ernest Becker, *The Denial of Death* (New York: The Free Press, 1973).
2. Charles H. Brown, *William Cullen Bryant* (New York: Charles Scribner's Sons, 1971), p. 59.
3. Stephen E. Whicher, "Whitman's Awakening to Death: Toward a Biographical Reading of 'Out of the Cradle Endlessly Rocking.'" In: *The Presence of Walt Whitman: Selected Papers from the English Institute*, ed. with a Foreward by R.W.B. Lewis (New York: Columbia Univ. Press, 1962), p. 3. Also see Clark Griffith, "Sex and Death: The Significance of Whitman's Calamus Themes," *Philological Quarterly*, 30, No. 1 (Jan., 1960), 18–38, and Edwin H. Miller, *Walt Whitman's Poetry: A Psychological Journey* (Boston: Houghton Mifflin Co., 1968). Both studies give excellent insights into Whitman's psychological death-tensions deriving from his need to deal with his homosexuality and insecurities. The number of studies dealing with this issue are too numerous for extended citation here.
4. Quoted in V.K. Chari, *Whitman in the Light of Vedantic Mysticism* (Lincoln: Univ. of Nebraska Press, 1962), p. 62.
5. See Becker's discussion of this term employed by Jean Wahl in *The Denial of Death*, p. 19.
6. Tremaine McDowell, *William Cullen Bryant: Representative Selections*, American Writers Series (New York, 1935), p. lxviii, footnote. Also, Joan D. Berbrich, *Three Voices From Paumanok: The Influence of Long*

Island on Cooper, Bryant, Whitman (New York: Ira J. Friedman, Inc., 1969), Ch. viii.

7. "Specimen Days & Collect," *The Works of Walt Whitman: The Collected Prose*, Vol. II, with a Prefatory Note by Malcolm Cowley (New York: Minerva Press, 1969). Originally titled *The Complete Poetry and Prose of Walt Whitman*, Vol. II. In my text cited as *SD & Collect.*.

8. Donald A. Ringe, "Bryant and Whitman: A Study in Artistic Affinities," *Boston University Studies in English*, 2 (1956), 85.

9. Albert F. McLean, Jr., *William Cullen Bryant* (New York: Twayne Publishers, Inc., 1964), p. 27.

10. Brown, pp. 78–79. For the text of this fragment, see McDowell, *Bryant*, p. 350. My own text for Bryant's poems, unless otherwise noted, will be *The Poetical Works of William Cullen Bryant*, Roslyn ed., With Chronologies of Bryant's Life and Poems, etc., by Henry C. Sturges (rpt. 1903; New York: AMS Press, 1969). Since most of the poems are short and can easily be located in this edition, I am not giving the page number of quoted lines in my text.

11. David E. Stannard, *The Puritan Way of Death* (New York: Oxford Univ. Press, 1977), Ch. 6.

12. Philippe Ariès, *Western Attitudes Toward Death* (Baltimore: Johns Hopkins Univ. Press, 1974), pp. 55–65, passim.

13. Becker, p. 21.

14. Quoted in Brown, p. 87.

15. *Leaves of Grass*, Comprehensive Reader's Ed., Harold W. Blodgett and Sculley Bradley, eds. (New York: W.W. Norton & Co., 1965). Hereafter *LG* in my text.

16. McDowell, *Bryant*, Introduction, passim.

17. For a study of the texts see Tremaine McDowell, "Bryant's Practise in Composition and Revision," *PMLA*, LII (June, 1937), 474–502; and William Cullen Bryant II, "The Genesis of 'Thanatopsis,'" *New England Quarterly*, 21 (June, 1948), 163–84.

18. McLean, *Bryant*, pp. 77–78. Also see chapter 3 as a whole, which gives an excellent analysis of Bryant's death poetry and its historical context. Particularly interesting is McLean's article, "Bryant's 'Thanatopsis': A Sermon in Stone," *American Literature*, XXXI (Jan., 1960), 474–79, which shows the probable influence of the three-part structure of a Puritan sermon on the poem.

19. *The Prose Writings of William Cullen Bryant*, ed. Parke Godwin, Vol. I (rpt. 1884; New York: Russell & Russell, Inc., 1964), pp. 163–75.

20. Brown, p. 90.

21. Interestingly, this painting was influenced by Bishop Porteus' poem, "Death, A Poetical Essay," which also contributed to Bryant's "Thanatopsis." For a brief discussion of Peale's work see E.P. Richardson, *A Short History of Painting in America* (New York: Thomas Y. Crowell Co., 1963), pp. 111–13.

22. Donald A. Ringe, "William Cullen Bryant and the Science of Geology," *American Literature*, 26 (Jan.,1955), 507–14.

23. Quoted in Brown, p. 517.
24. Whitman, of course, is our great Civil War poet, and in his poetry about the War he confronted the whole dimension of death in its relationship to the affirmation of American democracy. Bryant, who as a journalist was so politically involved in War, nevertheless kept the conflict at least overtly out of his poetry with the exception of his commemorative poem, "The Death Of Lincoln" (1871). Unlike Whitman, Bryant does not use Lincoln's death as an occasion to explore the problem of death itself; rather, he gives us a traditional lament over the noble leader who freed the slaves and died "Among the noble host of those/Who perished in the cause of Right." It is a poem in the tradition of "Oh Captain, My Captain" rather than the mythic "Lilacs" elegy.
25. *Uncollected Poetry and Prose*, ed. Emory Holloway, Vol. II (New York: Doubleday & Co., 1922), 63 ff.

"Thanatopsis" and the Development of American Literature

R. RIO-JELLIFFE
University of Redlands

On reading an anonymous poem brought by Willard Phillips, his co-editor with Edward Channing of the *North American Review*, Richard Henry Dana, Jr. is said to have exclaimed: "Ah! Phillips, you have been imposed upon; no one on this side of the Atlantic is capable of writing such verses" (I.150).[1] Dana's skeptical remark identifies in the unknown author, soon discovered as the young William Cullen Bryant, the presence of a new voice, the promise of a new direction in American letters. Other critics have since concurred with Dana's estimate. H.M. Jones takes the first publication of "Thanatopsis" in 1817 as "the landmark . . . from which many are inclined to date the beginnings of a truly national American letters." In Bryant's first collection and Cooper's *The Spy*, both published in 1821, F.O. Matthiessen detects "the literature of the new nation, as distinct from colonial literature, [beginning] to find its voice."[2]

"Thanatopsis" is also significant for adumbrating a concept of nature and art which generated over half a century a coherent poetic theory and practice denoting the character of the yet unborn American literature. While the historical significance of "Thanatopsis" is generally acknowledged, its artistic structure and the relation of that structure to the development of American literature remain undefined. This paper examines the artistic structure of "Thanatopsis," a pattern of tension created by contradiction and paradox (I); and notes the relation of that structure to Bryant's theory of poetry and language, and of his theory and poetry to the development of American literature (II). Limited by space to a summary of my evidence, the paper is based on a full-length study of Bryant's concept of nature and its relation to poetic theory and practice.[3]

133

Literary historians detect in the attempts of early nineteenth century writers to assimilate and order a confusion of inherited and indigenous literary crosscurrents the beginnings of an American literature. The works of Brown, Irving, Cooper, Bryant, and others record the propaedeutic struggle toward artistic independence. Bryant's precursive discovery of a subjective locus for synthesizing borrowed and native elements, of an aesthetic for giving voice to innate experience of American nature, points the way to artistic identity and integrity. His coherent system of poetics and poetry, probably the first in America, exemplifies the process of assimilation and naturalization indispensable for the advent of the great writers in the "renaissance."

At a time when American "criticism was preoccupied with the social implications of literature" and "questions of art and technique were too often neglected,"[4] Bryant discoursed on literary technique, language, and form. Contradictory assessments of Bryant's critical position and tenets require a coherent and thorough consideration of his theory and poetry. For Bryant, like Wordsworth, is a transitional writer who sets traditional material in new orientations and thus recasts them with fresh significance. Both show the influence of associational writers, the English poet primarily of the mechanist Hartley, and the American of the later intuitive-idealist Alison, whose theories anticipate romantic aesthetics.[5] Bryant's critical and poetic works center around and are informed by an innate feeling for American nature and its implications for art.[6] His poetic theory and practice, founded on romantic principles of emotional expression, naturalness, simplicity, spontaneity, irregularity, and freedom, set him squarely in the romantic movement which he anticipates in America by over a decade.

I

After the first publication of the body of the poem in 1817, generally assumed to be a fair copy of the original draft,[7] two other versions preceded the 1821 "Thanatopsis" with its now famous introduction and conclusion. Two manuscripts, dated 1813–1815 and 1818–1820, contain prototypal versions of the introduction and conclusion.[8] These variants contravene assumptions made by some readers that the 1821 introduction and conclusion were "additions . . . hastily composed" under Wordsworth's influence for the collection Dana had commissioned.[9] The variants give evidence of an evolving view of nature which structures and informs the poem, and lies at the heart of Bryant's poetic theory and practice.

The introduction of the 1821 "Thanatopsis" opens with a general statement on nature's "various language" which breaks down into detailed components of gladness, beauty, sympathy, and consolation:

> To him who in the love of Nature holds
> Communion with her visible forms, she speaks
> A various language; for his gayer hours
> She has a voice of gladness, and a smile
> And eloquence of beauty, and she glides   5
> Into his darker musings, with a mild
> And gentle sympathy, that steals away
> Their sharpness, ere he is aware. When thoughts
> Of the last bitter hour come like a blight
> Over thy spirit, and sad images   10
> Of the stern agony, and shroud, and pall,
> And breathless darkness, and the narrow house,
> Make thee to shudder, and grow sick at heart;—
> Go forth, under the open sky, and list
> To Nature's teachings, while from all around—   15
> Earth and her waters, and the depths of air—
> Comes a still voice—

The next abstract reference to "thoughts of the last bitter hour" modulate from the vague "sad images" and "stern agony" to the concrete "shroud, and pall" and "narrow house." Embedded in these concrete images, and countering the impersonal generalization, are feelings of terror and grief. Material objects convert universal fact into personal experience. The movement from abstract generalities to sensuous, emotionally connotative particulars is a structural pattern reenforced by contrasting tones of detachment and involvement, and by rhythm congruent with imagery: gentle cadence among cheerful images in the first half, spasmodic rhythm among sorrowful, harsh images in the second half. These contrastive patterns recur consistently throughout the poem in various forms of expansion and development.

The body of the 1821 "Thanatopsis" (17–73) originally published in 1817,[10] likewise opens on an impersonal assertion of universal fact which shades into details connoting loss and grief: "cold ground," "lost each human trace," "brother to th'insensible rock." Kinetic imagery in "The oak / Shall send his roots abroad, and pierce thy mould" (29–30) renders general truth into dread. No emotions are overtly named; they are inherent in particularized or concrete images. Discourse enunciates an objective cognition of ultimate doom, while poetic texture sounds undertones of feeling.

The paradoxical interplay of intellectual and emotional elements is reenforced by the contrast in landscape of eternal cosmos and transient being doomed to dissolution:

> Yet a few days, and thee
> The all-beholding sun shall see no more
> In all his course; nor yet in the cold ground,
> Where thy pale form was laid with many tears,   20
> Nor in the embrace of ocean shall exist
> Thy image. Earth, that nourished thee, shall claim
> Thy growth, to be resolv'd to earth again;
> And, lost each human trace, surrend'ring up
> Thine individual being, shalt thou go   25
> To mix forever with the elements,
> To be a brother to th'insensible rock
> And to the sluggish clod, which the rude swain
> Turns with his share, and treads upon. The oak
> Shall send his roots abroad, and pierce thy mould.   30

Nature the consoler in the introduction turns in this section of the body into an enemy. Imagery corroborates antithetical design in yet another way. Large natural entities of sun, ocean, earth dwindle to rock, clod, roots. The living body fades into pale form and vanishes in "mould." Contracting immensity and reducing "individual being" to mere shade underscore the sense of subsidence and deprivation.

The same contrastive patterns structure the second section which argue against grief and fear (31–48). The generalization on the magnificent sepulcher of the dead break down into component images of hills, woods, rivers, brooks, and sun, planets, stars. Yet their glory make them no less the "sad abodes of death." In the third section (48–57), the general abstraction on the infinite dead crystallizes in images of time and space whose grandeur, again paradoxically, intensifies the human being's sense of loss. The remote, impersonal background modulates to felt life in sensuous objects. In the concluding section, an abstract common destiny takes substantial form in specific details.

The conclusion of the poem repeats the pattern in preceding sections with an impersonal injunction and vague "pale realms of shade" which resolve into kinetic images celebrating nature's triumph over man's enemy:

So live, that when thy summons comes to join
The innumerable caravan, that moves 75
To the pale realms of shade, where each shall take
His chamber in the silent halls of death,
Thou go not, like the quarry-slave at night,
Scourged to his dungeon; but sustain'd and sooth'd
By an unfaltering trust, approach thy grave, 80
Like one who wraps the drapery of his couch
About him, and lies down to pleasant dreams.[11]

Two obverse images render the theme of the whole poem: negatively in the quarry slave, and positively in actions encapsulating nature's lessons on how to die and how to live.

The tensional interplay of intellectual abstraction and sensuous emotional objects, general and particular, detachment and involvement, eternal and transient, converts the poem from a versified disquisition on death, a commonplace at the time, to a record of dissonances in mind and heart. A structural pattern of contrast and paradox transforms intellectual discourse into a "structure of emotion" where, in Alison's terms, external objects function as "emotion-bearing" vehicles.

Consistent with the structural pattern, the dialectic, which centers on the role of nature, hinges as well on opposition and paradox. Postulated in the introduction as premise of the whole poem, nature is benefactor of human spirit, particularly in the extremity of death. Yet in the first verse paragraph of the body, the benign comforter disappears behind an indifferent cosmos threatening the individual with loss of every "human trace." The "all-beholding Sun" the transient Self "shall see no more." In the premise set by the introduction, the end of consciousness turns into the ultimate deprivation of nature herself, of access to spiritual aid. The role of nature in the first section of the poem contradicts her role premised in the introduction.

The temporary reversal in nature's role reflects the way the human being, overwhelmed with fear, views the natural universe. In contrast, nature's cosmic, timeless perspective subsumes human fear and grief in the common destiny of all things. This universal vision counters the individual's view of nature as an impersonal threat. Natural beauty, magnified in detail after concrete detail, is a metaphor of nature's all-encompassing beneficence. The sun, symbol of individual extinction in the first section now glorifies man's eternal home. Forbidding immensity and solitude on earth and sky, as in "Take the wings of morning . . ." (45–54), are transformed into nature's enthralling world. Changes in descriptive mood reflect the individual's subjective alteration from fear and regret to assurance.

With this development the major paradox of the poem becomes clear. For over these natural scenes of beauty lies the shadow of grief and loss evoked in the first section. Enhancing nature's grandeur heightens the attractiveness of man's final resting place, but contrarily, intensifies rather than mitigates feelings of sorrow and loss which, from the start, imbues natural objects in the body of the poem. Working against nature's rational precepts are countersignals of feeling embedded in imagistic particulars. The rhetorical question in the final section of the body (58–60) reiterates the loneliness and bitter regret of one cut off from the living. Nature's arguments address human reason, but the language of the poem betrays instinctual undertones of dismay and terror past rational argument.

The intellectual reasoning culminates in the concluding image of one who "lies down to pleasant dreams." The understructure of counter-feeling climaxes in the opposite image of a quarry slave "Scourged to his dungeon." Both, not one or the other, encapsulate the paradoxical theme of "Thanatopsis." This conclusion may not be what the poet had consciously intended to leave with the reader. But Bryant's own theory of language, of imagery in particular, and the preeminent role of emotion in the creative process, recognizes the power of words as accessible only to partial control. "Symbols of words," Bryant says, "suggest both the sensible object and the association" (V.5). It is those associations that could undermine sense.

In style, technique, and thought, the 1821 introduction is more successfully integrated with the body than earlier variants. In the variants, a "better genius" mediates for nature whose ministry on spirit is contingent on the poet's voluntary return to the "repose of nature," a condition that holds in the later work. For the surrogate, a being with complex attributes appears in the 1821 poem, attesting to the poet's increased faith in nature as generative source of his art. This inner history is recorded in the early poems and confirmed in the centrality of nature in Bryant's critical theory.[12]

An incremental dialectic from the introduction through the body rises to a point in the conclusion. Considered by many readers as a didactic excrescence, the conclusion brings nature's injunctions to its logical issue: in life alone man may learn how to die. To complete the lesson on death, nature must instruct man to "so live" that he dies in peace. The lesson on dying, the conclusion establishes, is primarily a lesson on living. In the context of the whole poem, from nature's ministry on spirit in the introduction to the influence of her "still voice" in the body, the conclusion clearly affirms "an unfaltering trust" in nature alone. From beginning to end, man's ultimate recourse in life or death is nature's benign government.

The introduction, body, and conclusion are integrally joined to one another with consistent structural patterns and antithetical stresses in technique and dialectic. Balanced contrast is reflected as well in diction which deviates markedly from Bryant's immediate legacies of English poetic tradition and its transplants in America. The language of "Thanatopsis" demonstrates the American poet's functional naturalization of poetic diction and more recent realistic modes from favorites like Cooper, Burns, and Wordsworth. In the descriptive passages, the realistic "Rock-ribb'd" operates with formulas, "ancient as the sun" and "venerable woods" (38-40). Inert epithets like "th'insensible rock" obtain conceptual and affective life in the vivid actions of the "rude swain" who "turns with his share and treads upon" the "sluggish clod." In contrast to flaccid images of "cold ground" and "pale form," kinetic energy in the image of oak roots spreading out and piercing the human mould sharpens the sense of horror (19-30). Interacting with sensuous immediacy in natural or human actions, poetic diction acquires fresh viability.

Bryant prunes poetic convention to its functional essence, using formulaic simplicity to reinforce imagistic impression and consonant thought. Prosopopoeia, the preeminent figure of late eighteenth-century ornamental poetry, is transformed in Bryant's handling of personified nature into a functional device to set the premise of the poem and inform the whole structure.[13]

Strategic placement of conventional phrases also contributes to unfolding dialectic and mood, as the infinite hosts of heaven (45-48) convey as well immensity of space and eternal time; and "the continuous woods/Where rolls the Oregon" (52-53) picture infinity and solitude of the dead. The two modes of language function conjointly to intensify paradoxical dissonance of universal fate and individual resistance to it in design and thought.

What might appear to modern readers as an unusual handling of nineteenth century poetic language and form sets Bryant apart from the prevailing practice of his time. "Thanatopsis" diverges markedly from antecedent traditions in England. The most direct lines are the graveyard school, and the didactic strains of popular nature poetry with their sentimental, hyperbolic rhetoric, excessive analogizing of nature and human life; deliberate elevation of language with cumulative similes; periphrases, abstract personifications, extended descriptions; and loose, discursive form.[14]

At a time when poetic diction was of universal currency, and pre-romantic and romantic writers like Cowper, Burns, Wordsworth, and Coleridge were generally unknown or unwelcome to American readers, Bryant fashions a multivalent langauge closer to the bone of American experience. Tempered language, restrained, dignified tone, and controlled structure distinguishes "Thanatopsis" from the prevailing poetic practice of the period. In this literary phenomenon, Bryant forges material and form, both inherited and original, in the shape of an American artist's vision of life and death.

The artistic qualities of "Thanatopsis" confirm the unique position accorded to it in the history of American literature. The poem is important in other ways not generally recognized. It adumbrates fundamental principles of Bryant's theory and poetic practice, a congruent system based on his concept of nature and its implications for poetic form portending the character of a national literature. The discussion below outlines basic theoretical principles of Bryant's theory of language and related techniques.

II

The original draft of "Thanatopsis" (1811) precedes by almost a decade and a half, the 1821 version by four years, Bryant's formulation of his critical theory. The four "Lectures on Poetry" (1825–1826) is a comprehensive statement of theory drawing together dispersed ideas, and in the next five decades, consistently applied and reaffirmed in criticism and poetry.[15] The concept of nature which unifies "Thanatopsis" becomes the fundamental principle of theory and practice grounded on the "premise of feeling" in associational and romantic aesthetics.[16] Already germinal in the early poem are principles and tenets which bear on the development of American literature.

Bryant echoes an associational principle in postulating that the "great spring of poetry is emotion" (V. 10); but he locates the "living and inexhaustible sources of poetic inspiration" (V.40) in nature. The creative process generated by nature-inspired feelings mirrors the spontaneity of natural processes. Poetry is the product of mind quickened by nature. On these premises lies the touchstone for poetic language, style, and structure: the "natural." Bryant's organic view of mind and art prefigures the principle of organicism central to American critical theory from the renaissance to later periods.[17]

The coadunation of mind and nature in Bryant's theory occasions a concept of poetic form now known as the doctrine of analogies or correspondences. Over a decade before the doctrine becomes central to American criticism, Bryant defines a poetic technique which exhibits "analogies and correspondences . . . between the things of the moral and of the natural worlds," and "connects all the varieties of human feelings with the works of creation" (V.19), "moral associations with inanimate objects."[18] Metaphoric analogy combines at once the main elements of Bryant's poetics: instigating and unifying emotion; nature, source, and norm of art; language and technique congruent to union of feeling and nature. It also achieves the immediate and ultimate ends of poetry, aesthetic experience and moral elevation.

The poetic structure blueprinted in the doctrine of analogies opens on a natural scene imbued with congruous feelings and thoughts, or posits an idea associated with feelings which permeate natural objects in the poem, as in "Thanatopsis." The fusion conjures up analogous scenes embodying inner responses. Poetic form emerges with the accretion of congruent details reenforcing the original fusion, and by accumulation grows in intensity. The "leitmotif of romantic thought about art," the doctrine is an aesthetic formulation of the romantic vindication of mind over physical world, and outlines romantic structural forms.[19]

In theory the doctrine of analogies combines discrete elements. In Bryant's practice, intense feeling inundates natural objects, and natural images are infused with feeling-thought. A new reality transcends the objective-subjective dualism. Irradiated with mind and feeling, imagery speaks the language of the inner world. The majestic beauty of the prairies becomes an agency of mind for projecting its own life. Under the fusion force of emotion, material and immaterial conjoin, and words function polysemously.

Anticipating in theory the metaphoric and symbolic modes of later poetry, Bryant applies the doctrine of analogies in poetic form distinguishing his nature poems from traditional descriptive-mediative types, where natural scene provides the setting for moral or intellectual reflections, or occasions a literal, often mechanical analogizing of nature. In most Bryant nature poems (except in the rare instance of a work like "Monument Mountain"), emotion unifies natural scene and sujective experience. From early works like "I Cannot Forget the High Spell" (1815) to great middle period works like "A Forest Hymn" (1825) and "The Prairies" (1832), landscape and cogitation mingle and illuminate one another.

All other components of Bryant's theory stem from the principle of emotion as unifier of mind and art. Since emotion and other mental constituents are "embodied in language" so as to affect another mind, the nature of poetic language engages Bryant over several decades. Emotion, he postulates, is the unfailing guide to poetic expression analogous to originating experience.

Bryant defines language as "the symbols of thought." Poetry selects and arranges these "arbitrary symbols" which are "as unlike as possible to the things with which it deals," and by this very limitation may render the immaterial in material "images" and "pictures" (V.5–6). This view of poetic language as symbol advances beyond the associationists toward the romantic theory of Coleridge. It also suggests modern views on the nonrepresentational character of language.

Images or pictures are the heart of poetic language. Emotion opens up "the storehouse where the mind has laid up its images" (V.10); while imagination "shapes materials . . . into pictures of majesty and beauty" (V.26). The poet's "sketches of beauty" are transformed in the reader's imagination to "noblest images" brought forward "from its own stores" (V.6–7). Bryant, however, dissenting from writers of the time, distinguishes a poem "affluent" with "mere imagery" from the "language of passion" framed in "spontaneity or excitement" (V.8–10). Supplanting the vogue of ornamental language and extended pictorial description, Bryant's imagism relies on a "few touches to delineate both external reality and subjective response, and thus to activate simultaneously sense, imagination, feeling, and moral sensibility. Imagery whose materiality calls up "the idea of certain emotions" (V.7) exemplifies Bryant's principle of synchronous operation in creative mind and poem.

The image, furthermore, concretizes general "lessons of wisdom" or "moral truth" in objects or particulars (V.11). Like Wordsworth, Bryant regards universal and permanent features of human and natural life as proper subjects of poetry, but requires that they be manifested in the particular or specific.

In depicting both particular and universal, outer and inner worlds, transient and permanent, imagery achieves the suggestive and effective ends of poetry. Both "picturesque and impassioned," a well-wrought image "touches the heart and kindles the imagination" (V.52). The polyphonic function of imagery adumbrated in "Thanatopsis" appears in varying degrees of concentration in nature poems of the following decades. Bryant's view of image prefigures a line of thought from the renaissance to the present, as in Pound's definition of image as "an intellectual and emotional complex in an instant of time."

In accord with the informing principle of his thought and art, Bryant locates the source of functional imagery in nature, the "original fountain" and "standard of perfection" for poetry. He urges the poet to "go directly to nature" for original imagery true to experience, instead of the current dependence on "the common stock of the guild of poets" (V.158).

Related to these tenets is Bryant's contention that only brief poems or those of moderate length may touch mind and heart. Despite the popular taste for epics of the revolutionary poets, or tales such as those he himself composed, Bryant asserts, "There is no such thing as a long poem" (I.186). Presaging Poe's famous dictum by a decade,[20] Bryant sets down a primary tenet of early nineteenth-century poetics on the lyric.

While Bryant advocates "simplicity and clearness" in language (V.19), he would admit "obscurity . . . in the phrase" and "recondite or remote allusions" (V.157) to heighten poetic effect. He allows poetry to "transgress arbitrary rules" so long as it "speaks a language which reaches the heart" (V.10). The end of poetry, to make the "fullest effect upon the mind," is thus attained "no matter by what system of rules" (V.45). His radical prescriptions for prosody abrogate current rules and open the way for freer forms.[21]

Even more revolutionary for his age where "artificial elevation of style" with "meretricious decorations" prevailed in poetic practice (V.51–52) is Bryant's vehement advocacy of "simple and severe" style (V.51), or "simple and natural . . . style" (V.155). He repeatedly inveighs against "strained, violent contrivances," "florid and stately" imagery and epithet popular with American poets. "Too far removed from the common idiom of our tongue" (V.157–158), the "false sublime" subverts "pathos and feeling" (V.52–53), and is therefore—a heinous sin in the Bryant creed—"out of nature" or "unnatural" (V.49). Like Wordsworth, Bryant believes "the language of poetry is naturally figurative," but figures must be used only "to heighten the intensity of expression . . ." Unless forged in the heat of feeling they turn into "cold conceits" or "extravagance" (V.10).

Bryant's obsessive demand for "simple and natural" language rests on a principle of marked historical significance: the organic correlation of verbal expression to originating emotion. From early to late critical works, he censures the "artificial and mechanical" in poetic language, and recommends "a natural and becoming dress for the conceptions of the writer" (V.54), an "honest expresion of meaning."[22] Only "natural" language gains the end Bryant extols, as did Coleridge before and Poe after him, "unity of effect."[23] As no American writer of the time held so inflexibly, Bryant requires the language of poetry to be an organic expression of and commensurate to the originating subjective state.

Bryant locates the sources of "natural" language "in the organic expression of the people," in "the vernacular language of the poet" (V.36-37). Consistent with his organicism, Bryant resolves the fundamental issue in the search for national literature. For all the causes adduced to account for its absence, and all the solutions to bring it about, the problem hinges primarily on locating an indigenous language to give intrinsic expression to American experience.[24] An advanced pioneer on this question, Bryant renounces the prevailing dependence on English heritage, and locates an American language in "the copious and flexible dialect we speak" (V.36). "It has grown up . . . among a simple and unlettered people," and has "accommodated itself, in the first place to things of nature, and, as civilization advanced, to the things of art . . ." It has thus "become a language full of picturesque forms of expression . . ." (V.34). While the language of "Thanatopsis" is hardly the vernacular, still its chaste diction and controlled form deviates markedly from ornate expression and loose structure in similar works. Nature poems after "Thanatopsis" move closer to common speech in diction and rhythm. Departing from contemporary theory and poetic practice, Bryant's views on language presage the language of the emergent American literature.

Bryant addresses another question in the search for national literature when he directs American writers to draw "their subjects from modern manners and the simple occurrences of common life" (V.33). He anticipates the shift at about the fourth decade from elegant or sublime subjects to "real life" (V.55), to "familiar and domestic life."[25] Portending the practice of many American novelists, he claims romance puts "familiar things in a new and striking yet natural light," for its subject is not the "supernatural and the marvelous" but the "manners of our countrymen" (V.55). The romancer is an "anatomist of the human heart," a title befitting such writers as Hawthorne, Melville, James, and Faulkner. Bryant grounds both language and subject matter in the life of "human beings, placed among the things of this earth" (V.29).

As the demand for American literature rose in the early decades, the idea of an indigenous literature became increasingly identified with romantic spirit and modes. A complex of ideas and trends—elevation of feeling and imagination over reason; power of mind to link man and nature; with democratic socio-political ideals, the rise of the common man, and the divinity of common things; resurgence of American nature as source of poetic inspiration and expression; location of literary language rooted in American soil; subsidence of neoclassicism in literary art and taste; shifts in critical norms from absolute universal standards to historic relativism and subjective or impressionistic appeal; the moral ends of literature balanced with aesthetic pleasure; the turn from nationalism to universalism; the concept of organicism in government and art—these constituents of Bryant's thought and art identify the search for national literature with romantic confluences.

Enunciating romantic tenets in the twenties, Bryant may have promoted the shift from the rational-mechanistic to an organic view of mind and art. His poetics, grounded on emotion as the unitary creative principle, and poetry as analogue of mind quickened by nature, prefigure other major statements of organicism in America, and precede the belated reception of Alison and romantic theorists like Wordsworth and Coleridge. From the forties on, when romanticism had become "the positive movement of the time,"[26] organic unity and its allied doctrine of analogies echo in the works of Emerson, Melville, Lowell, Whitman, and others. Holding to the life principle as spirit, and to objects as symbols of inner or higher reality, Bryant prefigures transcendental organicism.

His organicism, however, falls short of the radical totality of All in Each espoused by Emerson and some contemporaries. Still relying on the human imagination to unite nature and mind, and to effect the same unity in the poem, Bryant adumbrates only in part the metaphysics to come. Similarly, his poetry in general merely foreshadows the symbolic mode after him. Still dwelling on natural beauty for its own sake as well as for its spiritual significance, the poems are essentially metaphoric in function. The nature poems nonetheless inaugurate "the organic union of art, nature, and mind of man," the salient mark of organicism in American literature.[27]

Bryant's theory and art typifies one of two contemporaneous streams of American romanticism: an "organic emotional romanticism . . . of a slow but indigenous growth," and the imitative romanticism of Freneau, Halleck, Willis, Drake, Percival, and somewhat later, Poe, who exploited medievalism, the gothic, and other exotic trends in Europe.[28] Two main branches of American poetry stem from Bryant and Poe, the first important poets of early nineteenth century. Poe initiates art for art's sake, the use of technique to achieve supernal beauty transcending mundane reality. Bryant inaugurates a poetic tradition founded on a total view of reality encompassing natural world and human mind. Where Poe in his poetic practice bypasses nature, Bryant takes nature for the main constituent of his art.

Bryant keeps faith in the literary potential of America when writers, misled by early associational thought, despair over a landscape empty of hoary legend and history. Virtually alone among the poets of the first three decades, he makes American landscape viable for poetry, not by drumming up external attributes of historic or mythic values, but by recreating natural scene in the crucible of impassioned imagination. For Bryant, the quest for nationality is the quest for personal artistic integrity. He discovers an inner locus for assimilating American nature and life, and for rendering it in art forms accordant to its spirit. His philosophy, aesthetics, and poetry offer a way to release American writers "from the sterile obligation to express what their own experience had not nurtured."[29] Within the limited scope of his vision and achievement lay the seeds of the future.

Readers of his day find Bryant's poetry "complex and difficult," a testimony to the unique character of his work.[30] For modern readers, Bryant's poems are loosely knit, lacking the tension of paradox, the oblique curve of irony, the concentration of symbol, the power of Adamic self-parturitions in Emerson, Whitman, Melville, and Dickinson. Yet for all their faults, the poems manifest a viable synthesis of tradition and innovation which prepares the ambience necessary for the great writers to come. His poetry describes and states, like poetry of the past; it also embodies, like much of the poetry to come. His "organic style,"[31] issuing from his search for language commensurate with his experience of American landscape and life, opens the way to an American literature sought after in his age, and claimed with pride in our own.

NOTES

1. All references to Parke A. Godwin, *The Life and Works of William Cullen Bryant* (New York, 1883), 6 volumes, are indicated in this manner, with Roman numeral for volume and Arabic numeral for page.

2. Howard Mumford Jones, *Ideas in America* (Cambridge,1944), 15. Francis O. Matthiessen, *American Renaissance* (New York,1941), 372n.

3. This paper is based on my unpublished dissertation, "The Poetry of William Cullen Bryant: Theory and Practice" (University of California, Berkeley,1964), which examines fully Bryant's theoretical system, the relation of theory to poetic practice, the philosophical and historical backgrounds of his thought and art, and the implications of his work for the development of American literature. A brief treatment of the subject is in my article, "Bryant's Concept of Nature in Relation to Poetic Theory and Practice," *Massachusetts Studies in English*, Vol.5 no.3.

4. William Charvat, *The Origins of American Critical Thought, 1810–1835* (Pennsylvania,1936),6.

5. A radical difference in psychology and its resultant aesthetics separate early and later associationists. Charvat records the pervasive influence of Scottish psychology and rhetoric in America at the turn of the century. He does not, however, distinguish the empiricism and Augustan standards of the early school from the idealistic "Common Sense" school of Reid, Stewart, and Campbell, and the intuitive emotionalism of aestheticians like Alison, Knight, and with reservations, Jeffrey. The mechanistic psychologists postulate a Lockean mind, essentially atomistic, which develops from primary experiences to more complex associations of ideas. Later organicists accept Shaftesbury's postulate of the moral sense as "first principle" of mind deploying and integrating materials of experience; and of emotion as governor of the moral sense. The shift from atomistic to organic concept of mind parallels the intellectual revolution elevating emotion over reason. A fragmented Humean world coalesces once more under the unifying force of emotion which, from a minor stylistic device in neoclassicism, becomes the chief requisite of poetic creation. Pursuing the aesthetic implications of the new psychology, the organic intuitionists formulate a poetics prefiguring romantic theory and poetic form. Alison, the leading organistic aesthetician, was unknown to most American critics and writers at the time of Bryant's "Lectures" (1825–1826).

    The associational backgrounds of Bryant and Wordsworth, similarities and differences in their memory and poetry are discussed in detail in Chapters I and II of my unpublished dissertation, and briefly in my article on "Bryant's Concept of Nature in Relation to Poetic Theory and Practice" (n.3). Although Bryant is often associated with Wordsworth, Bryant's theory corresponds more closely to Coleridge whose principle of organic form entails the fusion of inner and outer worlds through impassioned imagination.

6. A passage in the unfinished autobiography testifies to Bryant's innate sensitivity to natural beauty which is reenforced by his readings:

I was always from my earliest years a delighted observer of external nature—the splendors of a winter daybreak over the wide wastes of snow seen from the windows, the glories of the autumnal woods, the gloomy

approaches of the thunderstorm, and its departure amid sunshine and
rainbows, the return of spring, with its flowers, and the first snowfall of
winter. The poets fostered this taste in me, and though at the time I
rarely heard such things spoken of, it was none the less cherished in my
secret mind. (I.25)

7. The date of the original composition of "Thanatopsis" is indeterminate.
The exact time is immaterial for the concerns of this paper. William Cullen Bryant II ("The Genesis of 'Thanatopsis,'" *New England Quarterly,*
June,1948) sets it around 1815. Charles Henry Brown in his biography,
William Cullen Bryant (New York,1971), or favors the 1813–1814
period. Bryant himself refers in the autobiography to an 1811 of 1812
period. At another occasion he refers to his seventeenth or eighteenth
year, the latter being 1813. With all this uncertainty, I shall retain the
earliest date (1811) as a convenient historical maker.
8. The four existing complete versions of "Thanatopsis" and some variants
from the Goddard-Roslyn Estate collection, are printed in Tremaine
McDowell, "Bryant's Practice in Composition and Revision," *PMLA,*
LII (June,1937). "On the evidence of the handwriting," he dates Ms.A
1813–1815, Ms.B 1818–1820. Here are two variants of the introduction:

Ms. A. c.1813–1815
It was his better genius that was wont
To steal upon the bard what time his steps
Sought the repose of nature, lone and still
And unfrequented walks—and in his ear
To whisper things of which it irks the mind   5
That clings to the dear fallacies of life
To think:—and gravely with his graver hours
Oft the benevolent and heedful one
Would thus commune—"Yet a few days, and thee
The all-beholding sun shall see no more . . .

Ms. B c.1818–1820
It was his better genius that was wont
To steal upon the bard what time his steps
Sought the repose of nature—lone and still
And unfrequented walks—and in his ear
To whisper things of which it irks the mind   5
That clings to the deawr fallacies of life
To think: and gravely with his graver hours
The heedful and benevolent spirit oft
Would thus commune. —"Yet a few days, and thee
The all-beholding sun shall see no more . . .

The 1821 "Thanatopsis" appeared in the *North American Review*
as follows:

To him who in the love of Nature holds
Communion with her visible forms, she speaks
A various language; for his gayer hours
She has a voice of gladness, and a smile
And eloquence of beauty, and she glides
Into his darker musings, with a mild
And gentle sympathy, that steals away
Their sharpness, ere he is aware. When thoughts
Of the last bitter hour come like a blight
Over thy spirit, and sad images   10
Of the stern agony, and shroud, and pall,
And breathless darkness, and the narrow house
Make thee to shudder, and grow sick at heart;—
Go forth, under the open sky, and list
To Nature's teachings, while from all around—
Earth and her waters, and the depths of air—
Comes a still voice—Yet a few days, and thee
The all-beholding sun shall see no more
In all his course; nor yet in the cold ground,
Where thy pale form was laid, with many tears,   20
Nor in the embrace of ocean shall exist
Thy image. Earth, that nourished thee, shall claim
Thy growth, to be resolv'd to earth again;
And, lost each human trace, surrend'ring up
Thine individual being, shalt thou go
To mix forever with the elements,
To be a brother to th'insensible rock
And to the sluggish clod, which the rude swain
Turns with his share, and treads upon. The oak
Shall send his roots abroad, and pierce thy mould,   30
Yet not to thy eternal resting-place
Shalt thou retire alone—nor couldst thou wish
Couch more magnificent. Thou shalt lie down
With patriarchs of the infant world—with kings,
The powerful of the earth—the wise, the good,
Fair forms, and hoary seers of ages past,
All in one mighty sepulchre.—The hills
Rock-ribb'd and ancient as the sun,—the vales
Stretching in pensive quietness between;
The venerable woods—rivers that move   40
In majesty, and the complaining brooks
That make the meadows green; and, pour'd round all,
Old ocean's grey and melancholy waste,—
Are but the solemn decorations all
Of the great tomb of man. The golden sun,
The planets, all the infinite host of heaven,
Are shining on the sad abodes of death,
Through the still lapse of ages. All that tread

The globe are but a handful to the tribes
That slumber in its bosom.—Take the wings   50
Of morning—and the Barcan desert pierce,
Or lose thyself in the continuous woods
Where rolls the Oregon, and hears no sound,
Save his own dashings—yet—the dead are there,
And millions in those solitudes, since first
The flight of years began, have laid them down
In their last sleep—the dead reign there alone.—
So shalt thou rest—and what if thou shalt fall
Unnoticed by the living—and no friend
Take note of thy departure? All that breathe   60
Will share thy destiny. The gay will laugh
When thou art gone, the solemn brood of care
Plod on, and each one as before will chase
His favourite phantom; yet all these shall leave
Their mirth and their employments, and shall come,
And make their bed with thee. As the long train
Of ages glide away, the sons of men,
The youth in life's green spring, and he who goes
In the full strength of years, matron, and maid,
The bow'd with age, the infant in the smiles   70
And beauty of its innocent age cut off,—
Shall one by one be gathered to thy side,
By those, who in their turn shall follow them.
So live, that when thy summons comes to join
The innumerable caravan, that moves
To the pale realms of shade, where each shall take
His chamber in the silent halls of death,
Thou go not, like the quarry-slave at night,
Scourged to his dungeon; but sustain'd and sooth'd
By an unfaltering trust, approach thy grave,   80
Like one who wraps the drapery of his couch
About him, and lies down to pleasant dreams.

9. See for example, Tremaine McDowell, *William Cullen Bryant: Representative Selections* (New York, 1935), 391n.
10. Without the introduction, the 1817 "Thanatopsis" is spoken by an un-
    known persona who neither invests objects with her beneficence, nor gen-
    erates unresolvable paradoxes in imagery and dialectic. That transient
    man is severed from the external cosmos is plain fact in the 1817 work.
    The entrance of beneficent nature in the 1821 introduction sets up the
    paradoxical interplay of universal fact and human feelings. The introduc-
    tion alters the function of natural beauty in the later work to heighten na-
    ture's arguments and her spell, and contrarily, to accentuate human loss.
    A new complexity of language and dialectic structures the later poem.

11. Generally regarded as a didactic excrescence, the conclusion appears to be Bryant's concession to a popular poetic mode. More deserving of the censure is an earlier variant (1818–1820) in which the poet labors to correct the label, "pagan," on the 1817 poem:

> So live that when thy summons comes to join
> The innumerable caravan, in crowds each day
> Descending to the earth, and lay thee down
> In thy chamber in her dark and silent halls—
> Thou go not like the quarry-slave at night
> Scourged to his dungeon—But sustained and soothed
> In th' extreme agony that nature dreads
> By the kind hope that mercy will accept
> Perfect the imperfect duties of thy life
> And pardon all thy errors approach thy grave
> Like one who wraps the drapery of his couch
> About him and lies down for pleasant dreams.
>
> (McDowell, 484)

Two appurtenances of the graveyard school with which "Thanatopsis" is identified appear in this variant: Nature dreading "th'extreme agony," and implied Christian "hope and mercy." In the tightly linked dialectic of the 1821 poem, Christian consolations of salvation or afterlife have no place. The traditional opposition of nature and death contravenes the poet's concept of nature whose ministry encompasses life and death. This variant never appeared in print.

12. For evidence in the poems, see Chapter III, Part 1 of my dissertation (n.3). Poems from the juvenile "The Spring's Walk" 1810) to "I Broke the Spell That Held Me Long" (1824) chronicle the poet's growing faith in nature's control over his mind and art. The first poem outlines a prototypal enunciation of his belief that poetry originates in the interaction of feeling and nature. After vacillating between acceptance and rejection, the poet establishes in the latter poem the central doctrine of his poetics: nature is the "original fountain" of poetry.

An unpublished third version of the introduction, possibly written after 1821, omits nature with small success. The flat discursive tone testifies to Bryant's distrust of egocentric subjectivism, and his dependence on union of mind and nature for artistic vitality and form:

> Such often in my solitary hours
> Strange thoughts that weave involuntary verse
> Still come till deeply moved the spirit grows
> Familiar with the grave and dresses it

With a sad beauty. Then the last dread hour
That recollected in the midst of joy
Drives back the bounding blood on the sick heart
Affrights me not. Calmly and unafraid
I think to yield me to the common fate
And trust myself with millions. As I look
On the low airless dwellings in the earth
Of those who went before me to their rest
A voice not in the ear but at the heart
Like an articulate silence gravely thus
Communes with me . . .

                                        (McDowell, 488)

13. Abstract personification became the chief device of a decadent strain of ornamental poetry in the late eighteenth century. Bryant decries the American imitators of Darwin and Hayley for their excessive dependence on "convenient" pieces of "standing pageantry" which subvert the "force and directness" of poetic expression (Review of Solyman Brown, *An Essay on American Poetry, North American Review* VII [July, 1818], 208; and Review of Henry Pickering, *The Ruins of Paestum and Athens, and Other Poems, North American Review* 29 ([July, 1824], 48). In "Thanatopsis" nature personified is a functional, not decorative, device to set the premise of the poem and inform its whole structure.

14. For a detailed discussion of the relations of "Thanatopsis" to poetic traditions in England and America, see Chapter I of my dissertation (n.3).

15. The four "Lectures on Poetry" (1825-1826) outline a congruent body of principles and tenets which are expanded in literary essays, illustrated in critical reviews, and practiced in the writing of poetry over the next half century. Published in Godwin, Vol. V.

16. The phrase is from Walter Jackson Bate, *From Classic to Romantic* (Cambridge, 1946), Chapter V.

17. For organicism in American literature and criticism, see for example, H.H. Clark, "Changing Attitudes in Early American Literary Criticism: 1800-1840" and more importantly, Richard H. Fogle, "Organic Form in American Criticism, 1840-1870" in *The Development of American Literary Criticism,* ed. Floyd Stovall (Chapel Hill, 1955). Also see Benjamin Spencer, *The Quest for Nationality* (Syracuse, 1957) for the shift in concept of government during this period (1815-1860) from balanced contrast to an organism growing out of the land and people, and its correlative concept of literature as an organic expression of national life.

18. Review of Catherine M. Sedgwick, *The Travellers,* New York Review 1 (June, 1825), 35.

19. See M.H. Abrams, *The Mirror and the Lamp* (New York, 1953), 51-52; and W.K. Wimsatt, Jr., *The Verbal Icon* (Lexington, 1954), 109-110.

20. The common source of Bryant and Poe may be A.W. Schlegel who was widely disseminated in American periodicals before 1820, although Bryant may have picked his idea from Longinus.
21. While the couplet still rules unchallenged in America, Bryant calls for variety and irregularity in prosody as early as in his first literary essay (1811). Aware that the "liberty" for which he contends has "often been censured and ridiculed," he advocates trisyllables in iambic verse. What appears to be a minor innovation of "trisyllabic substitution" becomes a major factor in bringing about "a new method of both writing and reading poetry" in early nineteenth century, according to Paul Fussell, Jr. in his *Theory of Prosody in Eighteenth Century England* (New London, 1954), 156. See also Chapters IV and V.
22. Quoted in John Bigelow, *William Cullen Bryant* (Boston, 1890), 74.
23. Review of Pickering, 43.
24. See Spencer, *Quest for Nationality* for backgrounsds.
25. Review of Catherine A. Sedgwick, *Redwood, North American Review* 20 (April, 1825), 248–249, 251–252.
26. Fogle, 72.
27. Fogle, 83–84.
28. A few medievalistic and gothic poems, several narratives, and some short poems like "The Knight's Epitaph" (1835) constitute a minor group peripheral to Bryant's poetic application of his theory.
29. Spencer, ix. See Bryant's third and fourth "Lectures," "On Poetry in its Relation to our Age and Country" and "On Originality and Imitation," in Godwin, Vol. V.
30. Robert E. Spiller, ed. *The Literary History of the United States* (New York, 1948), 304. Spiller considers Bryant's poems "unsurpassed of their kind in American poetry."
31. William Ellery Leonard, "Bryant," *Cambridge History of American Literature* (Cambridge, 1943), I, 264.

Progress and Dissolution
in Bryant's Poetry

ALBERT F. McLEAN
Point Part College

In April of 1848, the news from Europe was, for educated and informed men like William Cullen Bryant and Richard Henry Dana, most unsettling. The spirit of revolution appeared to be sweeping much of Europe toward political chaos. France, under the fading Louis Phillippe, had seen barricades and bloodshed in the streets during the preceding months, and the fate of the Republic was, at best, uncertain. Dana had written Bryant of his dismay with these developments and Bryant, in his reply, gave voice to his convictions about the process of history of which these events were a manifestation. "You are not to make melancholy faces at news from Europe. That earth is to become a paradise in consequence of any political changes that can be made I do not belive, but I believe it to be the order of Providence that republican institutions will come in with a higher and more general civilization, and that their effect is good and wholesome." And later in the same letter he stated, "As to what is going on in France, I confess that I am not without my apprehensions—but I am of a more hopeful temperament, I believe, than you are, and my hopes predominate.[1]

This appeal to a basic optimism was, in its moderation and firmness, quite characteristic of Bryant, both as a publicist and as a poet. In a number of poems like "The Greek Boy" and "The Antiquity of Freedom" Bryant had expressed this philosophical position, that human possibility within liberal societies, while not inevitable nor unlimited, was a rational premise upon which men could act. That such possibilities were greater in the United States, given its civil and religious liberties, protected by republican governments, and enhanced by its natural environment, was a reasonable extension of this proposition.

155

Bryant's observation to Dana, however, is explicit in disavowing the belief that "earth is to become a paradise" as a result of political change. With the heady optimism of contemporary utopian thought Bryant had little patience, and the evangelical fervor of millennialism was foreign to his temperament. The late nineteenth century had given rise to a variety of expectations that an earthly paradise lay ahead for humankind. Utopian communities like Brook Farm, and millennarian sects contributed to the prevailing thought of nineteenth century Americans. Traditional Calvinism had shed the provincial notion of a theocratic "city on the hill," and from Jonathan Edwards through the revivals of the nineteenth century, the faithful had been led to expect "the new heavens and the new earth." As Cushing Strout has pointed out, "millennialistic speculation was rife in the whole evangelical movement, and William Miller's Adventist prophecy of the Second Coming in 1843 and 1844 was only a more literal and premillennialist version of a common theme."[2] This heightened anticipation of a new social and religious order, as Professor Strout demonstrates, contributed to the evangelical crusade for the abolition of slavery, a movement to which William Cullen Bryant and the *Evening Post* gave their support.

In his role as a poet, however, Bryant would often strike an even more somber note. In going to nature for his inspiration he found signs and symbols of an ominous kind. Vast and formidable, Nature in her various voices told man of decay and dissolution as well as rebirth. Nature made no promises for republican societies and offered little encouragement to man other than that the grave stood ready to receive him. In his elegiac poetry he would, as in "The Death of Schiller," evoke the promise of an afterlife, unburdened by mortal limitations, and elsewhere, in such poems as "The Song of the Sower," he would praise the constantly generative force of Nature, yet the disturbing question as to the future of the race of mortal men haunts his poetry. On occasion a pessimistic vision is raised, as in "An Indian at the Burial Place of His Fathers," where the young man, witness to the sad fate of the Indian cultures, looks into the future:

> But I behold a fearful sign,
>   To which the white men's eyes are blind;
> Their race may vanish hence, like mine,
>   And leave no trace behind,
> Save ruins o'er the region spread,
>   And the white stones above the dead.[3]

Or in "The Fountain," where the poet speculates on what changes lie ahead for the woodland spring:

> Will not man
> Seek out strange arts to wither and deform
> The pleasant landscape which thou makest green.[4]

For Bryant the immutable laws of growth and decay were the lessons of Nature, and while they held forth prospects for the future, they could also serve to reenforce the melancholy tendencies of his thought.

That Bryant's visions of the future of mankind should reveal contradictions and inconsistencies, at least as seen from the perspectives of a systematic observer, should come as no surprise to students of the nineteenth century. Emerson's generation of hope contended with the tragic visions of Hawthorne and Melville. As literary culture itself maintained a persistent dialogue on these troubling problems, so Bryant in his creative moments explored the intricacies of his personal experience. It is the nature of genuine poetry that it crystallizes the emotional and intellectual life in moments of intense realization, and as the patterns of the poet's life change with time, so do his poetic formulations of this experience. Bryant's poems contribute to that self-consciousness of Americans of the noble experiment, that "last, best hope of man," in which they were the protagonists, or at least the participants, and his mission as a poet was, in part, to articulate the hopes and fears prompted by this self-consciousness.

For purposes of the moment, I shall focus on several poems, composed at various stages of Bryant's career, and attempt to bring into focus the major avenues by which he approached, and sometimes avoided, the confrontations between hope and despair, progress and dissolution. The poems I have selected are "The Ages," delivered at the commencement at Harvard University in 1821; "The Crowded Street," published in *Graham's Magazine* in 1843; "The Battlefield," which appreared in the *Democratic Review* in 1837; and "Sella," written at Roslyn in 1862 and published in the collection of 1864, titled *Thirty Poems.*

The long narrative poem, "The Ages," was avowedly a paean to human progress. The explanatory note which was to accompany the poem through successive editions set forth the author's purpose to "confirm the hopes of the philanthropist for the future destinies of the human race."[5] In thirty-five numbered stanzas consisting of eight rhymed lines in iambic pentameter, and capped with a ninth emphatic line in hexameter, the poet reviews the "days gone by," the golden days of old." In the opening stanzas he addresses the concern of those who go to their "common rest" still uncertain as to the future for their loved ones. The anxiety arises as "We think on what they were, with many fears/lest goodness die with them, and leave the coming years." Much as men may honor "the glorious record" of past virtues, there are still insistent questions as to the future.

> Has Nature, in her calm, majestic march,
> Faltered with age at last? does the bright sun
> Grow dim in heaven? or, in their far blue arch,
> Sparkle the crowd of stars, when day is done,
> Less brightly? when the dew-lipped Spring comes on,
> Breathes she with airs less soft, or scents the sky
> With flowers less fair than when her reign begun?
> Does prodigal Autumn, to our age, deny
> The plenty that once swelled beneath his sober eye?[6]

The response is not far to seek. The reader is exhorted to "look on this beautiful world and read the truth/in her fair page." Furthermore, God "the Merciful One" will not "leave a work so fair all blighted and accursed." And mankind, "who has tamed the elements" and "whose eye unwinds the eternal dances of the sky" shall discover God's will, so that "love and peace shall make their paradise with man." Having unequivocally announced the impending millennium, the poet invites his audiences to "sit at the feet of History" and review the progress of virtue.

What follows in progressive stanzas is the history of freedom subscribed to by Americans throughout the nineteeth century. From barbarism through early civilization mankind evolved a humane ethic, protecting the weak and establishing justice. The rise of ancient empires let loose "a boundless sea of blood" culminating in "a record in the desert" and the ruins of "the Cities of the Dead." Virtue fled to Greece, however, and "Liberty awoke." In spite of the devisive warfare of ancient Greece, its better deeds,

> . . . puts to shame
> Our chiller virtue; the high art to tame
> The whirlwind of the passions was thy own,
> And the pure ray, that from the bosom came,

> Far over many a land and age has shone,
> and mingles with the light that beams from
> God's own throne.

From Greece to Rome and then to "the Galilean Lake, the light of hope, the leading star of love," wended the course of human history. Through the years of early Christianity, when "priestly hands. . . were red with blood," and into the age during which "vice, beneath the mitre's kind control/sinned gayly on."

> But this unsteady progress came to its hour of decision:
> At last the earthquake came—the shock that hurled
> To dust, in many fragments dashed and strown,
> The throne, whose roots were in another world.

According to this chronicle, the "web" which had bound "prostrate Europe" for a thousand years "crumbled and fell, as fire dissolves the flaxen thread." And the post-Reformation era still persists: "The spirit of that day is still awake/spreads himself, and shall not sleep again," for "Truth survives" and "Earth has no shades to quench that beam of heaven." The history of freedom had moved inexorably from the Reformation toward the Great Migration and the American Revolution.

The historical panorama turns to scan the "Western shore, that morning chased/The Deep and ancient night." Visions of white sails, of "the broad and boundless mainland" that are a "youthful paradise," only marred by the brutality of Indian warfare.

> Here the free spirit of mankind at length
> Throws its last fetters off, and who shall place
> A limit to the giant's unchained strength
> Or curb his swiftness in the forward race?

Europe may still be caught in its "iron net," but America—"thou shalt never fall/save with thy children."

Having reached the happy heights of history the poet closes on his rhetorical question:

> Who shall then declare
> The date of thy deep-founded strength, or tell
> How happy, in thy lap, the sons of men shall dwell?

It is, of course, only a question. Here, Bryant, as he was to do in numerous other poems, avoids a conclusive prophecy. Through his historical myth of the progress of virtue his point has been made. The basis of hope, the eventual ascendency of freedom and virtue, and his vision of the happiness and gallantry of his contemporary America, leave little room for scepticism or despair. The environment protects and sustains the new society, and the ubiquity of Nature informs the American of the eternal law of rebirth and renewal. This civilization that he depicts is, of course, a largely agrarian one, built on homespun virtues and simple faith. It is a post-Reformation order dedicated to hard work in one's calling, domestic and familial values, and a libertarian political framework in which social power of all sorts is diffuse and permissive.

Whatever its shallowness as a vision of human history, "The Ages" works a profound vein in the American experience. It identifies positive and creative forces as providentially ordained and leaves the unpleasant aspects of humanity well buried in the past, or at least thirty-five hundred miles east of Long Island. It places significant weight on the influence of the American environment as a determinant of the destiny. And, by correlating the growth of political and religious liberty with *classical* virtue, rather than the Puritan notion of morality, it provides a comprehensive standard for human behavior against which social progress could be measured.

Each of the next two poems which I shall consider is of considerable interest in its own right, but they also provide an informative contrast with one another. The earlier of the two, "The Battlefield" (1837), starts out as one of Bryant's graveside meditations, but after a short bridge becomes a rather muscular exhortation to those who would, in the present age, battle for the truth.[7] The other, "The Crowded Street" (1843), is a poetic panorama of the "flitting figures" of the New York thoroughfares to which the poet adds his tentative conjectures as to their condition and fate.[8] "The Battlefield," though positing the "hurrying crowd" of battle, turns rapidly to the role of the individual in the perseverance of Truth. "The Crowded Street," on the other hand, is more like Whitman's poetry in its perspectives, viewing humanity "en masse," yet singling out representative types—the father, the ambitious youth, the pleasure-seeker, the mourner, and the beggar. As types, they are obscured in the heterogeniety of the mob. Their steps "beat the murmuring walks like autumn rain." The poet remarks on "how fast the flitting figures come," and observes that "they pass and heed each other not." If "The Battlefield" bears some resemblance in its militant tone to Tennyson's "Ulysses," one might consider "The Crowded Street" closer to Eliot's "The Waste Land" with its

> Unreal City
> Under the brown fog of a winter dawn
> A crowd flowed over London Bridge,
>   so many,
> I had not thought death had
>   undone so many.[9]

Both of these poems of Bryant's middle-aged mark encounters with contemporary life. If in "The Ages" the poet had mythologized a past to give credence to the present, in these poems he devises emotional strategies for fostering morale, in the one, and coping with the multiplicity of urban life in the other. From his pastoral vision of happy generations sustained by an accommodating environment, Bryant has turned to the confrontation with the trials of contemporary, urbanized existence. "The Battlefield," which could so easily have lapsed into nostalgic eclogue of the heroic ages, became the psychic reinforcement of the embattled editor of the *Evening Post,* beset by hostile Whig competitors on the one side and by equally hostile creditors on the other. As for "The Crowded Street," it could easily have been merely another exuberant "Hymn of the City," composed some thirteen years earlier, in which the poet exclaims that:

>   Not in the solitude
> Alone may man commune with Heaven . . .
>   Even her do I behold
> Thy steps, Almighty!—here amidst the crowd.[10]

In stressing the tone of melancholy and the sense of alienation in "The Crowded Street," I would not overlook the concluding stanzas, which give voice to a belief in a Providence, and affirm that: "There is who heeds, who holds them all." Although Bryant maintains the intellectual position of "Hymn of the City," that The Almighty lends His guiding hand to the motley urban crowd, the imaginative thrust has been radically tempered. What thirteen years earlier had been the "voices and footfalls of the numberless throng" have become "struggling tides of life that seem/in wayward, aimless course to tend." In

"The Hymn of the City," Providence had found glorious participation in the life of urban man, but by "The Crowded Street," Providence had become a neutralized and somewhat distant governor who, in some unspecified manner, directs the "eddies of the mighty stream" toward an unspecified fate—what the poet simply designates as the "appointed end."

The ringing finale of "The Battlefield" contains no such ambivalence: "Truth, crushed to earth, shall rise again." The protagonist can die "full of hope and manly trust" for "Another hand thy sword shall wield." Through the perseverance of the Truth shall eventually come the trumpet's "Blast of triumph o'er thy grave."

That these two poems of the middle period should display alternative postures toward the turmoil and conflict of urban society should come as no surprise to those familiar with Bryant. The profound acquiescence with the universe, almost fatalistic at times in his early poetry, was balanced by his activist and determined Yankee character. What both poems reveal, however, is Bryant's heightened perception of the complexity of human experience in an evolving urbanized and cosmopolitan society. As he came to closer grips with the historical process, the shape of the earthly paradise became less and less susceptible of definition.

One can observe a decided shift in emphasis in a fable in verse composed in 1868. This long narrative poem, "Sella," takes up the themes of youth and nature, and yet is more than a simple variation upon these themes.[11] Although it is a tale of a young woman and her fulfillment, it explicitly avoids romantic involvement, and it cloaks its contemporary relevance in dim history. In the opening line, the poet announces that what follows is, "a legend of the days of old," told for men who enjoyed a tale that was "wild and strange." The heroine is a maiden whose eye "was bright with venturous spirit," but whose "face was passionless, like those by sculptor graved for niches in a temple." Indifferent to her many suitors, she is drawn to the wells, streams, and rivers of her pastoral habitat, and spends her days rowing in her shallop. It is her fortune to come across a pair of magic slippers which give her fairy powers to travel beneath the sea. Guided by a female sprite, she wanders through the "mighty world of waters" exploring caverns and coral reefs, fascinated by the scenic magnificence and the creatures of the sea. After an initial excursion, her travels into the underworld of water become habitual for her. Her brothers would plead with not

to seek companions in that strange cold realm below
For which God made not us nor thee, but stay
To be the grace and glory of our home.

The brothers, fearful of her withdrawal from their domestic life, eventually discover the magic slippers where she has hidden them, and throw them irretrievably into the sea. Upon telling her what they have done, they claim their act was one of love for her. She grows pale, however, and shrieks:

She said, "gone—gone forever! cruel ones!
'Tis you who shut me out eternally
From that serener world which I had learned
To love so well. Why took ye not my life?"

In her dark night of the soul she laments her loss, remembering the "sweet company," the "creatures with calm eyes," and "sweet low prices of the sea." She asks that they think of her

With pity, as of one condemned
To haunt this upper world, with its harsh sounds
And glaring lights, its withering heats, its frosts,
Cruel and killing, its delirious strifes,
And all its feverish passions, till I die.

Such is Sella's lament for her paradise lost. She had made contact with the pristine natural world, as the romantic imagination would have it. In that experience, she had transcended the prosaic virtues of family life and her simple social environment. Like H. D. Thoreau in his two years at Walden Pond, she had undergone a ritual of cleansing and renewal, had transcended, as much as it is possible for human beings to transcend, the limitations of temporal life, and taken unto herself the mystic powers of the unearthly paradise.

But there is more to the tale, for Sella, after her night of mourning, "woke to a new life."

        Her days
Henceforth were given to quiet tasks of good
In the great world. Men hearkened to her words,
And wondered at their wisdom and obeyed,
And saw how beautiful the law of love
Can make the cares and toils of daily life.

What Bryant has accomplished here is an art that conceals art. He has written a nostalgic fantasy, which Godwin and others would undervalue as mere escapism. Composed during the dark days following Bull Run and the Peninsular Campaign, the poem avoids both the violence of battle and the imperatives of urban life. Its tone, alternately melancholy and rapturous, avoids the cycle of social promise and defeat. By assigning the focal role to a young female, Bryant has captured the attention of his sentimental, Victorian readers. By distracting her from the problems of sexual encounter and intimacy, he associates her with an ideal chastity. By leading her into an underwater world which he depicts as delightful and non-threatening (no Maldive sharks or moray eels here) he conjures up the nostalgic naturism of Rousseau and Wordsworth.

Yet the poem, for all these palatable trappings, addresses the issues raised by "The Ages," "The Battlefield," and "The Crowded Street." The progress of society within an hospitable environment may not be as assertively assured, but it remains a possibility. The heroine, Sella, rising above personal tragedy and initiated into her mortal condition, turns from aesthetic contemplation to good works. Like Plato's philosopher, liberated from the shadows of the cave, she is enabled to return to the less enlightened humankind in order to apprise them of the true nature of the world.

Sella's good works are most appropriately channeled. She teaches her fellow men "to pierce the soil and meet the veins/of clean cold water." She encourages men to build viaducts and fountains. She shows them how to harness the streams to drive mills, and to build aqueducts to store up water against draught. From personal poetic delight in nature, she turns to the utilization of natural resources and lives out her maturity in such service. One is reminded of Thoreau's observations on the cycle of forest growth and its application to the forest husbandry, and his measurement of bridges in anticipation of spring floods. With maturity, the nature lover becomes the ecologist, seeking human welfare through a symbiotic relationship with natural phenomena. Sella does not conquer nature, nor despoil it. Her hydromechanics are a realization of nature's power and beauty. By a profound knowledge of nature's capabilities and laws, man raises his own civilizations and fulfills his mortal mission.

The melancholy of the poem is not occasioned by dismal views of dissolution. In a decade of conflict and political upheaval, Bryant chooses to emphasize the loss of innocence which leads to wisdom. It is a speculative extrapolation at best, but one can analogize the loss of the magic slippers, which condemn Sella to the prosaic world of humanity, to the loss of common purpose in the United States of the 1840s and '50s, brought about by sectionalism and slavery. For the nation, like Sella, in the dark night of despair, the backward glances at the lost land of pleasure and tranquility serve to increase the anguish. But the process is a purgative one, and the catharsis leads to a renewal of life. From naturism to mobilization, from self-indulgence to social action, from solitude to participation, the poem instructs its wartime readers in a personal ethic of hope and achievement.

At Sella's death in advanced old age, as the old legends told it, "A hundred cities mourned her, and her death saddened the pastoral valleys." By the cottage of her birth her monument was raised. And then, in Nature's own tribute, the stream divides to make a tiny island of her grave.

And there the flowers that love the running stream,
Iris and orchis, and the cardinal flower,
Crowded and hung caressingly around
The stone engraved with Sella's honored name.

The message of "Thanatopsis," that the individual may meet his mortal end but that the race prevails, is given once again its poetic expression. The human community in this later poem, however, has been brought closer to earth through the wise awareness of its potential. Beauty persists and seeks its own renewal. Like the brook that flows past Sella's cottage into the wondrous sea, human life moves on into a future toward which empathetic individuals like Sella may make their personal imprint. His confidence in the efficacy of virtue and wisdom was manifested once more in this poem.

The themes of progress and dissolution were entwined once more in a later poem, "Among the Trees," written in 1868 and published in *Putnam's Magazine* in 1869. In large part a retrospective revery, the poet reiterates that, in contrast to men, the ancient trees "have no history," and that they have outlived "the flitting generations of mankind." Once more he poses a cautious question as to the future:

Idly I ask; yet may the eyes that look
Upon you, in your later, nobler growth,
Look also on a nobler age than ours;
An age when, in the eternal strife between

Evil and Good, the Power of Good shall win
A grander mastery . . .[12]

While Bryant hedged his prophecies in the interrogative mode, his steady and determined view of the possibilities of the human race was not to blink in the face of the challenges raised by the accelerating rate of progress. This optimism, considerably mellowed from his earlier poetry, tempered by the urbanization of his world and the fires of political strife, was as much a contribution to American letters as his earlier moralizing on man and nature. In the broad reaches of his poetry, William Cullen Bryant informed his times and those that followed of his own solid perception of the role of each man in human history. That the role had limitations, as well as its possibilities, had its demands upon each person as well as the promise of achievement, was never in question. While the world may seduce men to despair, Bryant's panoramic vision of the historical progress could teach the lessons of hope.

NOTES

1. Letter to Richard H. Dana, New York, April 8, 1849. Collected in *The Letters of William Cullen Bryant,* William Cullen Bryant II and Thomas S. Voss, eds. (New York, 1977), II, 521.
2. Cushing Strout, *The New Heavens and the New Earth: Political Religion in America* (New York, 1974), p. 151.
3. *The Poetical Works of William Cullen Bryant,* Roslyn Edition (1903; reprint ed., New York: AMS, 1969), p. 60.
4. *Ibid.,* p. 188.
5. *Ibid.,* p. 406.
6. *Ibid.,* pp. 10–21.
7. *Ibid.,* pp. 181–82.
8. *Ibid.,* pp. 206–8.
9. *The Oxford Book of American Verse,* F. O. Matthiessen, ed. (New York, 1950), p. 805.
10. *Poetical Works,* p. 129.
11. *Ibid.,* p. 268–81.
12. *Ibid.,* p. 325.

Bryant's Fiction:
The Problem of Perception

DONALD A. RINGE
University of Kentucky

Although William Cullen Bryant is well remembered a century after his death as poet and newpaper editor, other aspects of his many-sided career have received scant attention. Bryant the critic is less well-known than Bryant the poet, and Bryant the writer of fiction is all but forgotten. The few scholars and critics who have mentioned his narratives at all have usually dismissed them as derivative or treated them with condescension.[1] It is true, of course, that Bryant's "A Border Tradition" resembles Washington Irving's "The Legend of Sleepy Hollow," and that "The Cascade of Melsingah" may have been influenced by Cooper's Indian romances. It is probable, too, that the latter tale owes something to the Baron de la Motte Fouqué's *Undine*, for, like the water sprites in the German story, the apparition of the Indian spirit fades, when approached too closely, into the whiteness of the falling water. Bryant's narratives do indeed sometimes reveal their ancestry, but to overemphasize this aspect of the tale is to miss their true significance.

Bryant's fiction must be seen in a broader context if we are to understand his accomplishment. He wrote at a time—1825 to 1832—when a large number of cross influences were being felt by most authors, and he worked most often in a form—generally speaking, the tale of the supernatural—that was extremely popular at the time. German and English Gothic works had been imported wholesale into the country for at least a generation, and American writers, starting with Charles Brockden Brown, had followed the mode they had set. Bryant's life-long friend, Richard Henry Dana, wrote a fine example of the type in "Paul Felton," printed in *Idle Man* (1822); Washington Irving produced some of his most effective Gothic stories for *Tales of a Traveller*

(1824); and James Fenimore Cooper published the most Gothic of his romances, *Lionel Lincoln*, in 1825. The first collected edition of Brown's novels appeared in 1827 in a six-volume set that Dana reviewed for Bryant's *United States Review and Literary Gazette* in the same year. The time was right for the development of the American Gothic tale, and Bryant, like so many of his contemporaries, took up the form.

The philosophic disposition of the time, however, gave the writers a problem: how to lend credence to tales of specters, ghosts, goblins, devils, and water sprites in a thoroughly rationalistic age. Such tales were extremely popular. Everyone seemed to enjoy them. But the materials they developed ran counter to the professed beliefs of those, including the authors, who viewed such creatures as dying remnants of a more credulous age. Bryant faced the issue in "A Pennsylvanian Legend," one of his earliest stories. Assuming the role of one who half-regrets the fading of the old superstitions, the narrator writes: "Is the world to become altogether philosophical and rational? Are we to believe nothing that we cannot account for from natural causes? Are tales of supernatural warnings, of the interposition and visible appearance of disembodied spirits, to be laughed out of countenance and forgotten? . . . Alas! we shall soon learn to believe that the material world is the only world, and that the things which are the objects of our external senses are the only things which have an existence."[2]

In the face of rationalistic beliefs, Bryant, like other Gothic writers, needed some means to account for tales of the supernatural and for the pleasure that readers obviously took in them. If "supernatural interpositions" have vanished before "the incredulity of the age," and if "portents and prodigies are not shown to mockers, and spectres will not walk abroad to be made the subjects if philosophical analysis,"[3]—if, in other words, the writer cannot seriously present his materials as contemporary fact, he must set his tales in the distant past or in some remote region where the phenomena could be made consonant with the beliefs of those who witness them. The story itself, consistent within its own frame of reference, would pose no problem of belief or acceptance to the rationalistic reader. He could accept it as the faithful depiction of its own time and place. His pleasure in such a story, moreover, could be accounted for quite simply as the lingering effects of the pleasurable fear he had felt, when, as a child, "old nurses and servant maids" told him "tales of goblins and apparitions."[4]

In three of his stories, Bryant presents supernatural beliefs as integral parts of the culture he is describing. In "A Pennsylvanian Legend," for example, the transformation of a hunchback into a handsome, wealthy man by a wood sprite whose tree he had saved, and his reversion to his orginial condition when through greed and carelessness he destroys her tree are recounted as the authentic folk belief of the German settlers. In "A Narrative of Some Extraordinary Circumstances that Happened More than Twenty Years Since," the death of a deceitful impostor by a strange explosion that breaks from the ground as he crosses a field is depicted as a providential event, for the religious beliefs of the people permit the interpretation of unusual circumstances in that way.[5] And in "The Cascade of Melsingah," the narrator dismisses all modern associations that have clustered around the waterfall to retell an age-old Indian legend that accepts as actual the presence of a water spirit there.[6] Bryant locates these events in out-of-the-way and unfamiliar places, or throws them into the distant past, to make the tales acceptable to his sophisticated audience.

Like other Gothic writers, however, Bryant also used supernatural materials for quite a different purpose. He sometimes assumed the voice of a rationalist narrator who does not believe the tales he tells and explains away the strange phenomena as the misapprehensions of the superstitious. In "The Legend of the Devil's Pulpit," a terrified cockney tailor perceives a band of smugglers in Weehawken, New Jersey, as a group of devils, tells his experience in New York, and accompanies an expedition led by Dr. McGraw to investigate. The account of that expedition comes down from the past as a devil story in which the bluff doctor captures and punishes a goblin. Though some consider it only an allegory invented by McGraw to warn the people against the evils of materialism, the narrator, tongue in cheek, accepts the supernatural explanation. This version is attested to by many respectable people. It "accords with the received tradition, [and] with the formal account drawn up by Dominie De Ronda, and preserved in the archives of the Garden-street Dutch Church."[7] Rationalist doctor is set off against superstitious pastor, and although the narrator seems to side with the latter, his comic tone clearly implies that the tale is not to be taken at face value.

In "A Border Tradition," too, Bryant uses the Gothic for comic effect. Like Ichabod Crane in "The Legend of Sleepy Hollow," James Williams is a Connecticut Yankee of a rather superstitious turn, fond of reading Cotton Mather's *Magnalia*, and easily influenced by tales of the supernatural told by a Dutch girl, Geshie Suydam. When James breaks his troth to her sister Mary, Geshie plots to bring him back. She lies in wait for him near a spot which the villagers think is haunted, appears to him as a specter dressed in white, and frightens him into unconsciousness. James and his Yankee minister attribute the terrible visitation to the fact that the young man had broken faith with Mary, and they take it as a sign that he should return to her. Both men remain silent about the apparition; Geshie, of course, says nothing; James and Mary are married; and Geshie reveals what she did only after many years have passed. The story, clearly derived from Irving's, is based, like its source, on a fundamentally rationalistic view. What James perceived is merely a deceptive appearance that his superstitious nature will not permit him to penetrate.[8]

Yet comic as these tales undoubtedly are, they raise an important question about human beings that serious writers like Bryant could not ignore. Given sufficient provocation, the human mind can transform perfectly natural objects into visions of terror or perceive monstrous phenomena that have no basis in reality. The superstitious natives in "Story of the Island of Cuba" attacked by three murderous Indians who pass "from place to place as mutely and rapidly as ghosts of the dead," begin to perceive them as creatures "in a league with the powers of darkness," and the more they dwell on this idea, the more terrified they become.[9] And Le Maire, the vigorous frontiersman in "The Skeleton's Cave," interprets the faint flutter of a bird he hears while entrapped in the cavern as a supernatural manifestation. Indeed, an imprisonment of several days affects him to the point where he actually sees the skeleton, whose bones lie in the chamber, half raise itself up and beckon to him. The priest and the girl who are also entrapped, perceive no unusual phenomena, but Le Maire is convinced that voices are calling to him, and he says to the priest, "do you hear them yonder—do you hear how they mock me!"[10]

This is neither the simple retelling of pleasant legends drawn from the past nor the comic depiction of gullible folk like the cockney tailor and James Williams, but the serious exploration of an important element in human psychology, which, pursued to its logical extreme, raises serious questions about the theory of knowledge that Bryant shared with his contemporaries and which formed the basis for the entire corpus of his poetry. Bryant's poems are firmly based on sensationalist psychology. All his awareness of the physical world, all the knowledge he draws from it, and the faith he derives from the contem-

plation of the beauty and sublimity of nature are founded upon the belief that the poet can perceive correctly, that he sees in the physical
world what is actually there; in other words, that his senses—and especially those of sight and hearing—are reliable witnesses to the world of
things and the avenues by which he can relate in a trustworthy fashion
to what lies outside of himself. The world of these Gothic stories, on
the other hand, is one in which the mind of the perceiver can seriously
misinterpret the evidence of his senses and apprehend what is not physically present.

On the theoretical level, the issue is easily resolved. One need only
assert that the healthy mind perceives truly, that one who is alert, at-
tuned to the beauties of nature and humbly receptive to its influence
and its meaning, sees the world correctly. Misapprehensions of reality
can then be attributed to whatever disturbs that mental state. A man
beset by fear at twilight can transform " a white horse into a spectre
wrapt in its winding sheet,"[11] and fatigue, combined with a shimmer-
ing landscape and murmuring sound, can make one perceive visions.[12]
A diseased mind, moreover, like that of Dana's Paul Felton or Bryant's
Charles Medfield, can perceive such horrors as to be utterly destroyed
by them. The rational explanation of what has occured, however, does
little good to any of these victims. On the personal level, the problem
does not simply go away because of some abstract theory. Whatever
the cause, the person has seen or heard something that has just as
much reality to him as the common objects of nature and of everyday
living, and although he may be willing to admit the reasonableness of
the rationalist's theory, he cannot deny the evidence of his senses.

This is the problem faced by the protagonists of two of Bryant's best
tales, "Medfield" and "The Indian Spring." In both, the characters
who experience strange phenomena are allowed to tell their own stories
while they wrestle with their perceptual problems. To be sure, "Medfield" uses a framing device in which a rationalist narrator listens to
Medfield's story and tries to explain away the phenomena that he describes, and "The Indian Spring" permits the interpretation that what
has happened to the narrator is only a dream. But the emphasis in both
tales is not on the question of whether the phenomena are real. It hardly
matters whether they are or not. The fundamental problem is that faced
by the protagonists themselves. If the senses provide their sole access
to the external world, how can they ever know that the information
they receive through their sensations is accurate? How can they distinguish between the strange apparition or ghostly touch and the sights

and sounds of the material world that are always present to their senses? The problem is especially acute when the afflicted person is by all accounts a normal man living in an environment that ought to help him maintain his intellectual balance. Such a one is Charles Medfield. A man of education, refinement, and taste, Medfield lives on a farm amidst great natural beauty, holds opinions on politics and religion as rational as those of most men, and has nothing about him of the credulous or superstitious. His neighbors respect him as a man "of great judgment and equity, as well as benevolence," and although he no longer holds the office of magistrate, they still refer "their disputes to his friendly decision."[13] His single fault is a violence of temper that is quickly triggered by even slight opposition. His wife laments this failing and on her deathbed makes him promise to control himself in the future. Medfield accedes to her wishes, but slips at times into his old violent ways. Whenever he does, however, he feels a ghostly touch on his arm, and if he does not heed this admonition, he feels a firmer grasp take hold.

Medfield's experience is not a simple one nor does he lightly assume it to be a spiritual manifestation. He looks for physical causes when it occurs, and he even experiments to see if the phenomenon always appears under the same circumstances. When he touches the spot that seems to be held, he feels a hand beneath his, but one unattached to an arm, and the pressure always returns whenever he performs an intemperate or inhumane act. A grasp of iron invariably follows any resistance on his part to the gentle touch, and at the climactic point in the story when, infuriated by a lazy and insolent tenant, Medfield is about to horsewhip him, the hand becomes that of a skeleton, and he feels as if he were surrounded by a cage. When Medfield explores the phenomenon with his free hand, he realizes that he is surrounded by a group of invisible skeletons, one of which holds his arms while another presses its rib cage against him. After a short while, the pressure against him ceases, and Medfield is free to move his limbs. So strong has been the sensation, however, that Medfield vows never to incur the risk of experiencing it again.

Because he is a rational man, Medfield thinks much about his experience. To him, it can be nothing but "a reality . . . a substantial verity, whatever it might be, or appear, to the rest of the world." Yet as a philosophical realist, he will not believe at first "that what [he] had witnessed was owing to a cause above nature."[14] He knows that delusions exist—especially those of the fallible organs, the eye and the ear—that "disturbed nerves" or "a disordered mind" can cause a person to perceive definite forms or audible voices that have "the appearance of a supernatural interposition."[15] What bothers Medfield most is that the phenomenon manifests itself through the sense of touch, the one "least liable to delusion or mistake. It is the most direct of all our channels of perception; it brings its objects to the closest and minutest scrutiny; it is the least under the control of the imagination, the least liable to be acted upon by delicate and evanescent influences." Indeed, "the touch is the test by which we prove the truth of the information furnished us by the other senses, and in its decisons the mind acquiesces with undoubting confidence."[16]

Medfield could understand the experience if it fit any usual pattern of hallucination, but it does not. His sight and hearing are never deceived, even on those occasions when one might expect them to be. When he walks home at twilight after a frightening encounter with the ghostly hands, he half expects to perceive some indefinite form in the shadows, but nothing unnatural appears. His imagination refuses "to body forth a visionary shape from the indistinct outlines of things" that surround him.[17] The frightening experience had occurred, on the other hand, when the natural scene could not have been less fitted to suggest "the idea of communication with the supernatural world."[18] The woods of autumn were tinged with bright color, and a golden light so pervaded the forest as to create a glow that bathed everything in brightness. Medfield's experience is utterly different from anything that rationalist theory might have led him to expect. Small wonder, then, that the more he considers the problem, the more he comes to perceive himself as accompanied by unseen companions who keep so close a watch on him as to hold him in a prison from which there is no escape.

When the narrator of the story tries to reason with Medfield, to explain what has occurred as "only a delusion of the imagination, . . . a diseased relation between the mind and one of the senses, to which a man of the soundest and clearest judgment might be subject," Medfield dismisses the argument with the reasonable assertion that his companion can advance no view that he has not already considered. To accept his friend's opinion, Medfield would have to dismiss "the evidence of the most scrutinizing and least fallible of our senses, the sense which conveys to us the most certain information of the world about us." He refuses to discuss the matter further, and although the narrator remains convinced that Medfield's melancholy over the death of his wife "had produced some alienation of mind," Medfield himself can only maintain that what he has perceived is reality.[19] He has himself no basis on which to label it a delusion, for the evidence on which his conclusion rests is percisely that on which he has formed and tested his other ideas about the nature of the physical world. Though others may doubt, he can only affirm what his experience has been.

Bryant develops a similar theme in "The Indian Spring," a tale told through a first-person narrator who recounts a frightening experience of many years before. Hiking with a friend through a part of the wilderness just opened to cultivation, the narrator outdistances his companion and, after walking for several hours, stops to rest near a spring in a narrow glade, where the mouldering ruins of a wigwam turn his thoughts to the original inhabitants of the place. Suddenly becoming drowsy, he feels as if he had once or twice dozed off, but realizing that he had better things to do than take a nap, he gets up, walks across the glade, and suddenly catches sight of an armed Indian warrior, in whose stern face the eyes seem to burn with "an unpleasent brightness from their depths like twin stars of evil omen."[20] Deeply shaken, the narrator quickly leaves the spot, followed by the Indian who maintains a constant distance between them. The warrior cannot, apparently, follow him into a settler's clearing, reappearing only when he returns to the woods, and the red man disappears when the narrator, summoning courage, tries to approach him. Once he turns away, however, the Indian again materializes behind him.

Thoroughly frightened by his experience, the narrator retraces his steps to the glade, thinking to find his way home from there. He crosses a stream in the hope that the Indian will, like a witch, be unable to follow across running water, but the red man continues the pursuit and soon begins to narrow the distance between them. In near panic now, the white man loses his hat, shoes, and fowling piece in his headlong flight, articles which the Indian quickly appropriates. When they arrive at last at the glade, the Indian, with a "wild shout," seizes the narrator in his "strong and sudden gripe," and the white man sinks into unconsciousness. Some time later—he cannot say how long—he is aroused by someone shaking his body. His hiking companion has at last caught up with him after looking "for more than an hour." The narrator sits up, finds himself in the glade of the Indian spring, and notes that a red earth-newt, which he recalls having seen just before he grew drowsy, has "advanced at least a yard from the place where [he remembers] to have seen him."[21]

Presented thus baldly, the story would seem to be little more than the kind of Gothic tale in which all the terrifying adventures are dismissed as a dream. Indeed, the following day when the narrator tells his companion what he has experienced, his friend so dismisses it and, the narrator adds, "my readers may possibly be of the same opinion."[22] The story is obviously constructed to justify this conclusion. The last idea in the narrator's mind before he becomes drowsy concerns the Indians who once lived near the spring—hence, the dream—and the physical sensation of heat which seems to come from the Indian's eyes can be accounted for by the rays of the sun that fall on the man while he sleeps. Even the most frightening details—the shout of the Indian just as he overtakes and seizes the white man—may be attributed to the narrator's hiking companion, who has been hallooing in the woods and who grasps his shoulder to awaken him. The adventure has, therefore, a rational explanation which the narrator knows full well, but that explanation, satisfying though it perhaps may be to the reader, is of little use to the man who believes he has undergone the harrowing experience.

Like the deeply troubled Charles Medfield, the narrator of "The Indian Spring" ponders long over what has happened and considers the problem it raises for himself and, by implication, for anyone else whose experience runs counter to his rational convictions. He claims to be "as much a philosopher" with "as little of what is commonly called superstition" as most other persons, and he is well aware that sensory evidence can be "counterfeited by the tricks of fancy, the hallucinations of the nerves, and by our very dreams."[23] At times, therefore, when he is "in a philosophical mood," he is inclined to account for the phenomenon in the same way as his friend. But knowledge is one thing, direct experience another. Whatever his reason may say, the vivid impression remains after many years, and the narrator is left in the final analysis at an intellectual impasse. "When I recal [sic] to mind," he concludes, " the various images and feelings of that time, deeply and distinctly engraved on my memory, I find nothing in them which should lead me to class them with the illusions of sleep, and nothing to distinguish them from the waking experience of my life."[24]

Bryant never carried this theme to its logical conclusion: to see all men as trapped within their sensations and facing an illusory world where one could never be sure that what he perceived was true. To have done so would have entailed a complete revolution in his thinking and the abandonment of the intellectual basis of his poetry. Bryant remained firm in his belief that man could perceive truly the objects of external reality, and he continued to base his poetry on sensationalist theory. This did not prevent him, however, from exploring problems of human perception in his prose, especially "Medfield" and "The Indian Spring." Though the mental aberrations of both protagonists can be explained in rational terms, the characters themselves cannot escape the problems raised by their vivid sensory experiences, and by telling their own stories, they raise philosophical questions that were soon to be more fully developed in the works of Poe, Hawthorne, Melville, and James. Bryant did not reach the psychological depths of these writers—nor did he perhaps want to—but in "Medfield" and "The Indian Spring," he clearly foreshadowed the direction in which American fiction was soon to move.

NOTES

1. See, for example, Fred Lewis Pattee, *The Development of the American Short Story* (New York, 1923), pp. 23, 42–45; Tremaine McDowell, ed., *William Cullen Bryant, Representative Selections* (New York, 1935), pp. xlv–liii, 413–414; Charles I. Glicksberg, "New Contributions in Prose by William Cullen Bryant," *Americana,* XXX (Oct., 1936), 591–592; and Charles H. Brown, *William Cullen Bryant, A Biography* (New York, 1971), pp. 142–143, 155, 162–163, 166, 171, 182, 210.
2. "A Pennsylvanian Legend," *The New York Review and Atheneum Magazine,* II (Dec., 1825), 49.
3. "A Pennsylvania Legend," pp. 49–50.
4. "A Pennsylvania Legend," p. 50.
5. This story may be found in the *United States Review and Literary Gazette,* II (Sept., 1827), 447–459.
6. This story may be found in *The Talisman for MDCCCXXVIII* (New York, 1827), pp. 198–227.
7. "The legend of the Devil's Pulpit," *The Talisman for MDCCCXXVIII,* p. 271. Bryant's collaborators in *The Talisman,* Robert C. Sands and Gulian C. Verplanck, probably had a hand in this and other tales in that annual.
8. First published in the *United States Review and Literary Gazette,* I (Oct., 1826), 40–53, the story may also be found in *William Cullen Bryant, Representative Selections,* pp. 224–239.
9. "Story of the Island of Cuba," *The Talisman for MDCCCXXIX* (New York, 1828), pp. 188, 183. The story may also be found in *Prose Writings of William Cullen Bryant,* Parke Godwin, ed. (New York, 1884), I, 262–296.

10. "The Skeleton's Cave," *Tales of Glauber-Spa*, by Several American Authors (New York, 1832), I, 231–232. The story may also be found in *Prose Writings*, I, 222–261.
11. "Adventure in the East Indies," *The Talisman for MDCCCXXVIII*, p. 12.
12. See Bryant's poem, "The Hunter's Vision," one of the very few in which he treats the problem of mistaken perception. Others include "Catterskill Falls" and "A Day-Dream." See *Poems* (New York, 1876), pp. 253–254, 242–246, 369–371.
13. "Medfield," *Tales of Glauber-Spa*, I, 245.
14. "Medfield," p. 256.
15. "Medfield," p. 259.
16. "Medfield," pp. 258–259.
17. "Medfield," p. 268.
18. "Medfield," p. 267.
19. "Medfield," pp. 275–276.
20. "The Indian Spring," *The Talisman for MDCCCXXX* (New York, 1829), pp. 13–14. This story may also be found in *Prose Writings*, I, 176–189, and *William Cullen Bryant, Representative Selections*, pp. 245–257.
21. "The Indian Spring," pp. 24–25.
22. "The Indian Spring," p. 25.
23. "The Indian Spring," pp. 7–8.
24. "The Indian Spring," pp. 25–26.

Anglo-American Encounter: William Cullen Bryant, Dickens, and Others

ROBERT B. SARGENT
Hofstra University

In the "Introduction" to *The Bibliography of William Cullen Bryant and His Critics 1808-1972,* Judith Turner Phair asserts that "Bryant's place in American history is secure, but ill-defined."[1] She suggests that at the center of the problem is "the question of Bryant the poet versus Bryant the editor," that "to neglect either is to fail to draw a truly revealing portrait."[2] She concludes that, with the exception of Allan Nevins's study of *The Evening Post,* critics have tended to write about Bryant the poet and pass over "Bryant's career as publicist, in spite of the fact that his relative significance as a journalist among journalists is greater than his excellence as a poet among poets.[3] It is, however, the fact that Bryant was at the same time the leading American poet and one of the most influential newspaper editors that gave him the opportunity to play an important role in establishing the independence of American literary culture. An examination of the encounter between Bryant and Charles Dickens, and with two other English visitors to the United States during the years 1836–1842, shows the cultural significance of Bryant's dual identity as poet and newspaper editor. Although these English writers were more sympathetic to America than most visitors, the fact that they gave Bryant special respect as a newspaper editor mainly because they regarded him as the one genuine poet in the United States suggests that they continued to see American culture from the perspective of the Old World. On the other hand, Bryant, as a result of his encounter with them, though sympathetic to their claim that they had been injured by a lack of an international copyright agreement between the United States and Great Britain,

179

grew to believe that they misunderstood and underestimated the state of American letters. Bryant assumed the full responsibility of his position as poet and editor, proclaiming through *The Evening Post* that America had come of age.

As poet-editor Bryant represents what made American literary culture unique, different from that in Great Britain and Europe during the years 1830–1846, and perhaps permanently different. If we think of those writers who seem especially American, many of them are journalists as well as writers: Franklin, Whitman, Twain, Hemingway, and Mailer. In the Old World poetry came *first*, in the sense that it developed before the invention of the press and in the sense that it was regarded as higher in value. In America the reverse was the case: the newspaper was the democratic medium, speaking directly to the common man and preparing the way for a national literature that would follow in time. Social historian Russell Nye notes that by the beginning of the nineteenth century the newspaper "had developed in a uniquely American institution," and during the period 1830–1860 "it existed in greater number and variety than anywhere else in the world"; it was at this time "an educational and cultural medium of major importance."[4]

It is true that Bryant was first a poet and then became a journalist only because he realized that the United States would not support poets[5] and that some of Bryant's contemporaries felt that he had ruined his chance to become a great poet by becoming a journalist.[6] However, it seems that Bryant became an important spokesman for an American literature by stripping away Europeanized notions about the relationship between poetry and the press and by accepting the fact that, in America, newspapers, if they are good ones, play an extremely important function in educating and raising the cultural level of their readers. In an early essay Bryant states that "though the class of men . . . who figure in this country as the conductors of newspapers are not, for the most part, in high esteem with the community. . . . Yet the vocation of the newspaper editor is a useful and indispensable, and, if rightly exercised, a noble vocation. It possesses this essential dignity— that they who are engaged in it are occupied with questions of the highest importance to the happiness of mankind. We cannot see, for our part, why it should not attract men of the first talents and the most exalted virtues."[7]

An examination of the most important armful of the hundreds of travel books which were written by visitors to America during the first half of the nineteenth century reveals a common need to offer their response to the American press. These visitors were drawn to do so because they recognized that the press had a much more important function in the United States than it did in European society and because they were disturbed by the fact that it seemed to operate in a much less restrained manner.[8] They were shocked by the personal and political name-calling in much of the press, though they were also usually impressed by the fact that "throughout the Union the commonest people were surprisingly well-informed on political matters through poring over every paper which came their way."[9]

Though a few travel books mention Bryant as a promising poet, most are like Tocqueville's *Democracy in America* (1835) which suggests that "the inhabitants of the United States have . . . at present, properly speaking no literature." Tocqueville states that "the only authors which I acknowledge as American are the journalists"; however, he asserts that "to suppose they only serve to protect freedom would be to diminish their importance: They maintain civilization."[10] In *Domestic Manners of the Americans* (1832) Frances Trollope implies that she has restrained herself from criticizing Bryant's poetry—as it deserves—only because she has been told that he "ranks highest as the poet of the Union"; however, she manages to convey this judgment indirectly elsewhere in the same book, for she states that "where newspapers are the principal vehicles of wit and wisdom of a people the higher graces of composition can hardly be looked for. That there are many among them who can write well, is most certain; but it is at least equally so, that they have little encouragement to exercise the power in any manner more dignified than becoming the editor of a newspaper or a magazine. . . . The general taste is decidedly bad; this is obvious, not only from the mass of slip-slop poured forth by the daily and weekly press; but from the inflated tone of eulogy in which their insect authors are lauded."[11] Other more sympathetic observers noted that in an essentially undeveloped society the average man has little time in which to read, but that through the newspaper Americans could "pick up critical dictums or read snatches of English poetry in the intervals of work."[12] Frances Wright asserted that "there is not a conceivable topic in the whole range of human knowledge" that the newspapers "do not treat in some way or other, not unfrequently, I must observe, with considerable ability, while the facts that they contain and the general principles that they advocate are often highly serviceable to the community."[13]

Most visitors, however, were shocked by the willingness of many

American newspapers to print details from the private lives of individuals and to dramatize crime and violence in their reporting, pandering to the lowest level of taste in their readers. In short, "most visitors from abroad . . . considered the American press to be depraved."[14] Although they were also highly critical of the American press, British visitors like Buckingham, Martineau, and Dickens who came to know Bryant personally and had a genuine enthusiasm for his poetry, stressed that there were exceptions to the general rule. They were drawn to Bryant and granted his special authority as an editor not because he was, like themselves, a journalist-writer interested in social reform, but because, even before they came to the United States, they regarded him as one of the very few American writers that had been accepted in England.[15]

The least important of these three English visitors is James Silk Buckingham who came to the United States in 1837 and after an extended lecuture tour of about four years returned to London and wrote the first of his three books about his trip—*America: Historical, Statistic, and Descriptive.* Charles H. Brown offers brief quotations from its description of the New York press in his biography of Bryant.[16] Buckingham's praise of Bryant as the editor of the *Evening Post* is linked directly to his perception of him as the major American poet, comparable in quality with British authors familiar to Buckingham's audience: "The Evening Post, which is the leading paper of the Democrats, is at present under the editorship of one of the most celebrated poets of the country, William Cullen Bryant, who may rank with our Campbell, the author of the Pleasures of Hope; and, like other great poets, Milton Bryon, Campbell, and Moore, he is an extreme Liberal in his politics. In talent, wit, taste, and, above all, in the gentlemanly fairness of argument, this paper appeared to me to possess great superiority over most of its opponents."[17]

Though Bryant's letter to Julia Sands (on October 29, 1837) suggests that he believed that Buckingham had more talent than principle as a lecturer, his letter to Buckingham (on January 23, 1838) expressed his willingness to publish Buckingham's verse in the *Evening Post.*[18] Though the editors of the Fordham University Press Edition of Bryant's letters have found none identifiable as Buckingham's,[19] it is significant that Buckingham would want to have his poetry published in the *Evening Post.* This experience as well as Buckingham's admiration for Bryant's poetry may lie behind Buckingham's later assertion, that of all the New York papers, "the *Evening Post* and the *American* . . . gave 'the greatest attention to literary subjects.'"[20]

During the more than two years Harriet Martineau spent touring the United States after her arrival in 1834, she came to know Bryant through their mutual friend Catharine Sedgewick and her family. Bryant's references to Martineau in his letters to his wife grow increasingly critical, mirroring the response of Catherine Sedgewick to Martineau's public identification with Garrison and the Anti-Slavery Society in Boston during the latter part of her stay.[21] Bryant also worried about Martineau's relationship with Dr. Follon regarding him as having become embittered about America after he lost his professorship at Harvard for radical anti-slavery activities.[22] Later, in a letter to his wife after meeting Martineau in England in 1845, Bryant praises her "vivacity and fluency," but remarks that she is "as positive and dogmatical as ever."[23] Whatever Bryant thought about the soundness of Martineau's judgment, it is clear from the references she made to him in *Society in America* (1837) that she thought very highly of him both as editor and as a poet.

Unlike most British commentators on the American press Martineau acknowledges that the editorials in British newspapers contain "slanders and captiousness" and criticizes "the disgustingly jocose tone of their police reports, where crimes are treated as entertainment, and misery as jest"; however, she also asserts that, despite the universal "profligacy of newspapers," "of all newspaper presses, I never heard anyone deny that the American is the worst."[24] What most bothers her is the suppression of the news; she observes that many newspapers in America lack the courage required to print the truth if it goes counter to regional or special interests. After praising "a spirited newspaper at Louisville," she notes that "two New York papers, the New York American and the Evening Post, have gained themselves honour by intrepidity of the same kind, and by the comparative moderation and friendliness of their spirit."[25] Though Martineau hopes that "there may be many more" newspapers like Bryant's *Evening Post*, she is concerned that "the few newspapers conducted by men of truth and superior intelligence, are not yet encouraged in proportion to their merits." Recognizing the unique, symbiotic relationship that existed in American between journalism and literature, Martineau concludes that "there will be no great improvement in the literary character of the American newspaper till the literature of the country has improved."[26]

After making the bleak pronouncement that "if the American nation be judged by its literature, it may be pronounced to have no mind at all,"[27] Martineau proceeds to indicate that a national literature may be just about to emerge, acknowledging that the delay may have been caused by the difficulty of assimilating complex European and regional influences. Though she has words of praise for Catharine Sedgewick, Washington Irving, Cooper, and a few others, she is often highly critical as well. The reader of *Society in America* is, therefore, particularly struck by the following terse assertion: "The Americans have a poet." She is referring, of course, to William Cullen Bryant. She goes on to state that

> Bryant has not done anything like what he can and will do; but he has done some things that will live. Those of his poems which are the best known, or the most quoted, are smooth, sweet, faithful descriptions of nature, such as his own imagination delights in. I shall always remember the voice and manner with which he took up a casual remark of mine, about sights to be seen in the pine-barrens. When the visitors had all departed, his question "And what of the pine-barrens?" reveals the spirit of the poet. Of his poems of this class, "The Evening Wind" is to me the most delicious. But others,—"The Past," and "Thanatopsis"— indicate another kind, and a higher degree of power. If he would live for his gifts . . . he may be listened to as lovingly over the expanse of future time, as he already is over that of ocean.[28]

It is important to note that in this praise of Bryant, Martineau assumes that her British readers already know and admire Bryant and that they will appreciate the glimpse she gives them of her personal contact with the poet.

Though Martineau refuses to attribute "the non-existence of literature in America" solely to the lack of a law governing international copyright between Great Britain and the United States, she agrees that "the imperfection of these laws inflicts various discouragements on American writers . . . that American booksellers will not remunerate native authors while they can purloin the works of British writers . . . that in America, where every man must work for a living, it is a discouragement to the pursuit of literature that a living cannot, except in a few rare cases, be got by it." But, like Charles Dickens, she was less concerned about the plight of American writers than she was about her own situation as a successful British author losing potential income. It is, she remarks, "disgracefully injurious to foreign authors" especially since "the American public has a strong disposition to listen to the utterance of the English in preference to the prophets of their own country."[29]

During the same year in which she was writing these passages about international copyright (1836), having seen an editorial by Bryant in the *Evening Post* (On September 27th) that insisted "on an author's claim to his book as a 'natural right,'"[30] she wrote to Bryant explaining that on her return to England she had initiated a petition signed by important British writers urging the Congress of the United States to act on international copyright as the British government had done. To Bryant himself she added: "You can help us both as author and editor."[31]

Bryant had long been committed to international copyright, but as he felt himself more and more to be both an important poet and a spokesman for an American literature, it is natural that the angle of his argument for international copyright would be significantly different from that of British writers like Martineau and Dickens. In the beginning Bryant's argument is abstract—for example his editorial in the *Evening Post* for September 27, 1836, argues that books are like baggage and should be protected from being stolen whether the owner is a citizen or a visitor. But after Congress failed to act on international copyright in 1837, Bryant stresses that the lack of a copyright agreement with Great Britian "promotes the circulation of works of English origin in this country to the exclusion of our own, and to the discouragement of our authors" (March 2, 1837). By May 9, 1842, Bryant's confidence has grown as he senses that the literary balance of trade has begun to swing in the opposite direction. As a result, his argument for international copyright sounds like a declaration of literary independence:

> In a conversation which we had the other day with an eminent American author, now abroad he [probably Washington Irving; Bryant notes his leaving for Europe in *EP* on April 7th] remarked, that if American literature continued to make the same progress as it had done for twenty years past, the day was not very far distant, when the greater number of books designed for readers of the English language, would be produced in America. If we look back to the year 1820, and compare that state of authorship in our country, at that time, with what it is now; if we consider how barren our literature was then, and how prolific it has now become; if we look at the quality of the works produced at the two periods, and the rewards received by their authors, we shall find ourselves obliged to admit that the prediction is a very probable one.

> The plea against international copyright that it gives our publishers an advantage over those of Great Britain, is not true, or if true is true for the present moment only. If our publishers enrich themselves at the expense of British authors, British publishers enrich themselves at the expense of ours, and will continue to do so, from year to year, until the advantage will be shifted from our side to theirs. The policy of our country is to secure for its authors the benefit of an international copyright before that time comes. (*EP*, May 9, 1842)

The year Bryant chooses in his editorial to make the time of American inferiority, 1820, is, of course, a round number, but it reminds us that a year later Bryant's first slim volume of poems appeared. Ten years later these poems were reissued with eighty additional ones and in 1830 Bryant attempted to obtain a British publisher for his poetry through Washington Irving then living in London. Irving wrote to Bryant that it would give him "the greatest pleasure to be instrumental in bringing before the British public a volume so honorable to our national literature," but added that a British publisher "will not be disposed to offer you anything for a work in print for which they cannot secure a copyright."[32] At that time the prestige of being recognized as a poet in Great Britain was more than enough for Bryant, and he was happy to accept these rewards as payment. It was ten years after his volume appeared in England, then, that Bryant not only asserts that "within the past year, the number of books written by American authors, which have been successful in Britian, is greater than that of foreign works that have been successful in this country," but he proudly names them: "Robertson's work on Palestine, Stephens's Travels in Central America, Catlin's book on the North American Indians, Cooper's Deerslayer, the last volume of Bancroft's American History, several works prepared by Anthon for the schools" (*EP*, May 9, 1842). In order to convey the promise of American letters he then describes in some detail the work in progress of Cooper, Prescott, Bancroft, and others. Because Bryant was an important poet he could speak about the state of American letters in an authoritative manner in the pages of the *Evening Post*.

It is not surprising that Bryant's attitude towards the meaning of international copyright for American literature fully evolved during the first six months of 1842, for this was the period when Charles Dickens visited the United States and became involved in public discussion of international copyright. The general outlines of this controversy are fairly well known but are worth summarizing. In his first public speech in the United States in Boston on February 2, Dickens remarked to the after dinner audience that included Allston, Bancroft, and Bryant's friend Dana, that "you have in America great writers—writers who will live in all time and are so familiar to our lips as household words. Depriving . . . their inspiration from the stupendous country that gave them birth, they diffuse a better knowledge of it, and a higher love for it, all over the civilized world. I take leave to say, in the presence of some of those gentlemen, that I hope the time is not far distant when they, in America, will receive of right and some substantial profit and return in England from their labors; and when, we, in England shall receive some substantial profit and return in America from *ours*. . . . England has done her part; and I am confident that the time is not far distant when America will do hers. It becomes the character of a great country: Firstly, because it is justice; secondly, because without it you never can have, and keep, a literature of your own." News of the speech spread through excerpts reprinted in newspapers outside of Boston. The version quoted above appeared in Bryant's *Evening Post* in February 7, varying only in a very minor way from an account in the *Boston Advertiser*.[33] Although many newspapers attacked Dickens for being a rude guest by raising a matter involving his own economic interests at a dinner given to welcome him to America, a few like Bryant's *Evening Post* supported his right to speak on international copyright and his position on the issue, if not his particular line of argument for it. On February 11, Bryant argues that "if there is any justice at all in the copyright-law, as it seems to us there is, the composition which an author produces by the exercise of his talent and industry, be as much his own as his purse. . . . the people of foreign countries ought not to be allowed to plunder the foreigner." And on February 28, under the heading "Mr. Dickens on International Copyright," Bryant offers his readers an extensive excerpt from the *Charleston Mercury* describing Dickens's speech in New York at a dinner which Bryant attended as a guest of honor and hence may not have wanted to describe himself: "We are glad to see one thing, that he is not to be driven from this point about international copyright, because a few editors have called it indelicate, and all that. He is right. Dickens is received in this country as a literary man, and why should he not touch upon a topic which is a matter of lively interest and warm discussion to the whole literary world? He is himself interested to be sure in the extension of the right of authors, but so is every other writer." On May 9, Bryant prints a letter from Dickens (then in Niagara Falls) and the enclosed petition of British writers supporting Dickens's position on copyright and an individual letter from Thomas Carlyle that mentions his earlier support of a petition to Congress "under the auspices of Miss Martineau." The *Evening Post* was one of four papers selected by Dickens as a forum for these documents. In a letter to C. C. Felton on April 29, Dickens notes that "my . . . idea was—publicity being the object—to send one copy to you for a Boston newspaper—another to Bryant for his paper—a third to the New York Herald (because of its large circulation) —and a fourth to a highly respectable journal at Washington . . . which I think is called The Intelligencer."³⁴

Despite the support of Bryant and a few others, Dickens's attitude towards the United States and the American press in particular grew more and more critical. Admittedly, the causes of this are complex and debatable,³⁵ but certainly one thing that upset him was the very detailed and highly critical description of his manners and dress appearing in the many papers less restrained and sympathetic than Bryant's. The proverbial nail in the coffin as far as his attitude towards the American press was concerned seems to be an event that happened after he had returned to London and had written a printed circular of July 7 which he sent to many British journals and authors. This circular characterized the Americans who opposed his position on copyright as "persons who exert themselves to mislead the American public. . . . editors and proprietors of newspapers almost exclusively devoted to the republication of popular English works. They are, for the most part, men of very low attainments and of more than indifferent reputation."³⁶ Such a description of those in American press opposed to international copyright drew the *Evening Post's* first critical words on Dickens: "Now, this is a misrepresentation. We have ourselves taken the same view of the copy-right question as Mr. Dickens does; but we cannot suffer him to malign in this way, those of a different opinion. It is not true, that they are all governed by mercenary motives. We know many, very respectable in their attainments . . . who condemn the proposal to establish an international copy-right. . . . They do so on disinterested grounds. . . . It is extremely unjust, as Mr. Dickens has done, in his sweeping epistle, to class these with the parties of whom he ought to have spoken more definitely" (August 2, 1842).³⁷ Unfortunately, the New York *Evening Tattler,* instead of criticizing Dickens as the *Evening Post* had done, published a forged letter which combined paragraphs in the Dickens circular with paragraphs that were made up by an American who wanted to make Dickens look as bad as possible. The *Evening Post,* apparently taken in by the forgery, quoted from the *Tattler* and added: "We should like to know if these were Mr. Dickens's sentiments when he was flourishing his fine compliments at dinner tables. Either he was disreputably insincere then, or he is most lamentably inconsistent now" (August 3, 1842). The forgery in the *Tattler* (evidence suggests Walt Whitman was the editor at the time)³⁸ apparently confirmed Dickens's worst fears about the American press and played a role in the increasingly sharp satire directed against American newspapers from his *American Notes* (1842) to the American chapters of *Martin Chuzzlewit* (1843-1844). In *Martin Chuzzlewit* the New York newspapers are called the *Sewer,* the *Rowdy Journal,* and the *Popular Instructor*—the last of these, like the *Tattler,* publishes forged letters. Martin Chuzzlewit asks about "the national poets" and is informed that Americans are "too busy" for poems, but "don't mind 'em if they come to us in newspapers along with almighty strong stuff of another sort."[39]

The general consensus has been that the American chapters of *Martin Chuzzlewit* alienated many of Dickens's friends in the United States, including Washington Irving. Although there is no notice of the novel as a whole in the *Evening Post,* there is a highly critical response to the first American chapters, probably written by Bryant himself:

> The last number of Dickens's Martin Chuzzlewit, brought out by the Caledonia, has been reprinted here. We are admirers of Dickens's works in general, and are, therefore, sorry he should have written anything so very dull.

> Martin is represented as arriving in New York, and a variety of incidents and conversations are imagined to take place, with a view of satirizing our people and our national manners. The attempt fails for two reasons. In the first place, the author knows very little about us, and in the second place, the desire of being vehemently satirical seems to unfit him for what he wishes to do, and takes from him his wanted humor and invention. There are, no doubt, points in our national character from which a skillful writer might extract a good deal of ridicule, and practices in our country which deserve to be condemned, but whoever undertakes to deal with them, should be better acquainted with us than Dickens, and more at ease in the task then he appears to be. (*EP,* July 21, 1843)

Though this notice does not state in specific terms the subjects poorly treated by Dickens, an article by the London correspondent of the *Evening Post* that appeared two days earlier spells them out: "the editors, the boarding houses,—the colonels, majors and captains of the militia,—the manners, characteristics and feelings of certain coteries" (July 19, 1843). On September 21, 1843 the *Evening Post* prints a critical note from the London Correspondent about the later American chapters: "In the last number of 'Martin Chuzzlewit,' there is a sketch of a Repeal sympathizing meeting in the United States—perhaps the poorest thing that Boz has ever done. It is indeed difficult to realize

that it is from the pen of the author of Pickwick Papers." Though there
is no direct reference by Bryant to this section of *Martin Chuzzlewit,*
two days after the note by the London correspondent appeared, an article in the *Evening Post* entitled "What They Think of Us Abroad"
seeks to demonstrate that "the opinion of people so ignorant of our
condition" is not "worth the minding" (September 23, 1843).

The relationship of Bryant and Dickens is more complex and probably more significant than has been generally recognized. Several items
in the Goddard-Roslyn Collection in the New York Public Library are
apparently unknown to the editors of the Pilgrim Edition of the Dickens Letters (published by the Clarendon Press at Oxford), the edition
that has been regarded as definitive for the period covered so far (now
up to 1846). This edition has only one letter from Dickens to Bryant
(February 14, 1842), though there are several letters of Dickens to
others in which Bryant is mentioned. The Goddard-Roslyn Collection
has two additional letters of Dickens to Bryant (February 15th and
June 1st).[40] Though these are not especially important, they do suggest
a greater degree of intimacy than has been previously recognized. This
sense is reinforced by three undated calling cards of Dickens's wife;
the envelopes are addressed to W. C. Bryant, 326 Ninth Street and
signed by Dickens himself. These cards and letters, added to what we
already know about the meetings between Bryant and Dickens, suggest
that of the twenty-two days Dickens spent in New York, Bryant and
Dickens met on eight different days and on three additional days they
made contact through the letters that we now know about. Perhaps
this may help us to understand better the emphasis in Bryant's letter to
Dana on April 19, 1842: "You were right in what you said of Dickens:
I like him hugely; though he was besieged while he was here that I saw
little of him—little in comparison with what I could have wished."[41]
After this letter, however, in correspondence dated June 1, Dickens invites Bryant to dine with him on Monday evening, June 6, saying that
"no is not an admissible word, for on Tuesday we sail for England"
(Goddard-Roslyn Collection). In other words, Dickens chose to spend
his last evening in the United States with Bryant and his wife. It is
tempting on the basis of this new evidence, small as it is, to see an allusion to Bryant in Dickens's unusually warm description of his leave-
taking from his American friends in New York on returning to London in chapter seven of *American Notes:* "I never thought the name of
any place, so far away and so lately known, could ever associate itself
in my mind with the crowd of affectionate remembrances that now

cluster about it. There are those in this city who would brighten, to me, the darkest winter day that ever glimmered and went out in Lapland; and before whose presence even Home grew dim.''[42]

There are three essays heretofore known to Dickens scholars, but which have not been used before to help understand Dickens's attitude towards Bryant and regarding American newspapers and poetry. They appeared in a periodical published in London called *The Foreign Quarterly Review;* the first two essays are about the American press (1843) and the third is about American poetry (1844). Although they were published anonymously, there is very good reason to attribute them to John Forster, Dickens's confidant and literary advisor.[43] Given the relationship of Forster and Dickens at this time, it is probable that Forster was expressing ideas which Dickens wanted to be expressed but without being identified with them too directly himself. An important clue is to be found in the tone of a footnote Dickens evidently added to *American Notes* at the proof stage, the stage at which he normally consulted Forster. In the passage Dickens has been trying to convince his reader "accustomed to the leading English journals" that the newspapers in the United States are as "frightful" as he claims them to be. However, professing that he has "neither space for inclination" to document his assertion through extracts from the American newspapers, he notes in the footnote: "let him [the reader] refer to an able and perfectly truthful article, in *The Foreign Quarterly Review*, published in the present month of October; to which my attention has been attracted, since these sheets have been passing through the press. He will find some specimens there, by no means remarkable to any man who has been in America, but sufficiently sticking to one who has not.''[44]

These essays suggest the importance of the relationship of the press to poetry in America. The first two attack the American press in general, but they specifically name Bryant's *Evening Post* as one of the very few exceptions, as "able, respectable, and well conducted."[45] Such an emphasis is in keeping with Dickens's letters to friends in England during his visit to the States, that though the American press is "more mean and paltry and silly and disgraceful" than any other in the world, Bryant's is an exception, and that Bryant himself is often attacked in other newspapers because he is a good liberal journalist.[46] In the third essay, "The Poets of America," Forster, while generally adopting a skeptical air towards what passes in America for poetry and suggesting that the "degradation of the American press" has inhibited the support for poetry, proclaims that William Cullen Bryant's poetry is clearly of value and that he is the one truly American poet. The following is a brief selection from the long section Forster devotes to Bryant:

> We have been all along looking out for a purely American poet, who should be strictly national in the comprehensive sense of the term. The only man who approaches that character is William Cullen Bryant . . . Out of this national inspiration he draws universal sympathies. . . . He is the only one of the American poets who . . . lifts his theme above the earthy taint of biogotry and prejudice. . . . When America shall have given birth to a few such as Bryant, she may begin to build up a national literature to the recognition of which all the world will subscribe.[47]

This characterization of Bryant as the "purely American poet" by Forster makes explicit what was implied two years earlier in Dickens's first letter to Bryant: "With one exception (and that's Irving) you are the man I most wanted to see in America. . . . I have a thumbed book at home, so well worn that it has nothing upon the back but one gilt 'B,' and the remotest possible traces of a 'y.' My credentials are in my earnest admiration of its beautiful contents" (February 14, 1842, Goddard-Roslyn Collection).

Bryant's letters to Dana during this period show that he was aware of the tremendous increase in the amount of pirated British literature that was appearing in American magazines and newspapers and that he had been disturbed in the past by it also, believing it to be the major reason why he had had so much difficulty finding an American publisher for *Two Years Before the Mast* by the son of his friend. Thus, Bryant was aware of the situation that was so provoking to Dickens and certainly he had done what he could to assist Dickens. It is apparent, however, that he gradually came to believe that Dickens had lost his sense of proportion in his attacks on the American press. In his notice of *American Notes* in the *Evening Post* Bryant tries to restore a sense of balance and in doing so indirectly expresses deserved pride in being an example of the excellence to be found in the American press:

> In regard to the newspaper press, however, though its character is bad enough, he [Dickens] has overcharged his censures. The journals of several of our cities—Boston, Philadelphia, and Charleston—are quite as decorous, for ought we see, as the best of the English journals. In this city the newspaper press is worse than anywhere else in the United States; but the example of two or three presses in New York does not

prove general profligacy with which all the newspapers are conducted. It is true that the best of us, probably, have something to amend, and it is true, also, that the standard, of both morality and decorum, is not sufficiently high among the greater number of those who manage our newspapers. Without attempting to justify them by example of the London journals, which perhaps, would not be difficult, if comparisons were a fair mode of justification, we have no objection to see the scourge of reproof well laid on, and let those wince who feel the smart. (*EP,* November 9, 1842)

In the year following this temperate response to Dickens's slashing critique of the American press, the *Evening Post* takes on a much more aggressive stance towards English journals and publishers, pointing out, for example, "the narrowness and insolence with which the United States are treated even in liberal journals" (June 30, 1843) and accusing publishers of "literary robberies," printing "mutilated editions of works acknowledged to be transatlantic" (June 10, 1843). Even the argument for international copyright is stated in much more militant terms, using an analogy from the revolutionary war to suggest that if the Congress does not act, "English pamphlets may hold the day where British soldiers fell back" (November 27, 1843).

It is certain that Dickens had very high, too high expectations of America before he came—expecting it unreasonably to be the ideal republic of *his* imagination, free of the evils that so disturbed him in British social institutions. Instead he came to see it as "not the Republic of my imagination"[48] but as wild, lawless, and uncivilized. Recent Dickens criticism has argued that he had a nervous breakdown or a "psychic collapse"[49] while visiting the United States and that this accounts for his increasingly savage attacks on the press in *American Notes* and *Martin Chuzzlewit.* I believe that this interpretation is extreme. But the situation Dickens faced was extremely provoking, and I would agree that this period is crucial in his development. The main thing he learned in coming to America was how English he was; this realization had a lasting impact on his fiction.

In a similar way, I believe that this period, and in particular his encounter with Dickens, was important in Bryant's development. As a result he takes on fully the responsibility of being a major spokesman for American literature. In the face of Dickens's increasingly unreasonable attack on the American press Bryant cuts the last thread that tied him to what Hawthorne calls "Our Old Home." In an editorial on February 18, 1842, during the first weeks of Dickens's visit, Bryant argued that Dickens had been greeted with such enthusiasm by the American people because he had traits that "recommend him particularly to Americans. His sympathies seek out that class with which American institutions and laws sympathize most strongly. He has found subjects of thrilling interest in the passions, suffering, and virtue of the mass." However, like many other Americans since that time who were attracted to the works of Charles Dickens, Bryant did not understand at the moment he wrote this editorial just how English Dickens really was, or how important he [Bryant] had been and could be in putting American literature on a firm foundation, not only as a poet, but also as editor of the *Evening Post.* When Dickens returned to the United States in 1868, he declared that he was "astounded by the amazing changes," especially the "changes in the Press, without which no advancement can take place anywhere."[50] Although America was farther on the way in 1842 than Dickens recognized, Bryant as an example and a voice deserves a good deal of the credit for what Dickens discovered the second time around.

NOTES

1. Judith Turner Phair, *Bibliography of Bryant* (Troy, New York: The Whitstin Publishing Company, 1975), p. 23.
2. Phair, p. 21.
3. Phair, p. 23. The unpublished dissertation of Bruce Edward Petree, *"The Evening Post* and American Poetry: A Study of William Cullen Bryant's Influence" (University of Pennsylvania, 1974), concludes that Bryant as editor devoted considerable effort in helping to establish a national literature.
4. *Society and Culture in America* (New York: Harper & Row, 1974), pp. 366, 368.
5. Charles H. Brown, *William Cullen Bryant* (New York: Scribner's, 1971), pp. 141, 168; Parke Godwin, *A Biography of William Cullen Bryant* (New York: Appleton, 1883), I, 295.
6. Allan Nevins, *The Evening Post, A Century of Journalism* (New York: Boni and Liveright, 1922), pp. 136–137.
7. Godwin, *A Biography,* I, 252–253; Nevins, *Post,* p. 135.
8. See Jane Louise Mesick, *The English Traveller in America, 1785–1835* (1922; rpt. Westport, Conn.: Greenwood Press, 1970), pp. 227–229; Max Berger, *The British Traveller in America, 1836–1860* (Gloucester, Mass. Peter Smith, 1964), p. 68.
9. "Introduction," *American Notes For General Circulation,* John S. Whitley and Arnold Goldman, eds. (Harmondsworth, England: Penguin, 1972), p. 23.

10. *Democracy in America,* Richard D. Heffner, ed. (New York: New American Library, 1956), pp. 174, 202.
11. *Domestic Manners,* Donald Smalley, ed. (New York: Vintage, 1960), pp. 315, 311.
12. Mesick, p. 228.
13. *Views of Society and Manners in America,* Paul R. Baker, ed. (1821; rpt. Cambridge, Mass.: Belknap Press, 1963), p. 213.
14. Brown, p. 247.
15. See Clarence Gohdes, *American Literature in Nineteenth Century England* (Carbondale, Ill.: Southern Illinois Press, 1944), pp. 26, 51-2.
16. Brown, pp. 247-248.
17. *America* (London: Fisher, 1841), I, 66.
18. *The Letters of William Cullen Bryant,* William Cullen Bryant II and Thomas Voss, eds. (New York: Fordham University Press, 1977), II, 92.
19. *Letters,* II, 96n.
20. Brown, pp. 247, 255.
21. *Life and Letters of Catherine M. Sedgwick,* Mary E. Dewey, ed. (New York: Harpers, 1871), pp. 241-242, 242n.
22. *Letters,* II, 16; cf. I, 484 and II, 16.
23. Ibid., II, 344-45.
24. *Society in America,* Seymour Martin Lipset, ed. (Gloucester, Mass.: Peter Smith, 1968), pp. 104, 103.
25. Ibid., p. 106.
26. Ibid., p. 104.
27. *Society in America* (1837; reprinted. New York: AMS Press, 1966), III, 206.
28. Ibid., III, 214-15.
29. Ibid., III, 217.
30. Ibid., II, 246n.
31. Godwin, *A Biography,* I, 315.
32. Godwin, I, 265.
33. Cf. *Charles Dickens in America,* ed. William Glyde Wilkins (1911; rpt. New York: Haskell House, 1970), p. 33.
34. *The Letters of Charles Dickens,* ed. Madeline House, *et al* (Oxford: Clarendon Press, 1974), III, 214.
35. See Lawrence H. Houtchens, "Charles Dickens and International Copyright," *American Literature,* 13 (1941), 18-28 and Paul B. Davis, "Dickens and the American Press, 1842," *Dickens Studies,* 4 (March 1968), 32-78.
36. *Letters of Dickens,* III, 258-259.
37. Dr. William Cullen Bryant II pointed out at the Bryant Conference the difficulty of determining which material in the *Evening Post* was written by Bryant and which by others, such as Parke Godwin. In this essay I have used the Bryant letters as a means of determining whether or not it was possible for Bryant to have written the articles in question. For example, this reference to Dickens on August 2, 1842 and the one on the following day could not have been written by Bryant as he was in Rockport on vacation (*Letters,* II, 175-77; cf. Nevins, p. 215). On the other

hand, the notice of the first American chapters of *Martin Chuzzlewit* on July 21, 1843, could have been (*Letters,* II, 242, 248). Because so few articles have been conclusevely identified as Bryant's, the attribution of a particular piece of writing to Bryant is speculative and is a matter about which scholars may disagree. In the text I have tried to indicate the degree of confidence with which I have assigned a particular article to Bryant.

38. *Letters of Dickens,* III, 626n.
39. *The Life and Adventures of Martin Chuzzlewit* (London: Oxford University Press, 1951), p. 274.
40. Though a reference in the *Letters* (II, 172n) provided the clue that 'unknown' letters of Dickens to Bryant existed, the citation is incorrect and incomplete; it lists two letters, not three, and dates them February 27 and June 1, 1842, rather than February 14, February 15, and June 1, 1842 (Goddard-Roslyn Collection, New York Public Library).
41. *Letters,* II, 171.
42. *American Notes,* p. 144.
43. *Letters of Dickens,* III, 58n.
44. *American Notes,* pp. 288–289, 289n.
45. "The Answer of the American Newspaper Press," *The Foreign Quarterly Review,* 31 (April 1843), 266, 268.
46. *Letters of Dickens,* III, 156, 158.
47. "The Poets of America," *The Foreign Quarterly Review,* 32 (January 1844), 314-15.
48. *Letters of Dickens,* III, 156.
49. "Introduction," *American Notes,* p. 35.
50. "Postscript," *American Notes,* (May, 1868) p. 295.

"Not the Highest Praise": A Brief Reintroduction to William Cullen Bryant As a Translator of Homer

THOMAS G. VOSS
The University of Charleston

It is too often forgotten that William Cullen Bryant worked nine years completing a very successful and popular translation of Homer. At the age of sixty-nine, Bryant took up his Homer and at seventy-seven finished what was and still is considered by most classicists a very able English rendering of The *Iliad* and The *Odyssey*. His effort was greeted with favorable reviews and sales in his time, and while he generally portrayed the endeavor as an "exercise," he was surprised and delighted by his translation's success.

This short essay is to reintroduce Bryant's "exercise" as one of his major legacies to his English-reading posterity.

I. Bryant's Preparation

William Cullen Bryant's education in the literary and classical modes of his time is already well-researched and documented.[1] By way of a brief background to show something of his preparation for his later translation of Homer, let us recall that Cullen, as a boy, had read

I wish to thank Professor John Shea of Boston, Massachusetts for his assistance with some of the points which appear in this article.

Pope's *Iliad*; later, in 1808–09, he was trained in Latin for five months at North Brookfield, Massachusetts under the tutelage of his uncle, Thomas Snell, with whom he read Vergil, Horace, and Cicero. Also, in 1809, he studied Greek with Moses Hallock at Plainfield, where he mastered the New Testament in two months. In October of 1810, Bryant enrolled at Williams College, where he continued his classical education, translating Anacreon and Sophocles, among others. To show off his classical ability, he wrote a satire in which both the educational and environmental shortcomings of Williams are described in his "Descriptio Guliemopolis," which, no doubt, pleased his fellow members in the Philotechnian Society of the College, and, I am sure, greatly annoyed the president of the college.

During his days as an apprentice of the law under Samuel Howe in Worthington and William Baylies in West Bridgewater, he read William Cowper, as well as Byron, Southey, and Henry Kirke White, as antidotes to the legal tomes of his new vocation; he possibly first read Cowper's Homer then. In 1817, "Thanatopsis" appeared, and, when his change of careers brought him to New York City in 1825, he had already published about fifty poems. Some translations were among these, such as the two Odes from Horace which were published in *The North American Review* for September of 1817, the same issue in which "Thanatopsis" appeared.[2]

In New York he lived with the Evrard family, where he perfected his French, and later with the Salazars, with whom he learned Spanish. During his first trip to Europe in 1834, he polished his languages with particular thoroughness, especially during his stay at Heidelberg where he practiced German conversation with his fellow student and traveller, Henry Wadsworth Longfellow. By 1836, Bryant spoke and read French, Spanish, Italian, and German proficiently. Some thirty years later, with a heightened fluency in the European languages due to his travels abroad, he would still find his classical preparation sufficient to undertake what I think is his most major literary effort, the translation of Homer.

James Fenimore Cooper supposedly threw down *Pride and Prejudice* in Scarsdale and informed his wife he could write a better novel; William Cullen Bryant figuratively seems to have cast aside Cowper's *Translation of Homer* in Roslyn and declared to R. H. Dana that he could do better. But, unlike Cooper's *Precaution,* Bryant's Homer is better than Cowper's.

Bryant's first significant indication of his interest in translating

Homer is in the 14 May, 1863, letter to Dana where he writes:

> I have been looking over Cowper's Translation of Homer lately, and comparing it with the original. It has astonished me that one who wrote such a strong English as Cowper in his original compositions should have put Homer, who also wrote with simplicity and spirit, into such phraseology as he has done. For example, when Ulysses, in the Fifth Book of The *Odyssey,* asks, "What will become of me?", Cowper makes him say: "What destiny at last attends me?" and so on. The greater part is in such stilted phrase, and all the freedom and fire of the old poet is lost.[3]

But there may have been more involved than a distaste for Cowper's seventy-two-year-old translation of the Greek epic, which had been republished in 1836 and 1837. Starting in 1846 with William Munford's translation published in Boston, three other editions of Homer's *Iliad* appeared before Bryant began his translation: T. S. Brandeth (London, 1846); F. W. Newman (London, 1856); and Theodore Alois Buckley (London, 1857). Moreover, between Buckley's and Bryant's publication of The *Iliad* in 1870, seven others were published and Pope's, Derby's, and Buckley's were reprinted.[4] A definite market of interest among English-reading people existed which these various editions both served and fostered. Bryant's turning away from the *Odyssey* to the *Iliad* may have been based on this renewed interest since most of the eighteen translations in English had appeared within twenty-five years of his edition.

Bryant may have begun translating Homer, probably in the winter of 1863, as a respite from his journalistic absorption with the Civil War; or, as he is quoted by Godwin as saying, an exercise for his memory; "I was only trying my hand on the Greek to see how much of it I retained;[5] it might, too, have been a recollection of his attempt some forty-five years earlier at writing an epic poem, but now he would do it by way of translation.

Seven years later, upon finishing his *Iliad,* Bryant wrote Epes Sargent that this initial exercise grew into a full translation since Bryant "was not quite satisifed with any of the English translations of The *Iliad.*"[6] However, those translations had established a commercial reinterest in the epic, and the American Civil War may have added the social and political ambience for the retelling of the fall of the house of Priam for an American audience.

Bryant now began a task which would take him nine years to finish.

In his *Journal Of His Tour To Europe,* in the January to August, 1867 section, he indicates he spent time translating Homer almost daily. He also states he bought a copy of John Blackie's 1866 *Iliad* and read Jose Hermosilla's 1831 *Iliad.* We also know he had copies of Johann Heinrich Voss's 1793 *Iliad,* and Christian Heyne's 1802 translation. Moreover, he reread Pope's translation which he called a "jumble" in a letter to James Bradley Thayer on November 2, 1869.[7] Earlier, he had reviewed William Cowper's 1791 edition, and The Earl of Derby, Edward Stanley's 1864 translation; in Florence he had purchased Vincenzo Monti's adaption.[8] These, with George Chapman's 1610 edition, make up his known sources.

However, there is no clear reference by Bryant to the edition or editions of the Greek text he used. John Owens's *Odyssey of Homer* and *Iliad of Homer* had been published in 1844 and 1851, respectively, by Leavitt and Allen of New York, but these were primarily texts. They, in turn, were based upon Fredrick August Wolf's German translation, as was G. C. Felton's edition for J. Munroe & Co. of Boston in 1844.

But Parke Godwin gives a clue to Bryant's Text: "Going into his library about this time (summer of 1862 or 1863), I saw upon his table a fine edition of the *Iliad* and the *Odyssey* (an Oxford edition, I think) which some friend had kindly presented to him."[9] John Owens's prefaces include in *each* list an Oxford text: For the *Odyssey,* the Oxford edition of 1827 with Buttman's *Scholia*; and for the *Iliad*, the Oxford edition of 1849. These, or the two volumes of Frederich August Wolf printed in London in 1814, in both Greek and Latin, were probably the texts Bryant used.

II. The Translation

In his preface to the *Iliad* Bryant states he wanted a faithful, fluent, and accurate account of Homer "devoid of the awkward inversions of Pope."

In June of 1870, he wrote John Gourlie that he intended his translation to be easy to read: "I did not make it for those who are familiar with the original . . . but I intended it for the sake of English readers, and if I had not thought that I could give them a more satisfactory version than any of the previous ones, I would never have engaged in it."[10]

As his work progressed, he published sections of the *Iliad* in Field's *Atlantic Monthly* and the *Evening Post.*[11] Reading these excerpts,

Dana, as well as Longfellow and others, encouraged his labors. Bryant wrote John Durand:

> I am glad that you like my translation of Homer. It was an experiment on my part, and I have been curious to know how it appears to those who read it. It differs from all others in English by its greater simplicity. Cowper injured his by latinisms, pompous phrases, and harsh inversions. Lord Derby's is generally a fair rendering of the sense, but, as Halleck says, "he has made a good translation of the *Iliad* with the poetry left out." My own rendering is considerably closer to the original than either that of Cowper or Derby.[12]

Bryant completed *Iliad* Book I before sailing to Europe in the fall of 1866 and, while abroad, he worked through Book Five intermittently. As of November 30, 1867, he could write to Dana, "I trifle a little with Homer, whose poem I must confess does not seem to me the perfect work that critics have made it, notwithstanding its many undeniable beauties."[13]

Near the end of the sixth book he regretted that he had chosen to finish the *Odyssey,* since he felt little sympathy with Achilles and little admiration for the Gods: "I believe the Gods behave more shamefully in the *Iliad* than in the other poem and their conduct is so detestable that I am sometimes half-tempted to give them and Homer up altogether."[14]

But his pace quickened to forty lines a day, and by early 1869, he seems to have completed twelve books by devoting his mornings to Homer. This gain in facility can probably be attributed not only to Bryant's improved command of the Greek, but to his growing familiarity with the formulaic diction of his original. The second twelve books were published in June of 1870, and by July 1, the translator was immersed in the *Odyssey,* finishing twelve books by April of the next year, and being well into the second half as of June 19. On December 7, 1871, the twenty-fourth and final book was sent to the publisher and his *Odyssey* joined at least three others which were published in Britain during the preceding decade.[15]

But Bryant's progress did not preclude revision in detail. On March 8, 1871, Dana wrote of his delight with *Iliad* VI, especially the parting of Hector and Andromache, but suggested some revisions which were later followed: Bryant substituted "halter" for "cord" and, less happily, "scampers" for "prances."[16]

Unlike most of his predecessors, Bryant chose blank verse. Frederick H. J. Ritso (London, 1861), John Dart (London 1865), Edwin W. Simcox (London, 1865), and Sir John F. W. Hershel (Cambridge, 1866), had chosen hexameter in translating Homer; Charles Merivale in 1869 had rendered Homer into rhyme, Phillip S. Worsley and John Conington had done their Homer in Spenserian stanzas in 1865. While Bryant does not refer to their editions he, no doubt, could have had access to their works.

Bryant chose blank verse because it is probably the best way to render in natural Englsih meter a long succession of Greek hexameters; Fitzgerald has, in our generation, shown us that. Bryant acknowledged Voss's translation was better, but not Voss's use of hexameter in his excellent German translation;[17] nor would he abide Longfellow's suggestion about his verse translation:

> [Longfellow], who has spoken most kindly of my translation, had said that he wished I had chosen the hexameter instead of blank verse. I should like, for my part, to read the *Iliad* in such lines as those of his *Evangeline*, but I do not think that English readers, in general, would have liked *my* hexameters so well as my blank verse.[18]

Also, Bryant in his preface to the *Iliad* indicates he chose blank verse because "it enabled me to keep more closely to the original in my rendering, without any sacrifice either of ease or of spirit of expression." Indeed, in spite of the others who preceded him in hexameter and rhyme, I think he accomplished his translation better than they had and with more facility. However, his example and argument did not dissuade the American, James A. Martling, from translating the *Iliad* in hexameters nor, in 1877, R. P. Studley & Co. of St. Louis from publishing it.

In his preface to the *Iliad*, Bryant states: "I have endeavored to be strictly faithful in my rendering; to add nothing to my own, and to give the reader, so far as our language would allow, all that I found in the original." This is an heroic and noble task, the very attempting of which would be thought misguided by some, but it is achieved to an amazing degree by Bryant.

Additions of his own are almost nowhere to be found; "The Capitals of Many Nations" in the generally disappointing opening of the *Odyssey* adds a discordant overtone, but this is no doubt inadvertent; subtractions, or at least levelings, are more numerous. For example, in *Iliad* VII, 316 ff., when Hector and Ajax duel, "ponderous" and "massive" are fine words for their spears, and so they are described elsewhere, but Bryant gives up the Homeric "long-shadowed" with some poetic loss, but some metrical gain. "Death" is less than "black death"; lions "in their hunger" are at some poetic remove from lions "that eat raw flesh." Such instances can be multiplied, and this is obviously inevitable; however, Bryant can be called not just accurate but very accurate.

Bryant's decision to retain honorific epithets "in nearly all instances . . . making Achilles swift-footed and Ulysses fertile in resources, to the end of the poem," as he says in the preface, and to repeat in general where the formulaic diction of the original repeats (even in large scenes, e.g., preparing a banquet, donning armor, etc.), attests to both his accuracy and his feel for rhythm and spirit. The retention of epithets, in addition to the choice of a five-foot line, serves to explain also why Bryant's translation was longer than Homer's by about twenty-five percent, as was Cowper's.

Bryant strove for "simplicity of style," "such English as offers no violence to the ordinary usages and structures of our own [language]," and a "natural order of words." Again, his success is remarkable, but his diction is of course poetic and that of another century. One recent critic, Dorothea Wender, expresses much admiration for Bryant but thinks archaic diction is no longer a viable option for translators.[19] Indeed, expressions such as "strook" and "drave thither" have curtailed sales of Bryant's translations in our time. These archaisms reflect the influence of the King James Bible rather than stylistic deficencies on Bryant's part.

Paradoxically, a strong argument can be made for archaic diction in translating Homer. We know, as Bryant did,[20] that "Homer's technique was oral, and his formulae in some cases unchanged for centuries. He would not have sounded modern to his contemporaries and to this extent at least a "modern" Homer is a distorted Homer. But Bryant's diction is simple, rapid, and clear, and an infelicitous word such as "iliumward" (*Iliad* 1.94) rarely occurs.

A brief comparison with Cooper and with W. G. Caldcleugh (*Iliad*, Phila., 1870), in the same meter, will show Bryant's greater facility of expression and also indicate how much Caldcleugh had sacrificed in order to achieve parity with Homer in number of lines.

> To whom Achilles, swiftest of the swift.
> What thou hast learn'd in secret from the God
> That speak, and boldly. By the son of Jove,

Apollo, whom thou, Calchas, seek'st in prayer
Made for the Danai, and who thy soul
Fills with futurity, in all the host
The Grecian lives not, who while I shall breathe,
And see the light of day, shall in this camp
Oppress thee; no, not even if thou name
Him, Agamemnon, sovereign o'er us all.

Cowper, *Iliad* I. 101-110

Achilles, the swift-footed, answered thus:
"Fear nothing, but speak boldly out whate'er
Thou knowest, and declare the will of Heaven.
For by Apollo, dear to Jove, whom thou,
Calchas, dost pray to, when thought, givest forth
The sacred oracles to men of Greece,
No man, while yet I live, and see the light
Of day, shall lay a violent hand on thee
Among our roomy ships; no man of all
The Grecian armies, though thou name the name
Of Agamemnon, whose high boast it is to stand
In power and rank above them all."

Bryant, *Iliad* I. 107-118

Him answering, then Achilles thus replied:
Cheer up, and boldly speak thy prophecy,
For by Apollo, who inspires thy thoughts,
No one, whilst I 'm alive, shall do they harm;
Not e'en if Agamemnon thou namest,
Who boasts to be superior to us all.

W. G. Caldcleugh, *Iliad* I. 88-93

III. The Critical Reaction

Bryant's acknowledged and accepted criticism of mistakes in his translation, as when J. W. French offered the unsolicited correction of his diction (e.g. "file" for "rank"), which the translator states was indeed a "blunder."[21]

In spite of Bryant's recognition of his mistakes, others, friends, and critics alike, found this first major American verse translation remarkable. In 1866, with only the *Odyssey* V and the *Iliad* VI printed, the Boston *Daily Advertiser* on December 13, praised Bryant's felicitous choice of blank verse over Greek hexameter. The *Evening Post* (hereinafter EP) also praised their owner-publisher's work. Two articles, no doubt written by the literary editor, John Render Thompson, found the translation the most important work in verse that had appeared on the continent (*EP:* 2/10/70) and pronounced that Bryant's *Iliad* would become "the standard English version." (*EP:* 6/21/70). An article in the *Post* by Samuel Osgood (8/3/70) said the translation reflected Bryant's "Americanism" and "sense of nature" in this national edition of the epic, but James Hadley of Yale wrote (*EP:* 4/15/70 that while Bryant's American *Iliad* was more noble and beautiful than Pope's he thought the latter's rhyme would keep it more popular.

William Gilmore Simms had twice written his friend Bryant (on 3/2/70 and 4/9/70) to congratulate him on the "simplicity" and "directness" of his *Iliad;* moreover, he sent him in the second letter a copy of his article from the Charleston, South Carolina *Courier* of 2/26/70 in which he wrote that Bryant "is probably the one person . . . who could render Homer deservedly into the English language."[22]

The best article of the time was Charlton T. Lewis's critique in *Putman's Magazine* which appeared on the day of Bryant's publication of the *Iliad,* Volume I. Lewis, who one year later would join the *Evening Post*, compares the new edition with Cowper's, Chapman's (published 1610), and Blackie's and finds these foreign translations wanting. The same Lewis, in April, 1871, published a second article on Bryant's *Iliad* in the *North American Review* for April, 1871, upon the publication of Volume II, and found Bryant's work vastly superior to all others: "Mr. Bryant's translation will assuredly be recognized wherever our mother tongue is read as its best echo of the old Greek epic." J. B. Thayer in the Boston *Daily Advertiser* of Septemberr 28, 1871, stated that Bryant's *Odyssey* was the best English version and "no [other] version . . . . will bear comparison with it." John Bigelow in his *American Men of Letters* series found his friend's translation an exact rendering of the "genuine spirit of Homer, [and] . . . one of the finest specimens of pure Saxon English in our literature.

In mid-September of 1871, his publisher, James R. Osgood & Co. (Fields had sold out to his partner on January 2, 1871) offered a cheaper edition of the two volumes of the *Iliad* for five dollars, much to Bryant's delight.[23] With this acclaim and with encouragement from his friends, Bryant wrote R. H. Dana in June of 1870 that he finds "the work . . . takes well with the public. Is is commended in quarters where my original poems are not much thought of, and I sometimes fancy that possibly it is thought that I am more successful as a translator than in anything else, which you know is not the highest praise."[24]

With such a wave of acclaim, praise, and sales, Bryant returned to Homer and published Volume I of the *Odyssey* in September of 1871 and Volume II in March of 1872. It is the first known edition done by an American.

Modern critics agree with those of one hundred years ago about Bryant's work. F. Seymour in his *An American Guide To The Best Translations of The Greek and Latin Classics Into English* (London and New York, 1930) states that Bryant's edition is "on the whole a far more successful version than Cowper's which was in the same metre," and Dorothea Wender (*AJP,* 1975) ranks Bryant's *Iliad* among the best translations of previous centuries, and the most successful in his use of archaic poetic diction and formal metre.

These modern views should indeed have pleased the poet who, at seventy-six years of age, wrote his brother, John in 1870, that now he saw the task, as he was half-finished, as an "occupation . . . which will furnish me with a reason for declining other literary tasks, and a hundred engagements which I want some excuse besides old age for declining." Bryant received $2,000 for the *Iliad* and apparently the same amount for the *Odyssey.*[26] It was time and money indeed well spent.

Four years after the poet-translator's death, N. B. Kneas, Jr. and Co. brought out an edition in raised type for the blind, a suitable memorial and, in a real sense, "the highest praise" for the merit and popularity of the work of both Bryant and his blind mentor, Homer.

NOTES

1. Tremaine McDowell's: "Cullen Bryant Prepares for College" *SAQ, XXX* (April, 1931), 125–133. "Cullen Bryant at Williams College" *New England Quarterly* 1, *NEQ,* 1 (Oct., 1928), 443–466. "William Cullen Bryant and Yale" *NEQ,* 3 (Oct., 1930), 706–716. Of course, Parke Godwin's *A Biography of William Cullen Bryant, with Extracts from his Private Correspondence.* (New York: 1883) 2 Vols. (hereinafter, *Life*). chs. 1, 4 and 5. William Cullen Bryant II and Thomas G. Voss, *The Letters of William Cullen Bryant,* I (New York: 1975) ch. I, will furnish sufficient detail and additional dimension to Cullen's classical education and his familiarity with the major classical writings.
2. The odes were an imitation of Horace's "I, IX" and a translation of "Ode II, B., I." They appeared in *NAR* 5 (Sept., 1817), p. 336.
3. Letter in Goddard-Roslyn Collection of The New York Public Library (N.Y.P.L.) printed in *Life* II, p. 192. See also Bryant's critical note on Cowper's translation in *Thirty Poems* (New York, 1864) which is reprinted in *Life* II, pp. 193–194.

4. The seven were by T. S. Norgate, (London, 1864); Joseph H. Dart (London, 1865); Lord Derby's in 1865; Edwin W. Simcox (London, 1865); Philip S. Worsley and John Conington (Edinburgh, 1865–1868); Blackie's in 1866; John F. W. Hershel's in 1866.
5. *Life* II, 193.
6. Bryant to Epec Sargent, 3/29/70 (Massachusetts Historical Society).
7. *Life* II, 280
8. Bryant on Monti: "(He) translated the *Iliad* into excellent blank verse without any knowledge of Greek," Speech to Williams College Alumni, 2/22/70, in Parke Godwin's *The Prose Writings of William Cullen Bryant*, II (N. Y., 1884), p. 267.
9. *Life* II, 193.
10. *Life* II, 292, dated 6/27/70.
11. He had published part of Book VI of the *Iliad* on the *Evening Post's* front page on November 22, 1865 under the title of "The Parting of Hector & Andromache" and also in the *Atlantic Monthy* for December, 1865. On December 13, 1866, the *Post* carried the translation of the half of Book I of the *Iliad* which was published in the *Atlantic Monthly* in January of 1867, Book V of the *Iliad* appeared in the *Atlantic Monthly* in Janurary of 1868. This was his common practice since James T. Fields, of Fields & Osgood & Co., the future publishers of his Homer, was, until 1870, the editor of the *Atlantic Monthly*.
12. Bryant to Durand, 2/22/67; (N.Y.P.L., Berg Collection).
13. *Life* II, 267 dated 11/30/67.
14. Bryant to John Bryant, 1/24/68, (Amherst College Library Collection).
15. Philip Stanley Worsley (Edinburg 1861) did his in Spenserian stanzas; both T. S. Norgate's (London, 1863), and George Musgrave's (London, 1865) were rendered in blank verse.
16. *Life* II, 300–301.
17. See him preface to *Iliad* and Letter to John Gourlie in *Life* II, p. 192.
18. Bryant to James T. Fields, 6/20/70, (Massachusetts Historical Society); *Life* p. 287n.
19. "Plain in Diction, Plain in Thought: Some Criteria for Evaluating Translations of the *Iliad*" *American Journal of Philology*, (Vol. 96, no. 3). Pp. 239–255 (see pp. 250, 254).
20. *Prose Writings* II, p. 268.
21. Bryant to French 11/30/69 (University of Virginia); for his work's appeal and criticism, see *Life* II, 285–7.
22. M.C.S. Oliphant, *et alii*, *Letters of William Gilmore Simms* V, (Univ. of South Carolina, 1952) 299, 308–9, 311–312.
23. Bryant to Rev. Orville Dewey, *Life* II, 289–90, dated as 3/12/70.
24. *Life* II, 287 dated 6/20/70.
25. *Life* II, 296, dated 7/1/70.
26. Bryant to J. R. Osgood & Co. 3/20/71 and 3/27/71 (Huntington Library).

William Cullen Bryant and the Suggestive Image: Living Impact

DAVID J. MORIARTY
University of Wisconsin at Madison

One suspects that the literary critics have too often risen to defend a "denatured" Bryant, the one whose reputation as a poet has been assaulted by neglect and misunderstanding for the greater part of these one hundred years since his death. Acting as curators in a museum of dead ideas and forms, such critics do Bryant as much a disservice as the school teachers, who forced so many of us to memorize sections of William Cullen Bryant's "Thanatopsis," a poem on a subject of which we had but a dim awareness and written in an unfamiliar style, all to the effect of stilling our potential for appreciating "the Dear Old Poet" before it could be developed.

The critics, by inferring that Bryant's importance rests in his distinction as one of the first Americans to capture the spirit of English Romanticism and place that spirit in a distinctly American context,[1] only encourage a narrow view of his work, which denies the general reader access to Bryant's poetry and limits its appeal to those students of American Romanticism who would read a Bryant poem as a literary artifact. This, in turn, inevitably forces an unfair comparison of Bryant's work with that of the recognizably greater European Romantics. Leon Howard falls into just such a trap with his observation that "Bryant succeeded in naturalizing one of the great symbols of Romanticism by insisting that nature poetry make sense in terms of the American . . . experience, [but that] these symbols lost much of their power when transferred to a different cultural environment."[2] This statement is not arguable as it stands, yet is it relevant for the present-day reader's appreciation of Bryant's poetry? The misinterpretation of symbols primarily derives from a misinterpretation of context, but this very misinterpretation suggests a valid meaning and context all its own.

Another common critical opinion is that voiced by Hyatt Waggoner, who states that Bryant and his fellow New England poets, Longfellow, Lowell, Holmes, and Whittier, were regarded as symbolic "of America's coming of age culturally," but were not "outrageously overvalued" even in their own day. Such an evaluation leads one to conclude, with Waggoner, that these men were minor poets, too representative of the moods and manners of a simpler, more naive period of the American experience, and now "they are very hard for us to respond to sympathetically," often seeming "irrelevant or simply dull, when not ridiculous." It leaves one with the assumption that what is needed with regard to Bryant's work, as with that of any minor figure, is "an attempt to salvage something of value" from his prolific and inconsistent canon.[3]

Albert F. McLean, Jr., sounded a somewhat different note in 1964 when he wrote in the preface to his "ritual of criticism" of Bryant's work:

> It is time to change the format, to recast our characters, to build anew the sets. For beneath the calm, sonorous surface of his verse lie traces of discord and conflict, a drama of the inner life which has been politely ignored by the critics.[4]

In these "traces of discord and conflict" reside Bryant's appeal to the twentieth-century reader. How is one to detect such traces, what kind of posture must the modern reader assume toward Bryant's poetry in order that it elicit a sympathetic response? These are key questions whose validity depends ultimately on Bryant's own inherent modernity.

Because he was a pioneer on the frontiers of modernism, Bryant's poetic vision is not always clear and consistent. However, that he was a modern poet most critics are willing to grant. Howard recognizes this when he observes that Bryant, together with Washington Irving, "gave the lesser symbols of their language a greater vitality than can be found in their predecessors."[5] By his participation in this process of a breaking through the dead artificiality that afflicted much eighteenth-century verse, Bryant played a major role in initiating a tradition that finds its best expression, according to Waggoner, in the likes of Dickinson, Robinson, Frost, and Robert Lowell.[6]

There are other hints by the critics that imply Bryant's modernity, such as McLean's notion that his poetry "relates to the search for a style on the part of the modern artist," and that nature for him "becomes, in Baudelaire's famous phrase, *un forêt de symboles.*"[7] Howard indicates a psychological depth of the poetry in that "Bryant discovered . . . that he could make serious use of external nature if he adapted his treatment of it to the stream of associations he found in his own mind and could normally anticipate in the mind of his readers."[8]

These testimonials to the modern elements of Bryant's poetry find their justification or refutation in the poems themselves, which, of course, provide the primary source for any defense of Bryant's modernity. If Bryant's poetry foreshadows that of Robert Lowell, Frost, Dickinson, Robinson, and even that of Wallace Stevens, as McLean seems to propose at one point,[9] then we should be able to discover these incipient indications in his poetry. If the poetry relates to the modern artist's search for a style, then elements of such should surface in the poems, and if nature is a "forest of symbols," reflecting the association of ideas in the poet's mind, then, provided these associations are still vital and valid, we should be able to discern the clues in the poems.

We are constantly on the alert for the suggestive, vital, epiphanic image in the poetry of our contemporaries, as well as those poets whom we regard as speaking to the modern situation. The image is the essential element in the modern artist's search for a style. It is the living image that proves the seedling for the modern poet's forest of symbols. If we are to read Bryant sympathetically, it seems that we should allow and take with him the same liberties that we apply in the case of a Dickinson or a Frost.

In advocating a quest for the suggestive image in Bryant's poetry, we do it no vandalism or violence. Such a practice is consistent with Bryant's own theory of poetry, expressed in his *Lectures*, where he states that "poetry, by the symbols of words, suggests both the sensible object and the association."[10] Bryant, in fact, defines poetry as "a suggestive art" employing "arbitrary symbols," which work "like a spell upon the imagination," a faculty that is "by no means passive." The success of any poem, according to Bryant, relies on the reader's imaginative activity. The reader must take "a path which the poet only points out, and shape its visions from the scenes and allusions which he gives." It is the reader's imagination that completes the "sketches of beauty" supplied by the poet "with the noblest images its own stores can furnish."[11] Such a theory is true to the psychology of association that informs and structures much of Bryant's poetry,[12] making the poem "an exhibition of those analogies and correspondences which it beholds between the things of the moral and of the natural world." It is by "bringing images of visible beauty . . . to heighten the effect of moral sentiment," so that the poem "binds into one all the passages of human life and connects all the varieties of human feeling within the work of creation,"[13] that the poet accomplishes his aesthetic.

Bryant's aesthetic is quite similar to that of Whitman. It was Whitman's concept that the poem gives the clue, that the reader must involve himself or herself in a "gymnast's struggle" with an "alert creativity," thus making his own poem from the raw material of the poet's perceptions.[14] Such a concept is at the heart of any sympathetic response to Bryant's poetry, as well as Whitman's. Any modern reader of Bryant must meet him half way, come to him on equal terms, without the conventional critical preconceptions, without the patronizing attitude accorded the period figure, willing to allow Bryant his suggestive insights.

McLean notes Whitman's recognition of indebtedness to Bryant in "My Tribute to Four Poets," from *Specimen Days*. Whitman wrote of a "Bryant pulsing the first interior verse—throbs of a mighty world—bard of the river and wood, ever conveying a taste of the open air, with scents as from hay fields, grapes, birch-borders . . . ." Whitman found "here and there through all, poems of passages of poems, touching the highest universal truths . . . ."[15] Bryant is no symbolist poet. His idea of a poem is something that is not "merely a tissue of striking images," yet there is, even in this denial, an implicit realization that the "striking image" plays an important role in the poem's construct. Indeed, one detects in Bryant's poetry vestiges of the liberal Protestant imagination, that which informs the poetry of both Whitman and Blake, two poets attractive to the symbol seeker. It is a vision that reads the forms of images in nature as evidence of the types and symbols of the eternal verities. One finds this in Bryant's "A Forest Hymn" (1825), when the poet, entering the Temple of Nature, that repository of symbols, beholds there images that suggest the hand of the Master Artist. We do not need to share Bryant's idea of the Deity to appreciate the aesthetic ramifications of such a response to nature. In these moments, the poet becomes the priest-mediator observing and interpreting the forms and images in nature that correspond with the images in the mind of his reader. It is these images in the forest of nature that give evidence of the eternal, becoming analogues of the images in the forest of the mind, which are emanations of the "inner light," the God within, of liberal Protestant theology, or the shared racial consciousness of our modern Jungian psychology.

The secular metaphor is the poet as wizard, whose verse casts a spell over the receptive reader, enabling him or her to put aside the selfish concerns of the everyday life, a life that Bryant felt "begets desulatory habits of thought,"[17] and enter into the magical realm of poetic images. Bryant used this metaphor in "The Poet" (1864):

> What witchery hangs upon this poet's page!
> What art it his written spells to find
> That sway from mood to mood the willing mind!

We are less susceptible to this sense of self-abnegation, the ecstasy of the poet-priest and mystic, the magical mediator of the grandeur of God's creation, yet it is a theme that runs throughout Bryant's poetry and is captured especially well in an image from "A Forest Hymn," where the poet confronts a form suggesting stasis and permanence in the ancient religious totem of the Druids, "This mighty oak—By whose immovable stem I stand and seem/Almost annihilated—."

It is the modern reader, who has depleted to the point of exhaustion his store of noblest images, whose imagination has been lulled into a dull passivity by the uncontrolled onslaught of myriad sensations, who has experienced first hand man's alienation from nature, and whose moral sense is so lacking as to prevent him from distinguishing the correlations between the natural and the moral spheres, that has difficulty responding to the magic spell of Bryant's poetry. The fault is in ourselves, not in the poetry. As McLean perceives, we must struggle to recognize with Bryant "that his poetic dialogue was no simple dialectic between subject-Man and object-Nature; it was . . . an involved process of creation in which physical objects and poetic images were not easily distinguishable." In such instances, the best moments Bryant's poetry has to offer us, Mclean indicates, "the fine line which generally divides imagery from metaphor becomes gently obscured as all the phenomena of Nature assume the task of suggestion.[18]

This process of the blurring of distinctions between metaphor and image in Bryant's poetry is a counter to the charge of "imagistic incoherence" levelled at Bryant and said to parallel and/or reflect an "incoherence of vision."[19] Granted there are times when Bryant's imagery works suggestively and metaphorically and times when the images are only elaborately stated clichés. This is an "inconsistency of vision," an "imagistic inconsistency," the very thing that makes Bryant a minor poet, but it is not an incoherence. No critic would ever charge a modern poet in such a way, no matter how unintelligible the work. Rather, the critic would apply terms like paradox, tension, irony, and the like to the poetry.

The variety of images one finds in Bryant's poetry is impressive. The imagery not only reflects the profusiveness of his source, nature, but partakes of these modern qualities of irony and paradox, these "traces of discord and conflict" that McLean detects. Nature herself in Bryant's poetry is a paradox. At times it provides "an image of that calm life," that sense of repose from the bustling, grubbing rat race of life. The final stanza of "Green River" (1820) is a good example. Note how Bryant uses different consonant sounds to convey the contrast in mood from the first half of the stanza, where the sounds of dissonant d's and strident s's prevail to the last half of the stanza, dominated by fluffy f's, murmuring m's, and lovely l's.

> Though forced to drudge for the dregs of men,
> And scrawl strange words with the barbarous pen,
> And mingle among the justling crowd,
> Where the sons of strife are subtle and loud—
> I often come to this quiet place,
> To breathe the airs that ruffle thy face,
> And gaze upon thee in silent dream,
> For in thy lonely and lovely stream
> An image of that calm life appears
> That won my heart in greener years.

At other times, as in "The Prairies" (1832), "the encircling vastness" of nature diminishes, even threatens man. Initially the vastness of the prairie suggests the sensation of stasis, permanent motionlessness, stillness, which Bryant expresses with an image of the prairie as ocean, fixed and motionless, and there is a tension established between the vastness and the claustrophobic motionlessness.

> Lo! they stretch,
> In airy undulations, far away,
> As if the ocean, in his gentlest swell,
> Stood still, with all his rounded billows fixed,
> And motionless forever.

Indeed, this sense of motionlessness proves a momentary optical illusion as the poet's eye discerns all manner of movement.

> —Motionless?—
> No—they are all unchained again. The clouds
> Sweep over with their shadows, and, beneath,
> The surface rolls and fluctuates to the eye;
> Dark hollows seem to glide along and chase
> The sunny ridges.

Here the paradox is deepened by the image, since the very sense of movement in the landscape, created by the moving shadows of the clouds crossing the stationary ridges, is as much an illusion as the stillness. Another image, following immediately, reiterates this paradox of motionless motion, "the prairie-hawk that, poised on high,/Flaps his broad wings, yet moves not." This illusion is also undercut by the poet's concession, "ye have played/Among the palms of Mexico and vines/Of Texas, and have crisped the limpid brooks/That from the fountains of Sonora glide/Into the calm Pacific."

The hawk's vast range confirms the paradox in nature; beneath the seemingly still and motionless illusions of permanence and stasis in nature, ripples an energy, power, change, and evanescence that is suggested in the image of the hawk "crisping" the placid surface of some remote "limpid" brook. Before the paradox of nature, the poet stands in awe, "almost annihilated." Aware of his own insignificance in nature's scheme and his own limited range, the poet indulges in a reverie of images of changefulness, called up from the vast interior of his imagination: decay and death, the "sad images of the stern agony" that pervade "Thanatopsis." Images that formerly found their expression "In a forgotten language, and old tunes,/From instruments of unremembered form," which, like Bryant's own images, "Gave the soft winds a voice," and are subject to the change that all "the forms of being" undergo.

It must be admitted that such an awareness gives the lie to the grand illusions of Bryant's time: Progress, Manifest Destiny, and "rugged individualism." When the poet awakes from his reverie at the close of "The Prairies," he finds himself "in the wilderness alone," not "almost annihilated," but, in a sense, alienated from the forces of nature over which he has no control, a realistic statement of the consequences of "rugged individualism." In the poem there is a definite progression from the poet's intial discovery of the paradox in nature, to the reflections on the enigmatic forces of nature, to the final recognition that man has no tools to challenge this enigma, except the sad images and instruments of soon to be forgotten form.

If there is much irony implicit in Bryant's recognition that "the old tunes" are not immune to the vicissitudes of change, there is also irony in his sending his artist friend, Thomas Cole, off to Europe with a sonnet that envisions Cole as bearing in his heart "a living image of our own bright land" by way of preparing him for the images of decay and death that he will witness there:

> —everywhere the trace of men,
> Paths, homes, graves, ruins, from the lowest glen
> To where life shrinks from the fierce Alpine air.[20]

His exhortation to Cole to "keep that earlier, wilder image bright" amounts not only to a romantic vision of the mutual intent of their respective arts, to keep the preternaturally vivid image of the New World alive for as long as possible, but an equally romantic awareness that such preternatural images will eventually suffer decay and death as the source of civilization moves inexorably westward.

Bryant, one feels could not but appreciate the very irony inherent in the remarks of the critic who finds in his poetry "honesty, not irony in the modern manner," who proclaims that he wrote his best poetry before he was forty and who indicts him with the term "incoherent" because of his ability to celebrate Progress, while advocating the essential absurdity of human ideas of Progress in the face of an inexorable nature.[21] The final lines of his sonnet "Mutation" (1842) contain Bryant's response to such critics, "Weep not that the world changes— did it keep/A stable, changeless state, 'twere cause indeed to weep." Progress, after all, presumes an openness to change, and nature surely enforces the law of change without quarter, and man's response to nature is more timeless than his response to political ideas, though more complex and thus "inconsistent."

There is no perversion and no contradiction of Bryant's vision if critics, searching for signs of life among his literary remains, often ignore an early poem like "The Ages" (1821), based on the idea of Progress rather than the natural imagery of change. This is because there is an element of incipient self-destruction in the political poems that Bryant wrote for his contemporaries that is not present in his nature poems, where the natural, living image has "an enduring freshness and vividness,"[22] a longer "half-life," that outlives the mechanism of the personification of the abstract idea.

It is to Bryant's lasting credit that he was honestly aware of the irony in this idea of the evanescence of the image, it is this honesty that makes his poems which treat of the natural image more expressive of the human condition and more relevant for us now than any of the overtly political poems. Waggoner, who comments on "an almost classic simplicity and fitness about the images" in "To A Waterfowl" (1821),[23] seems impervious to the one image in the poem that conveys this ironic nature of Bryant's vision, that the ultimate image is inexpressible, "Thou art gone, the abyss of heaven/Hath swallowed up thy form." The image of the waterfowl, like other symbolic bird images, in its propensity to fade out, to disappear into the horizon, to be "swallowed up" in nature, is a fitting metaphor for the processes of art and the momentary epiphanic quality of the natural image.

As the individual grows old and the senses dim and are dulled and desensitized, the finely tuned ability to perceive the evanescent image fades. As Bryant noted in "Earth," written in Europe in 1835, "All in vain,/Turns the tired eye in search of form." Five years later, in "The Old Man's Counsel," Bryant wrote that life "Darts by so swiftly that [its] . . . images/Dwell not upon the mind, or only dwell/In dim confusion." Like Wordsworth, the British poet Bryant is most often compared with, he experienced this loss of the visionary gleam, and this failure of the vision was even more devastating to the American poet's reputation because he supposedly had access to the preternatural forms of the New World, through a proximity and an experience not available to a European Romantic. Because the "living image" seemed so accessible, so near, so real, to Bryant, in contrast to the Europeans, for whom the preternatural was more an abstract idea than a vital image, the death of the imagination, the decay of the poetic vision, the sense of loss is also more real and more tragic. For this reason, that Bryant turned, like Wordsworth, in his later years to poetry dealing with the abstract idea, becomes more forgivable, but all of this only indicates how easily one falls into this trap of reading Bryant in terms of the Romantic mythology.

What should be considered are the images themselves, those that are still alive, renewable, suggestive, for the reader of today, and it is the natural images, the ones that sparkle and furnish a momentary, evanescent vision of the human condition before they fade and are swallowed up in the abyss of eternity, that are this. These images that have outlived their percipient are surrounded by much "dead wood" in the poetry, and they require of the reader, who wishes to perceive them anew, an almost childlike openness to the wonder and surprise and epiphanic joy that Bryant himself felt when he came upon the yellow violet in the still dead forest of April, or the fringed gentian, its "blossom bright" in the dying Autumn wood.[24] This is not to indicate that such images must be taken out of context. In truth, they have a life of their own, and thus provide their own context, and, as I stated previously, they must be sought with alert senses, not dimmed by the light of common day.

In "Inscription for the Entrance to a Wood" (1821), the following lines appear: ". . . The primal curse/Fell, it is true, upon the unsinning earth/But not in vengeance." These lines contain the essence of Bryant's double-edged and ironic vision of nature. The whole of nature is innocent and blameless. "We observe no sin in her grander operations and vicissitudes," Bryant once mused;[25] and yet nature is cursed by the sin of man and subject to the very law of decay and death that it is called upon to enforce. However, such is not laid on "in vengeance," as it is with man, and nature has a reprieve not granted man. It is apparently renewable. The cyclical process in nature affords the natural image the chance to renew itself for readers of all time so that, as Bryant assures us, "The cool wind,/That stirs the stream in play, shall come to thee,/Like one that loves thee nor will let thee pass/Ungreeted, and shall give its light embrace." There is a delicate irony in this "light embrace" for we are all chilled by the melancholy "cool wind" of change and the cold wind of death that constitutes the primal curse.

There is this same kind of irony, the "equivocation" that McLean notices[26] in "Oh Fairest of the Rural Maids" (1820). By making a particular individual, Frances Fairchild, his future wife, an expression of the natural image, a "child of nature," Bryant grants her the same exemption, in her innocence, that nature holds, "The forest depths, by foot unpressed,/Are not more sinless than thy breast." Frances has long ago been annihilated by the primal curse, but the natural image of her beauty is still vital because, "Thy sports, thy wanderings, when a child,/Were ever in the sylvan wild;/And all the beauty of the place/Is in thy heart and on thy face."

The final result of the primal curse, man's severance from nature, sets up a tension in Bryant's best poems between the processes of nature and her temporal artifice, when a tentative and ephemeral bond is reset and a glimpse of the preternatural state, when the bond was permanent and fixed, is allowed. A fine example of this is "A Winter Piece" (1821) where an image like ". . . the clouds from their still skirts,/Had shaken down on earth the feathery snow,/And all was white,'' skirts, if you will, a line of delicate balance between the static and artificial personification of nature prevalent in the eighteenth century and the more modern natural image, striking and suggestive, and evidencing this tension. Particularly fortunate is the use of "still," implying the paradox and the tension, and indicating both a temporalness and a frozen stasis. The image itself is stiff, yet intimate, the formality of nature's dress undercut by the informality of the gesture, and the "ambiguity of the word" is reinforced further by the punning on "down" and "feathery" in the next line, and by the fact that "all was white," that most suggestive and ambiguous of colors, containing the potentiality of everything, lacking the actuality of anything.

This initial image prepares the way for an even more ambiguous image, one offering a glimpse of preternatural stasis and brightness, a moment when

> . . . the wildered fancy dreams
> Of spouting fountains, frozen as they rose,
> And fixed, with all their branching jets, in air,
> And all their sluices sealed. All, all is light;
> Light without shade.

Such an image succinctly prefigures the later nineteenth century's preoccupation with form and style. It is a photographic image of nature frozen and evicerated, in an attitude that celebrates the superiority of art over nature, while denying the reality, and it is this reality that Bryant reinforces as he shatters this precise, frozen, and pristine image, immediately, dissolving all in a confusion of melting, dissonance, and impending darkness:

> But all shall pass away
> With the next sun. From numberless vast trunks,
> Loosened, the crashing ice shall make a sound
> Like the far roar of rivers, and the eve
> Shall close o'er the brown woods as it was wont.

Near the close of this "Winter Piece," Bryant gives us the physical object as metaphor, that is the essential expression of the way the suggestive image operates in his poetry.

> Lodged in sunny cleft,
> Where the cold breezes come not, blooms alone
> The little wind-flower, whose just opened eye

Is blue as the spring heaven it gazes at—
Startling the loiterer in the naked groves
With unexpected beauty. . . .

There are poems of Bryant in which the sacred bond between man
and nature is shown as irretrievable, the preternatural state where all is
"sweetness and light" as irrecoverable. In these poems the death of
man and the decay of nature intermingle in a prophetic and apocalyp-
tic way that is especially compelling for the modern reader. The later
poem, "The Crowded Street," is an example. Here urban existence is
depicted as cut off from nature, and Godless and dead due to this separation. In their deadened state, the city dwellers evidence a "sense of
futility and indifference," to use McLean's phrase.[27] Man is victim,
nature no better than a survivor, but in "An Indian at the Burial-
Ground of His Fathers" (1824), man and nature guarantee each
other's doom. The Indian narrator of this work is not the "noble savage" of the European Romantics, but, rather, he is the poet's persona
and the alter ego of us all. As a displaced alien, he is able to see clearly
from his distanced perspective the disease of modern society, which is
a threat to all of us.

If an ecological balance existed between the Indian and the land, it
was because the Indian considered nature "sacred when the soil was
ours," but now Bryant's Indian sees the land as having been defiled by
the usurping, death-dealing white race, "the pale race who waste us
now. . . . They waste us—ay—like April snow/In the warm noon, we
shrink away." These lines have a poignant topicality for, just five
years after they were written, Andrew Jackson's infamous Indian Removal Act opened up the "Trail of Tears" and forced thousands of
Indians from the Southeast to migrate to the Oklahoma Territory, a
march that "wasted" many.

Bryant's Indian gives substance to the vision that we of the "pale
race" often feel but are too horrified to express, that there is a "fearful
sign" to behold in "the white stones above the dead." The headstones
in the Caucasian churchyard suggest a veritable "thanatopolis," a
metaphor in miniature of the city of the dead. There is an implicit tension between the more natural image of the white April snow melting
away in the noon sun, and the equally ironic, more pretentious, because it appears permanent, whiteness and artifice of the man-crafted
grave stones. Our own contemporary, Allen Ginsberg, can extend and
transvalue such imagery to indicate that the stone skyscrapers, built on
the Indian's sacred ground and Whitman's beloved Manahatta, are

also pretentious cenotaphs to the deadness of modern man.[28] A vision of nature dying, of course, presumes the death of poetry because it is exceedingly more difficult, if not impossible, to make poetry out of the attempts of others, their art and craft, than it is to make poetry about nature. One is all coldness and style, the other has warmth and vitality. One is the image of a cold, dead thing, the other a living image of the bright land.

As the Indian interprets the signs of the white man's violation of nature, he conjures a vision of nature polluted, corrupted, dying, a vision that has supplied Rachel Carson with the controlling metaphor for her telling book on the ecological catastrophe, *The Silent Spring.* It is a time when Bryant's future horror becomes our present reality:

> . . . grateful sound are heard no more,
>   The springs are silent in the sun;
> The rivers, by the blackened shore,
>   With lessening current run;
> The realm our tribes are crushed to get
> May be a barren desert yet.

It is a vision that anyone who has been in certain parts of New Jersey can confirm as prophetic; it is the dying image of our now tarnished land.

William Cullen Bryant, in his Indian mask, stands apart from the pretentiousness that too often blocks our true appreciation of his vision and accomplishment. All that Bryant ever sought from his dear nature, as he tells us in "November" (1824), was a coax "Yet one smile more . . ./Yet one rich smile, and we will try to bear/The piercing winter frost, and winds, and darkened air." Likewise, all that the suggestive image in the poetry seeks to elicit is a wry, Gioconda-like, smile of joy, surprise, discovery, what you will, when we loiterers come upon those "little wind-flowers" and are unexpectedly startled in the "naked groves" of poetry, before, that is, the cold wind of the critic blows all away.

NOTES

1. Cf. Marius Bewley in *Major Writers of America,* Perry Miller, ed. (New York: Harcourt, Brace, and World, 1962), I, 367.
2. Leon Howard, *Literature and the American Tradition,* (Garden City: Doubleday, 1960), p. 93.

3. Hyatt Waggoner, *American Poets from the Puritans to the Present,* (Boston: Houghton Mifflin, 1968), p. 34.
4. Albert F. McLean, Jr., *William Cullen Bryant,* (New York: Twayne, 1964), p. 7.
5. Howard, p. 93.
6. Waggoner, p. 34.
7. McLean, pp. 64, 76.
8. Howard, p. 93.
9. McLean, p. 128.
10. Cf. "On the Nature of Poetry" in *Prose Writings of William Cullen Bryant,* edited by Parke Godwin, (1884; reprinted New York: Russell and Russell, 1964), I, 5.
11. *Ibid.,* pp. 5-7.
12. McLean, p. 29 and p. 126.
13. Bryant, "On the Value and Uses of Poetry," *Prose Writings,* p. 19.
14. For a discussion of this concept see James E. Miller, Jr., "Introduction" to *Walt Whitman's Complete Poetry and Selected Prose,* edited and selected by Miller, (Boston: Houghton Mifflin, 1959), p. xi.
15. Cf. Walt Whitman's *Complete Prose Works,* (New York: M. Kennerley, 1914), p. 173.
16. Bryant, "On the Nature of Poetry," *Prose Writings,* p. 7.
17. Cf. "Reminiscences of the 'Evening Post,'" in John Bigelow's *William Cullen Bryant,* (Boston and New York: Houghton Mifflin, 1890), p. 341.
18. McLean, p. 76 and p. 127.
19. Waggoner, p. 42.
20. Bryant, "To Cole, The Painter, Departing for Europe," 1830.
21. Waggoner, p. 36 and p. 42.
22. Bryant, "On Originality and Imitation," *Prose Writings,* p. 35.
23. Waggoner, p. 41.
24. Bryant, "The Yellow Violet," 1821, and "To the Fringed Gentian," 1829.
25. Bryant, "On the Value and Uses of Poetry," *Prose Writings,* p. 19.
26. McLean, p. 52.
27. McLean, p. 62.
28. As an example see "Bayonne Entering N.Y.C." (1966) in Allen Ginsberg's *The Fall of America,* (San Francisco: City Lights, 1972), pp. 35-39.

Bibliography

Alder, J. H. "A Milton-Bryant Parallel." *New England Quarterly* 24 (1951): 377–380.

Amoruso, Vito. "La poesie de Bryant." *Studi Americani* 9 (1963): 39–67.

Arms, George. "William Cullen Bryant: A Respectable Station on Parnassus." *University of Kansas City Review* 15 (1949): 215–223.

Bancroft, George. *The Bryant Festival at the Century.* New York: D. Appleton, 1865.

Baxter, David J. "Timothy Flint and Bryant's 'The Prairies.'" *American Notes and Queries* 16 (1977): 52–54.

Berbrick, John D. *Three Voices From Paumanok: The Influence of Long Island on James Fenimore Cooper, William Cullen Bryant, and Walt Whitman.* Port Washington, N.Y.: Ira J. Friedman, 1969.

Bigelow, John. *William Cullen Bryant.* American Men of Letters Series. Boston: Houghton Mifflin, 1890.

Birdsall R. D. "William Cullen Bryant and Catherine Sedgwick: Their Debt to Berkshire." *New England Quarterly* 28 (1955): 349–371.

Booher, Edwin R. "The Garden Myth in 'The Prairies.'" *Western Illinois Regional Studies* 1, No. 1 (1977): 15–26.

Bradley, William Aspewall, *William Cullen Bryant.* English Men of Letters Series. New York: Macmillan, 1905.

Brown, Charles H. *William Cullen Bryant.* New York: Scribner's, 1971.

Bryant, William Cullen II. "The Genesis of 'Thanatopsis.'" *New England Quarterly* 21 (1948): 163–184.

———. "Bryant: The Middle Years; A Study in Cultural Fellowship." *Dissertation Abstracts,* (Abstract of Columbia Univ. diss.) 14 (1954): 1218.

223

————. "'The Waterfowl' in Retrospect." *New England Quarterly* 30 (1957): 181–189.

————. "Poetry and Painting: A Love Affair of Long Ago." *American Quarterly* 22 (1970): 859–882.

————, and Thomas G. Voss, eds. *The Letters of William Cullen Bryant, I: 1809–1836,* II: 1836–1849. New York: Fordham University Press, 1975.

Budick, Miller E. "'Visible' Images and the 'Still Voice': Transcendental Vision in Bryant's 'Thanatopsis.'" *Emerson Society Quarterly* 22 (1976): 71–77.

————. "The Disappearing Image in William Cullen Bryant's 'To a Waterfowl.'" *Concerning Poetry* (West. Wash. State Coll.) 2, No. 2 (1977): 13–16.

Callow, James T. *Kindred Spirits: Knickerbocker Writers and American Artists, 1807–1855.* Chapel Hill, N.C.: The University of North Carolina Press, 1967.

Cameron, Kenneth Walter. "An Early English Review of Bryant's Poems." *Emerson Society Quarterly* 13 (1958): 91.

————. "An Early English Review of Bryant's Poems." *Emerson Society Quarterly* 13 (1958): 91.

Casale, Ottavio M. "Bryant's Proposed Address to the Emperor of Brazil." *Emerson Society Quarterly* 63 (1971): 10–12.

Christensen, Norman Ferdinand. "The Imagery of William Cullen Bryant." *Dissertation Abstracts,* 21 (1960): 195.

Cody, Sherwin. *Four American Poets: William Cullen Bryant, Henry Wadsworth Longfellow, John Greenleaf Whittier, Oliver Wendell Holmes: A Book for Young Americans.* 1899. Reprinted, Folcroft, PA: Folcroft Library Eds., 1977.

Coleman, Earle E. "The Exhibition of the Palace: A Bibliographical Essay." *Bulletin of the New York Public Library* 64 (1960): 450–477.

Crapo, Paul. "Bryant on Slavery, Copyright, and Capital Punishment." *Emerson Society Quarterly* 47 (1967): 139–140.

Crino, Anna Maria. *Echi, temi e motivi nella poesia di William Cullen Bryant.* Verona: Linotipia Ghidini e Fiorini, 1963.

Dahl, Curtis. "Mound-Builders, Mormons, and William Cullen Bryant." *New England Quarterly* 34 (1961): 178–190.

Donovan, Alan B. "William Cullen Bryant: 'Father of American Song,'" *New England Quarterly* (December, 1968).

Duffey, Bernard. *Poetry in America: Expression and Its Values in the* ✓ *Times of Bryant, Whitman, and Pound.* Durham: Duke Univ. Press, 1978.

Duffey, Bernard. "Romantic Coherence and Romantic Incoherence in American Poetry," *Centennial Review* (Spring, 1963; Fall 1964).

Eby, Cecil D., Jr. "Bryant's 'The Prairies': Notes on Date and Text." *Papers of the Bibliographical Society of America* 56 (1962): 356–357.

Floan, Howard R. "The New York *Evening Post* and the Ante-bellum South." *American Quarterly* 8 (1956): 243–253.

Free, William J. "William Cullen Bryant on Nationalism, Imitation, and Originality in Poetry." *Studies in Philology* 66 (1960): 672–687.

Friedland, Louis S. "Bryant's Schooling in the Liberties of Oratory." *American Notes and Queries* 7 (1947): 27.

Glicksberg, Charles I. "William Cullen Bryant and Fanny Wright." *American Literature* 6 (1935): 427–432.

———. "From the 'Pathetic' to the 'Classical': Bryant's Schooling in the Liberties of Oratory." *American Notes and Queries* 6 (1947): 179–182.

———. "William Cullen Bryant: Champion of Simple English," *New England Quarterly* 26 (1949): 299–303.

———. "William Cullen Bryant and Nineteenth-Century Science." *New England Quarterly* 23 (1950): 91–96.

Godwin, Parke, ed. *A Biography of William Cullen Bryant, With Extracts from His Private Correspondence.* (Published as Vols. I and II of *The Life and Writings of William Cullen Bryant.*) 2 Vols. New York: D. Appleton & Co., 1883.

Gonzalez, Manuel P. "Two Great Pioneers of Inter-American Cultural Relations." *Hispania* (Univ. of Conn.) 42 (1959): 175–185.

Griffin, Max L. "Bryant and the South." *Tulane Studies in English* 1 (1949): 53–80.

Gross, Seymour L. "An Uncollected Bryant Poem." *Notes and Queries* 4 (1957): 358-359.

Grubbs, Henry A. "Mallarme and Bryant." *Modern Language Notes* 62 (1947): 410-412.

Guilds, John C. "Bryant in the South: A New Letter to Simms." Georgia History Quarterly 37 (1952): 142-146.

Harrington, Evans. "Sensousness in the Poetry of William Cullen Bryant." *University of Mississippi Studies in English* 7 (1966): 25-42.

Jelliffe, Rebecca Rio. "The Poetry of William Cullen Bryant: Theory and Practice." *Dissertation Abstracts* 25 (1965): 4148-4149.

Johnson, Curtiss S. *Politics and a Belly-full: Journalistic Career of William Cullen Bryant: Civil War Editor of the New York Evening Post.* New York: Vantage, 1962.

Lazzerini, Edward J. "Bryant as a Writer of Friendly Letters." *Emerson Society Quarterly* 48 (1967): 125-131.

Lease, Benjamin. "William Cullen Bryant: An Unpublished Letter." *Notes and Queries* 197 (1953): 396-397.

Leonard, W. E. "Bryant." *Cambridge History of American Literature,* I. New York: G. P. Putnam's Sons, 1917.

Long, H. P. "The Alden Lineage of William Cullen Bryant." *New England History and Gen. Reg.* 102 (1948): 82-86.

Mabbott, Thomas O., ed. *The Embargo.* (Facs. Reproductions of the Eds. of 1808 and 1809, With Introd. and Notes.) Gainesville, Florida: Scholars' Facsimilies and Reprints, 1955.

———. "Bryant's 'Thanatopsis.'" *Explicator* 11 (1952): 15.

Matthews, J. Chesley. "Bryant and Dante: A Word More." *Italica* 35 (1958), 176.

McDowell, Tremaine. "Cullen Bryant at Williams College." *New England Quarterly* 1 (1928): 443-466.

———. "William Cullen Bryant and Yale." *New England Quarterly* 3 (1930): 706-716.

————. *William Cullen Bryant.* American Writers Series. New York: American Book Co., 1935.

————. "Bryant's Practice in Composition and Revision." *Publications of the Modern Language Association* 52 (1937): 474–502.

————. "The Ancestry of William Cullen Bryant." *Americana* 22 (1928): 408–420.

McLean, Albert F., Jr. "Bryant's 'Thanatopsis': A Sermon in Stone." *American Literature* 31 (1960): 474–479.

————. *William Cullen Bryant.* New York: Twayne, 1964.

McMartin, Gaines Noble. "A Perspective on Unity in the Poems of Bryant, Longfellow, Emerson, and Whitman: The Use of Analogy and Example in Metaphor." *Dissertation Abstracts International* 36 (1976): 4494A.

Miller, Ralph N. "Nationalism in Bryant's 'The Prairies.'" *American Literature* 21 (1949): 227–232.

Monteiro, George. "The Patriarchal Mr. Bryant: Some New Letters." *Notes and Queries* 22 (1975): 440–441.

Morrill, Peter B. "Unpublished Letters of William Cullen Bryant." *Emerson Society Quarterly* 27 (1962): 47–48.

Murray, Donald M. "Dr. Peter Bryant: Preceptor in Poetry to William Cullen Bryant." *New England Quarterly* 33 (1960): 513–522.

Nevins, Allen. *The Evening Post: A Century of Journalism.* New York: Boni and Liveright, 1922.

Onis, Jose de. "The Alleged Acquaintance of William Cullen Bryant and Jose-Maria Heredia." *Hispanic Review* 25 (1957): 217–220.

————. "William Cullen Bryant y Jose Maria Heredia, vieja y nueva polemica." *Cuandernos Americanos* 17, ii (1958): 154–161.

Ornato, Joseph G. "Bryant and the United States Literary Gazette," *Emerson Society Quarterly* 48 (1961): 135–139.

Parrington, Vernon L. "William Cullen Bryant, Puritan Liberal." *The Romantic Revolution in America.* New York: Harcourt, Brace and Co., 1927.

Pattee, F. L. "The Centenary of Bryant's Poetry." *Sidelights on American Literature.* New York: The Century Co., 1922.

Peck, Richard E. "Two Lost Bryant Poems: Evidence of Thomson's Influence." *American Literature;* 39 (1967): 88–94.

Peckham, Henry Houston. *Gotham Yankee: A Biography of William Cullen Bryant.* New York: Vantage Press, 1950.

Phair, Judith Turner. *A Bibliography of William Cullen Bryant and His Critics: 1808–1972.* Troy, New York: Whitston, 1975.

Poger, Sidney. "William Cullen Bryant: Emblem Poet." *Emerson Society Quarterly* 43 (1966): 103–106.

Rebmann, David R. "Unpublished Letters of William Cullen Bryant." *Emerson Society Quarterly* 48 (1967): 131–135.

Ringe, Donald A. *Poetry and the Cosmos: William Cullen Bryant.* Harvard University, 1953.

————. "Kindred Spirits: Bryant and Cole." *American Quarterly* 6 (1954): 233–244.

————. "William Cullen Bryant and the Science of Geology." *American Literature* 26 (1955): 507–514.

————. "William Cullen Bryant's Account of Michigan in 1846." *Michigan History Mind* 40 (1956): 317–327.

————. "Two Items of Midwest Folklore Noted By William Cullen Bryant." *Midwest Folklore* 6 (1956): 141–146.

————. "Bryant's Use of the American Past." *Papers of the Michigan Academy of Science, Arts, and Letters* 41 (1956): 323–331.

————. "Bryant Criticism of the Fine Arts." *College Art Journal* 17 (1957): 43–54.

————. "Bryant and Whitman: A Study in Artistic Affinities." *Boston University Studies in English Byzantion* 2 (1956): 85–94.

Ringe, Donald A. "Painting as Poem in the Hudson River Aesthetic," *American Quarterly* 12 (1960): 71–83.

————. *The Pictorial Mode: Space and Time in the Art of Bryant, Irving and Cooper.* Lexington: University Press of Kentucky, 1971.

Rocks, James E. "William Cullen Bryant." *Fifteen American Authors Before 1900: Bibliographical Essays on Research and Criticism,* Robert A. Res and Earl N. Hurbert, eds. Madison University Press, 1971, 37-62.

Sanford, Charles L. "The Concept of the Sublime in the Works of Thomas Cole and William Cullen Bryant." *American Literature* 37 (1957): 434-448.

Scheich, William J. "Bryant's River Imagery." *College Language Association Journal* (Morgan State College, Baltimore) 20 (1976): 205-209.

Smith, Gerald J. "Bryant's 'Thanatopsis': A Possible Source." *American Notes and Queries* 13 (1975): 149-151.

Snow, Vernon F. "'Where Rolls the Oregon. . . .'" *Western Humanities Review* 10 (1956): 289-292.

Spann, Edward K. "Bryant and Verplanck, The Yankee and the Yorker, 1821-1870." *New York History* 49 (1968): 11-28.

Spivey, Herman E. "Bryant Cautions and Counsels Lincoln." *Tennessee Studies in Literature* 6 (1961): 1-13.

―――. "William Cullen Bryant Changes His Mind: An Unpublished Letter About Thomas Jefferson." *New England Quarterly* 22 (1949): 528-529.

―――. "Manuscript Resources of the Study of William Cullen Bryant." Papers of the Bibliographical Society of America 44: 254-268.

Stimson, Fredserick S., and Robert J. Biniger. "Studies of Bryant as Hispanophile: Another Translation." *American Literature* 31 (1959): 189-191.

Van Doren, Cari. "The Growth of 'Thanatopsis.'" *Nation* 101 (1915): 432-433.

Voss, Thomas G. "William Cullen Bryant's New York *Evening Post* and the South: 1847-1856." *Dissertation Abstracts* 28 (1967): 698A-699A.

―――. *William Cullen Bryant, an Annotated Checklist of the Exhibit Held in the Mullen Library of the Catholic University of America,*

October 30–November 10, 1967. Washington, D.C.: Catholic University of America, 1967. (18 p. pamphlet).

Weinstein, Bernard. "Bryant, Annexation, and the Mexican War." *Emerson Society Quarterly* 63 (1971): 19–24.

"William Cullen Bryant: Illinois Landowner." *Western Illinois Regional Studies* 1 (1977): 1–14. (Foll. by "Appendix: William Cullen Bryant's Land Transactions in Illinois Compiled from Bureau County Court Records, Princeton, Illinois." 10–13.)

Wilson, James G. *Bryant and His Friends: Some Reminiscences of the Knickerbocker Writers.* New York: Fords, Howard and Halbert, 1886.

Woodward, Robert H. "Bryant and Elizabeth Oakes Smith. An Unpublished Bryant letter." *Colby Library Quarterly* 5 (1959): 69–74.

———. "Bryant and the Oriskany Centennial." *Emerson Society Quarterly* 63 (1971): 19–24.

———. "'The Wings of Morning' in 'Thanatopsis.'" *Emerson Society Quarterly* 58 (1970): 153.

Yates, Norris. "Four Plantation Songs Noted by William Cullen Bryant." *Southern Folklore Quarterly* 15 (1951): 251–253.

Author Index

Subject Index